You and Your Windows 10 Computer

Studio Visual Steps

You and Your Windows 10 Computer

Everything you need to know about your computer, Internet, digital photos and more

www.visualsteps.com

This book has been written using the Visual Steps™ method.
Cover design by Studio Willemien Haagsma bNO

© 2015 Visual Steps
Author: Studio Visual Steps

First printing: November 2015
ISBN 978 90 5905 432 5

Resources used: Some of the computer terms and definitions seen here in this book have been taken from descriptions found online at the Windows Help website.

Do you have questions or suggestions?
Email: info@visualsteps.com

Would you like more information?
www.visualsteps.com

Website for this book:
www.visualsteps.com/your10computer

Table of Contents

Appendices

Foreword

Are you taking full advantage of what a computer has to offer? Only if you really know what can be done with a computer and the Internet, will you be able to benefit from the fun and convenience it can give you.

This comprehensive book discusses many topics such as managing files, making useful settings, using email securely, working with *Skype* and social media services such as *Facebook* and *Twitter*. You will also get acquainted with photo and video editing and learn more about the safe use of the Internet and online shopping. But this is not all, there are plenty of other tips on offer in this user-friendly book. Get started right away and discover what is possible.

We hope you will enjoy reading this book!

The Studio Visual Steps authors

P.S. Your comments and suggestions are most welcome. Our email address is: mail@visualsteps.com

Visual Steps Newsletter

All Visual Steps books follow the same methodology: clear and concise step-by-step instructions with screen shots to demonstrate each task.
A complete list of all our books can be found on our website **www.visualsteps.com**

You can also sign up to receive our **free Visual Steps Newsletter** on the web page **www.visualsteps.com/newsletter.php**

In this Newsletter you will receive periodic information by email regarding:
- the latest titles and previously released books;
- special offers, supplemental chapters, tips and free informative booklets.

Also, our Newsletter subscribers may download any of the documents listed on the web page **www.visualsteps.com/info_downloads**

When you subscribe to our Newsletter you can be assured that we will never use your email address for any purpose other than sending you the information as previously described. We will not share this address with any third-party. Each Newsletter also contains a one-click link to unsubscribe.

Introduction to Visual Steps™

The Visual Steps handbooks and manuals are the best instructional materials available for learning how to work with the computer. Nowhere else can you find better support for getting to know your *Windows* computer or Mac, your iPad or iPhone, Samsung Galaxy Tab, the Internet and a variety of computer applications.

Properties of the Visual Steps books:
- **Comprehensible contents**
  Addresses the needs of the beginner or intermediate user for a manual written in simple, straight-forward English.
- **Clear structure**
  Precise, easy to follow instructions. The material is broken down into small enough segments to allow for easy absorption.
- **Screen shots of every step**
  Quickly compare what you see on your screen with the screen shots in the book. Pointers and tips guide you when new windows or alert boxes are opened so you always know what to do next.
- **Get started right away**
  All you have to do is turn on your computer or laptop and have your book at hand. Perform each operation as indicated on your own device.
- **Layout**
  The text is printed in a large size font and is clearly legible.

In short, I believe these manuals will be excellent guides for you.

dr. H. van der Meij
Faculty of Applied Education, Department of Instructional Technology, University of Twente, the Netherlands

What You Will Need

To be able to work through this book, you will need a number of things:

The primary requirement for working with this book is having the US or English version of *Windows 10* installed on your computer or laptop. *Windows* comes equipped with all the programs you need to work with this book.

Please note: The screen shots shown in this book have been made using a local user account. It is also possible to login with a *Microsoft* account. Since this is a book for beginning computer users, we have chosen to not to use this type of account. If you are working with a *Microsoft* account, you will sometimes see different windows and other options.

It's also important to work with an up-to-date computer. You will learn how to update in *section 11.1 Windows Update*.

A functioning Internet connection.

Furthermore, you will need to have:

A digital photo/video camera, a portable device with a camera or SD card for transferring photos and/or videos to your computer. In this book you will learn how to use the programs by using a number of sample photos and videos.

Prior Computer Experience

In this book we assume you already have some computer skills and can work with *Windows*.

These are the basic skills you need to have:

- starting up and shutting down *Windows*;
- clicking the mouse;
- opening and closing programs;
- typing text;
- opening web pages;
- sending and receiving emails;
- adjusting settings on your computer.

How To Use This Book

This book has been written using the Visual Steps™ method. The method is simple: just place the book next to your computer or laptop and execute all the tasks step by step, directly on your own device. With the clear instructions and the multitude of screen shots, you will always know exactly what to do. This is the quickest way to become familiar with *Windows 10* and use the various programs and services it offers.

In this Visual Steps™ book, you will see various icons. This is what they mean:

Techniques
These icons indicate an action to be carried out:

 The mouse icon means you need to do something with the mouse.

 The keyboard icon means you should type something on your keyboard.

 The hand icon means you should do something else, for example, turn on the computer or carry out a task previously learned.

In addition to these icons, in some areas of this book extra assistance is provided to help you successfully work through each chapter.

Help
These icons indicate that extra help is available:

 The arrow icon warns you about something.

 The bandage icon will help you if something has gone wrong.

1 Have you forgotten how to do something? The number next to the footsteps tells you where to look it up at the end of the book in the appendix *How Do I Do That Again?*

In this book you will also find a lot of general information, and tips. This information is displayed in separate boxes.

Extra information
Information boxes are denoted by these icons:

 The book icon gives you extra background information that you can read at your convenience. This extra information is not necessary for working through the book.

 The light bulb icon indicates an extra tip for using a program or service.

The Website Accompanying This Book

On the website that accompanies this book, you will find additional information about this book along with practice files. Please, take a look at the website from time to time. The website is **www.visualsteps.com/your10computer**

The Screen Shots

The screen shots used in this book indicate which button, folder, file or hyperlink you need to click on your computer screen. In the instruction text (in **bold** letters) you will see a small image of the item you need to click. The line will point you to the right place on your screen.

The small screen shots that are printed in this book are not meant to be completely legible all the time. This is not necessary, as you will see these images on your own computer screen in real size and fully legible.

Here you see an example of an instruction text and a screen shot. The line indicates where to find this item on your own computer screen:

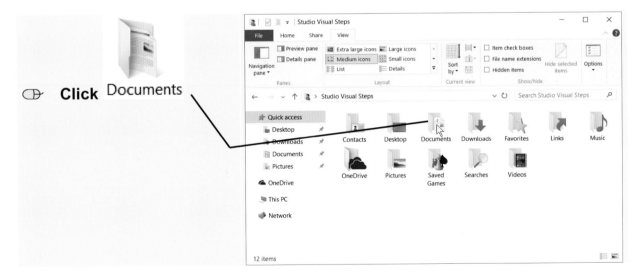

Sometimes the screen shot shows only a portion of a window. Here is an example:

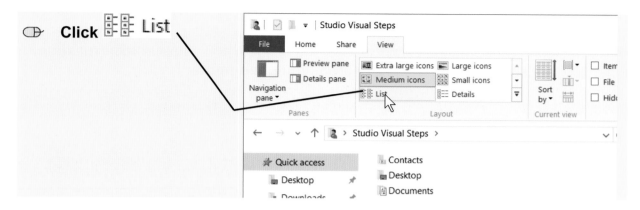

It really will **not be necessary** for you to read all the information in the screen shots in this book. Always use the screen shots in combination with the image you see on your own computer screen.

1. Basic Computer Knowledge

The computer can give you a lot of pleasure. It is so easy to stay in touch with your friends, children or grandchildren with email, for example. And what about all the interesting websites you can visit while surfing the Internet?

On the other hand, it has become more and more of a necessity these days to have some basic computer skills in order to participate in modern day-to-day life. Such things as managing a bank account or making travel arrangements are mostly done online using the Internet. You can carry out all these practical and useful tasks if you have some basic computer skills.

In this chapter you will read about opening and closing programs, the Internet, *Mail*, the folder window in *Windows*, and the *Settings* app. You need this app to customize your computer's settings. By working through this chapter, you can check your level of basic computer knowledge, and possibly expand it.

In this chapter you will read about:

- opening and closing programs;
- the Internet;
- email;
- *File Explorer*;
- changing settings.

1.1 Opening and Closing Programs

Almost everything you do on a computer requires the use of a computer program. A computer program is usually just called a program, or an app. A computer program is a set of commands or instructions that tells the computer what to do in order to carry out certain tasks. There are many different kinds of programs and apps. The *Paint* graphics program, the text editing program called *WordPad* and the *Solitaire* game are just a few examples.

In this book you will come across two different names for a computer program: program and app. *App* is short for *application*, which actually means program. So an app is just another name for a program.

The Start menu provides access to the programs and apps on your computer. In order to open the Start menu, you use the Start button:

Click the Start button

Once you have clicked the Start button you will see the Start menu:

Name of the user account:

On the right you will see square and rectangular icons. These are called *tiles*:

Most frequently used programs and apps:

File Explorer window and *Settings*:

Options to restart or shut down *Windows*:

All programs and apps:

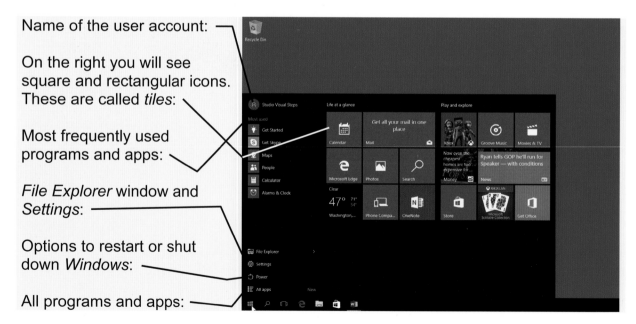

The Start menu may look a bit different on your computer. You can adjust the Start menu the way you wish. This will be discussed later in this book.

The Start menu is a combination of programs and apps and *Windows* functions on the left side and tiles on the right side.

The evenly colored icons on the right side of the Start menu are called tiles. A tile can open a program, a website, a setting or a folder. Initially, you will see tiles for apps in the Start menu, but you can also add new tiles for other programs, files, folders, and even settings.

An app is a program designed for use on a tablet or smartphone. But in *Windows 10* you can also use apps on the computer. One of the main differences between the two, is that an app is often less extensive than a full blown program and a lot of apps only work if you have a working Internet connection.

You can open installed programs and apps directly from the Start menu. You can search for a program in the *All apps* menu. In this long, scrollable list, you will find all the apps installed on your computer. In this example we will look for the program called *WordPad* and open it:

Click ⊞

Click **All apps**

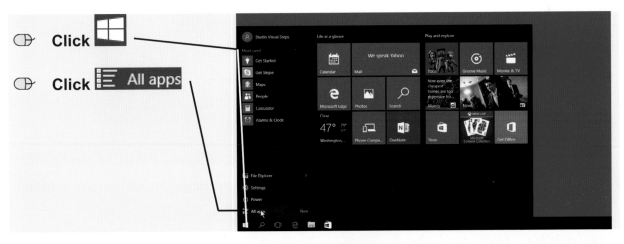

You see a list of all the programs and apps on your computer in alphabetical order: ———

You can scroll through the programs with the scroll box:

Drag the scroll box downwards

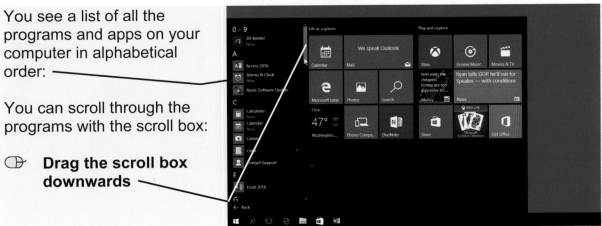

You will see more apps:

Some programs are placed in a collective folder, along with other programs and files. You can recognize these by the

folder and the ⌄ arrow:

A number of programs that come with *Windows 10*, such as *WordPad*, have been grouped together in a folder called *Windows Accessories*.

☞ **If necessary, drag the scroll box downwards**

☞ **Click**

Windows Accessories

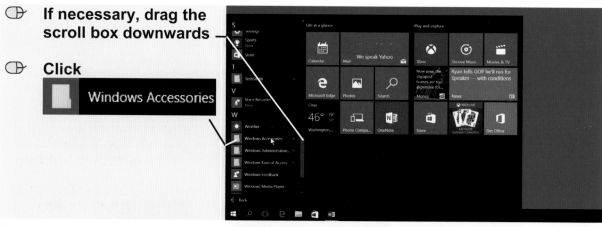

You will see the programs in the *Windows Accessories* folder:

To open a program:

☞ **If necessary, drag the scroll box downwards a little more**

☞ **Click** **WordPad**

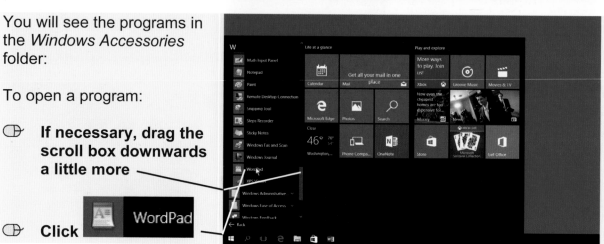

WordPad will be opened on the desktop:

On the taskbar you will see a

taskbar button 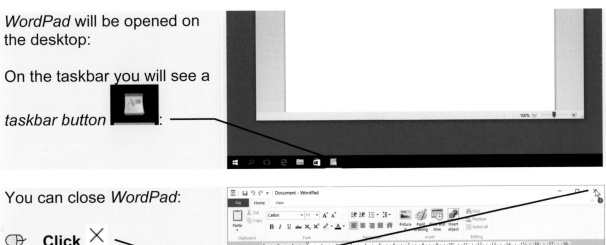 :

You can close *WordPad*:

⊕ **Click** ✕

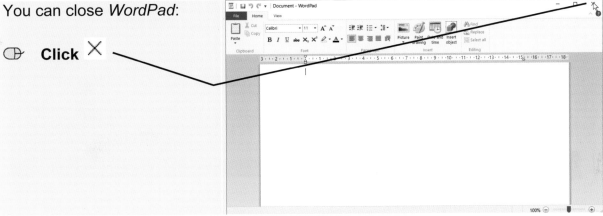

You can also use the search function on the taskbar to find programs, apps and files on your computer and on the Internet. You can open an app with the search function:

⊕ **Click**

HELP! I see a search box.

If you see a search box on the taskbar instead of , then click the search box
Search the web and Windows.

Type: `weather`

You will see search results in different categories:

Programs and apps:

Settings in *Windows*:

Search in documents and files:

To open the app:

Click

Weather
Trusted Windows Store

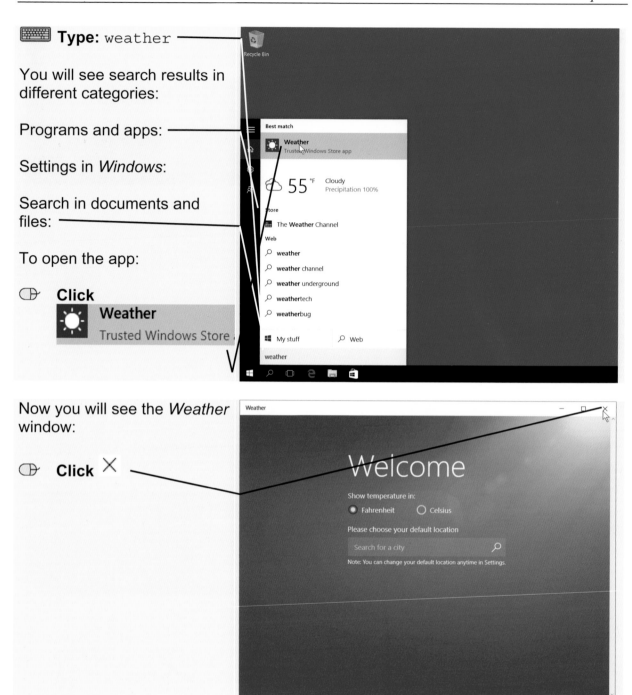

Now you will see the *Weather* window:

Click ✕

The window is now closed. Notice that the taskbar button for this program has disappeared from the taskbar. The program has been completely closed.

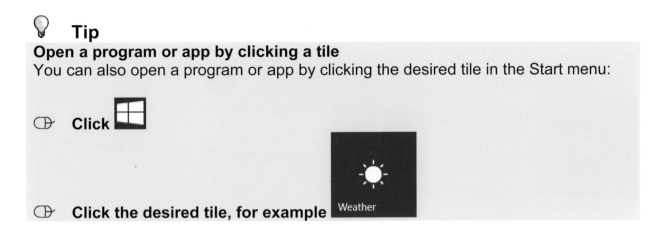

Tip
Open a program or app by clicking a tile
You can also open a program or app by clicking the desired tile in the Start menu:

☞ **Click**

☞ **Click the desired tile, for example**   Weather

1.2 Internet

You can find lots of information on the Internet. It is very easy to use the Internet. Just type a web address (URL) in the address bar, for example, type

www.visualsteps.com, then press the **Enter** key and the website will appear on the screen. You can use other hyperlinks to surf from one web page to another. In this section you will read about some important options and functions of the *Edge* program. *Edge* is *Windows 10* default browser program for viewing pages on the Internet.

It is important to check whether the websites you visit are safe. You can adjust several safety settings in the *Edge* browser program. In *Chapter 5 Safely Using Email and Purchasing Items on the Internet* you can read more about these settings.

This is how you open *Edge*:

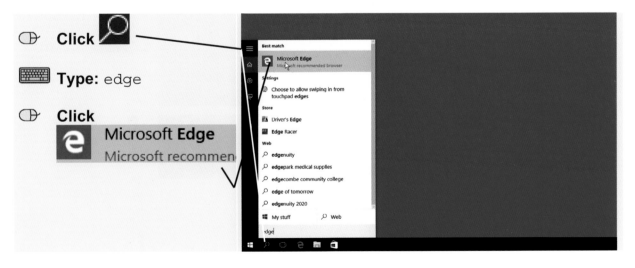

☞ **Click**

⌨ **Type:** edge

☞ **Click**

Microsoft Edge
Microsoft recommen

Tip

Other ways to open Edge

You can also launch *Edge* by clicking the taskbar button 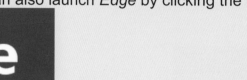, or by clicking the tile

in the Start menu.

Your screen will be filled with a *home page*:

This will usually be a page with news items. Along with some news, you may also see several advertisements on this page.

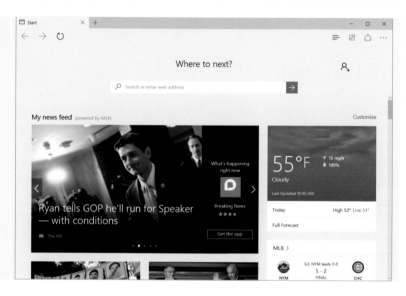

By typing a web address in the address bar and then

Enter

pressing ![Enter key], you can open web pages:

Initially, you may see the address bar in the middle of the window.

The *Edge* window contains a number of important buttons (also called icons):

Arrow buttons will take you back to the previously visited web page, or forward to the next web page:

There are also buttons with which you can display favorites ☆ / ☰, take web notes 🖉, or share a web page 🖒. The button on the far right ··· opens a list of other settings and options:

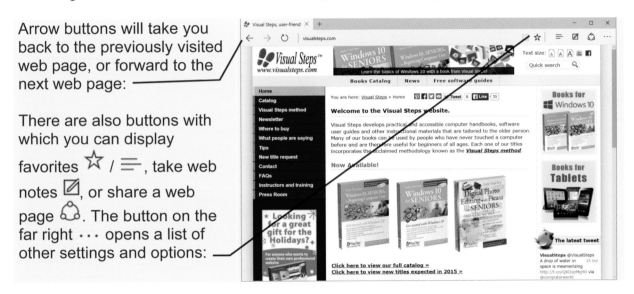

You can open multiple web pages by using tabs. To open a new tab, you simply click the ➕ button, type the web address, and the second web page will be opened. You can switch between the web pages by clicking the tabs.

Take a look now at the options available with the Hub ☰ button:

👈 **Click** ☰

The star button allows you to view your favorites:
Favorites are the web addresses you have saved.

The Reading List button ≣ lets you open the reading list. You can add pages to this list and read them later on offline without being connected to the Internet.

The History button 🕘 lets you view your browsing history. It shows you a list of hyperlinks from the websites you have recently visited.

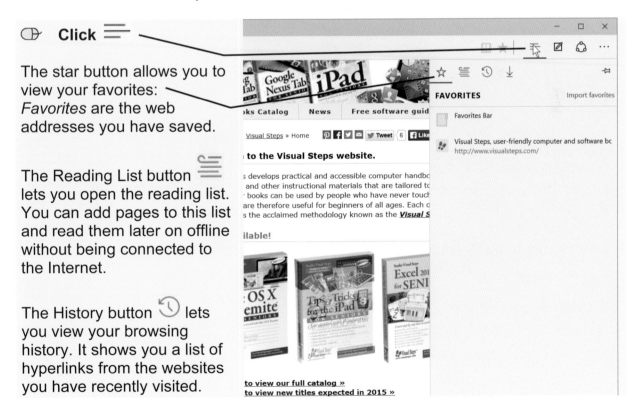

Some of the functions, such as printing or zooming in and out, can be accessed by clicking the • • • (More actions) button:

Click • • •

You see lots of additional options when you click this button:

You will learn more about this further on in the book.

You close the window:

In the upper right corner of the window:

Click ✕

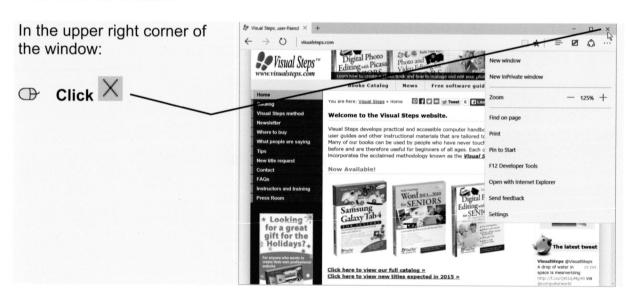

In later chapters of this book you can read more about using the Internet.

1.3 Email

Email has simplified many forms of communication. Sending and receiving messages through an email program or online web service has become especially popular in the business community, but also in private life. In this book we will discuss the *Mail* app. The *Mail* app is one of the standard apps installed on your *Windows 10* computer.

This is how you open *Mail*:

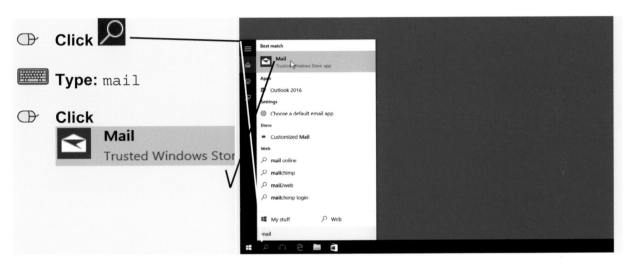

You may see this window:

You will see one or more email accounts you have set up:

If necessary, click the desired account

If necessary, click Ready to go

If you do not see an account, you can set it up by clicking Add account, if you wish:

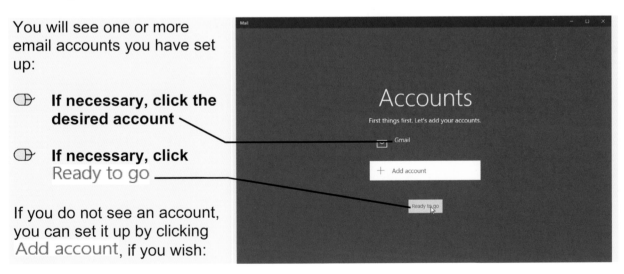

Below you will find a summary of the components in the *Mail* window. Your own window may look a bit different:

On the left side you will see the message list. This contains the sent and received email messages:

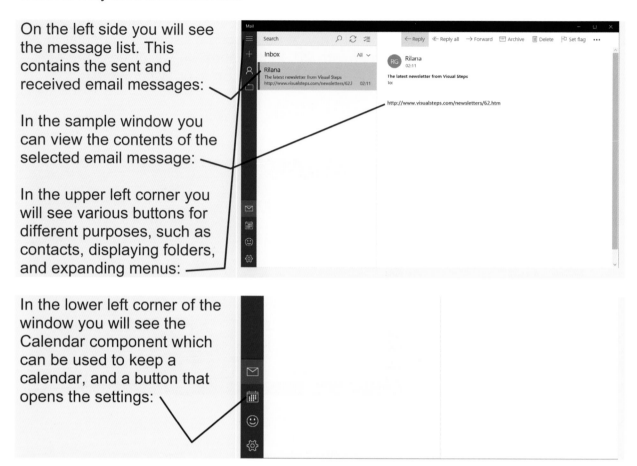

In the sample window you can view the contents of the selected email message:

In the upper left corner you will see various buttons for different purposes, such as contacts, displaying folders, and expanding menus:

In the lower left corner of the window you will see the Calendar component which can be used to keep a calendar, and a button that opens the settings:

✖ HELP! My window looks different.

If your window looks different, you can widen the window by dragging the window border. Then you will see a window more similar to the one above.

Your computer is probably set to automatically retrieve new email messages, but you can also click the ⟳ button to fetch new messages manually.

You can compose and send email messages. Take a closer look at the window:

In the upper left corner of the window:

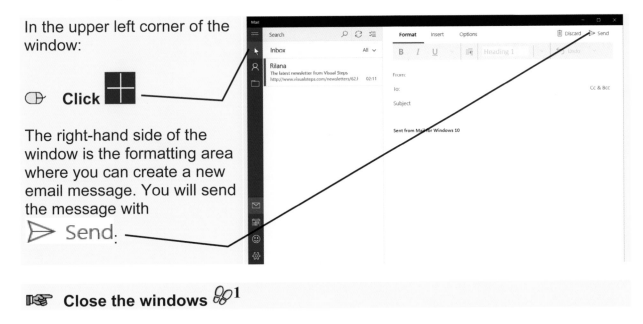

Click ▦

The right-hand side of the window is the formatting area where you can create a new email message. You will send the message with

▷ Send.

☞ **Close the windows** ✂¹

1.4 File Explorer

The program with which you can view the content of your computer and the connected devices in a folder window is called *Windows File Explorer*. In *File Explorer*, all the files are arranged in folders. A folder is a storage place where you can manage files. Every file on your computer is stored in a folder, and folders may also contain other (sub)folders.

Windows 10 also contains libraries. In a library, you can link folders and files. Then these folders and files will be displayed in the library. In this way you can easily find your files.

In *File Explorer* you can copy and move files or folders, and create new folders and libraries. You can also adjust the view according to your own preferences. In *Chapter 2 Folders and Files* you will learn more about this function.

You can open the *File Explorer* window like this:

On the taskbar:

Click 🗀

In the *File Explorer* window, you will see a number of standard folders that *Windows 10* has created on your computer:

This window is also called a *folder window.*

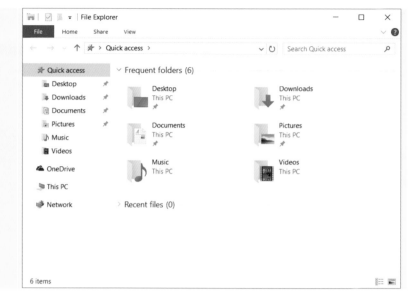

You can open a folder or a file by double-clicking it. If it is a file, it will then be opened in the corresponding program.

☞ **Close** *File Explorer* 👣¹

1.5 Adjusting Settings

In *Chapter 3 Making Useful Settings* you can read how to adjust various settings. The *Settings* app is the app you use to make adjustments. In this app, all sorts of *Windows* settings can be changed, such as hardware settings, security settings, and screen display settings.

This is how you open *Settings:*

The *Settings* window will be opened:

The window is filled with all sorts of subjects, arranged by category:

Each category is indicated by an icon:

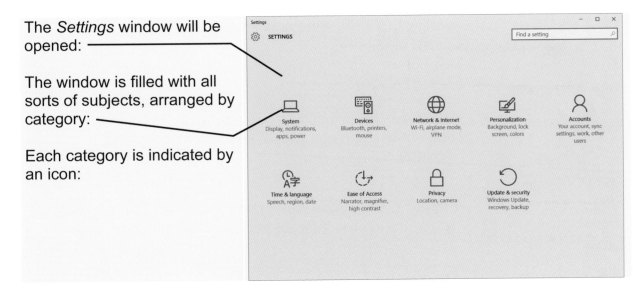

These are the various components:

System

Here you can find various settings for the screen, notifications, and apps.

Devices

Here you can view settings for printers, scanners, and the mouse, for instance. You can also determine what action to take when you insert a USB stick, for example.

Network & Internet

Here you can configure the Internet settings on your computer, and also find information regarding the amount of data you have used.

Accounts

Here you can manage user accounts and add a new account. You can also determine how you sign in and which components are to be synchronized when you sign in with a *Microsoft* account.

Personalization

This component contains the settings for the desktop background and the colors used in the borders of windows and the Start menu, among other things.

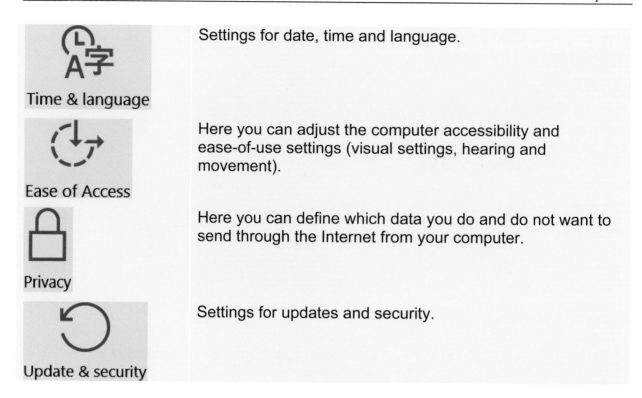

Time & language	Settings for date, time and language.
Ease of Access	Here you can adjust the computer accessibility and ease-of-use settings (visual settings, hearing and movement).
Privacy	Here you can define which data you do and do not want to send through the Internet from your computer.
Update & security	Settings for updates and security.

When you change settings, be sure to pay attention to the settings you select. Always remember the original setting, so you can revert back to it, if necessary.

In *Chapter 3 Making Useful Settings* you can read more on this subject.

☞ **Close** *Settings* ✔️[1]

In this chapter, you have read information about some of the basic but important operations necessary to work with your computer. In the next chapters we will expand your knowledge further.

1.6 Background Information

Dictionary

App	Short for *application*, which means a program. Originally, an app was a program designed for use on a tablet or a smartphone. But in *Windows 10* you can also use apps on the computer.
Browser, Web browser	A program used to display web pages and to navigate the Internet. *Edge* is a web browser.
Edge	Microsoft's own web browser program.
Email	Short for *electronic mail*. These are messages sent and received through the Internet.
File	The generic name for everything saved on the computer. A file can be a program, a data file with names, text you have written, a photo, a video or a piece of music. Actually, everything located on the hard drive of your computer is called a *file*.
File Explorer	The program that allows you to access, save and manage your files and folders.
Folder	A folder is a container that helps you organize your files. Every file on your computer is stored in a folder, and folders can also hold other folders.
Home page	The web page that is displayed each time you open *Edge*.
Hyperlink, Link	A hyperlink or link is a navigational element on a web page that when clicked lets the user browse to a new web page or to an area further down on the same web page. A hyperlink can be text or images such as buttons, icons or pictures.
Internet	A network of computer networks which operates worldwide using a common set of communication protocols. The part of the Internet that most people are familiar with, is the World Wide Web (WWW). Also called web.

- Continue on the next page -

Library	A library looks like a folder, but the difference is that in a folder, the files are actually stored there. There are no files stored in a library, but only the links to various folders. A library displays files that are actually stored in several different folders distributed all over the computer.
Maximize	Enlarging a window, so it will fill the entire screen.
Microsoft account	A *Microsoft* account consists of an email address ending in hotmail.com, outlook.com or live.com in combination with a password.
Minimize	Reducing the size of a window so it does not take up any screen space. You will then only see the program button on the taskbar.
Program	A set of instructions that a computer uses to perform a specific task, such as word processing or calculating.
Settings	In *Settings* you can change all sort of settings for your computer.
Start button	You can open the Start menu with the Start button.
Start menu	The Start menu is a gateway to the programs, apps, folders and settings on your computer.
Surfing	Displaying one web page after the other by clicking various hyperlinks.
Tab	Part of the *Edge* window on which you can open a new website or web page.
User account	A collection of data that provides information to *Windows* about which files and folders you are allowed to access, which changes you can make to your computer and its settings, and which personal preferences you have. By having a user account you can share a computer with other people and still have your own unique files and settings.
Website	A website is a collection of interconnected web pages, typically common to a particular domain name on the on the Internet.
Window	A rectangular box or frame on a computer screen in which programs and content appear.
Windows 10	The operating system that manages all the other programs and apps on the computer. It allows you to save files, enables the use of programs and apps, and lets you use other devices, such as a keyboard, mouse and printer.

Source: Windows Help

2. Folders and Files

In this chapter you will learn how to work with the *files, folders,* and *libraries* stored on your computer. A file is a collective term for everything that is saved on the computer. It might be a program, an address book, a text document, or a photo.

If you have many stacks of documents on your desk, it becomes much harder to find the document you are looking for. That is why paper documents are often stored in a filing cabinet. By arranging the documents in a logical order, finding a specific document becomes a lot easier. The folders on your computer have a similar function.

A folder does not only contain files, but can contain other folders as well. A folder that is saved within another folder is called a *subfolder*. You can create as many subfolders as you like, and in each subfolder you can save any number of files and additional subfolders.

In this chapter you will also learn how to work with libraries. The advantage of a library is that you can link folders and files so that they can be displayed all in one place. In this way you can easily find your files.

In this chapter you will learn how to:

- use *File Explorer* and create a new folder;
- adjust the view of the *File Explorer* window, the folders, and the files;
- copy, move, and delete folders and files;
- create and save a new file;
- change the name of a folder and a file;
- empty the *Recycle Bin*;
- create a compressed folder;
- add and delete files;
- connect a USB stick or external hard drive;
- copy files to a USB stick or external hard drive;
- delete a USB stick or external hard drive;
- create and delete a library;
- about *OneDrive*.

Please note:

In order to work through all the exercises in this chapter, you will need to use the practice files made for this book. You can download these files from the website accompanying the book **www.visualsteps.com/your10computer**
In *Appendix B Downloading the Practice Files* you can read how to do this.

2.1 Opening File Explorer

By opening a folder in *File Explorer* you can work with the folders and files saved on your computer. In that window you can delete, copy, and move files and folders. The program that is used to view the folder window with its folders and files is called *File Explorer*. This program will automatically open when you open a folder. Fortunately, you do not need to arrange all the items on your computer yourself. *Windows* has already created a number of standard folders for you. Among these are: *Documents*, *Pictures*, *Music*, *Videos*, and *Downloads*.

You can open your *Personal folder*, in which the folders mentioned above are all arranged. First you open *File Explorer*:

On the left-hand side of the taskbar:

👆 **Click**

You can now see that the *File Explorer* window shows the most important folders on the computer:

This window is also called a *folder window*.

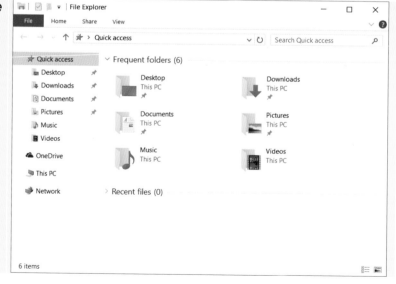

You can start by working with your *Personal folder*. The window with the content of your *Personal folder* will then be opened. In this window you can find the folders that have already been created by *Windows*. The content of this folder will vary on each computer.

Click

Click your profile name

In this example, it is 'Studio Visual Steps'.

You will see a window with the content of your *Personal folder*. Here you find the folders that have already been created for you:

The content of the *Personal folder* can be different on each computer.

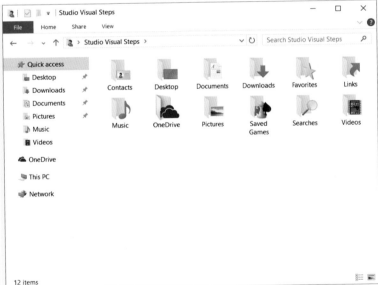

2.2 The Ribbon

Just as in *WordPad*, you will be working with the ribbon located in the top section of the window. You can think of the ribbon as a very extensive taskbar containing all of the options and commands you need to manage your files and folders. You cannot see all of these options at once. The ribbon is organized into tabs. By clicking a given tab, the tab will expand downward and all of the tab's commands will become visible.

The window consists of a number of tabs:

Take a look at one of these tabs:

☞ **Click the** Home **tab**

The corresponding groups and their commands are displayed:

☞ **Click an empty area of the window**

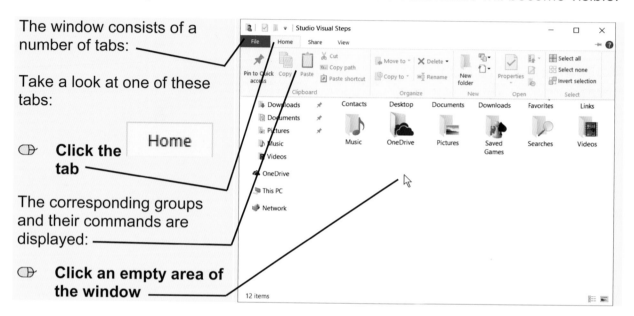

The ribbon will disappear. It is also possible to show the ribbon permanently:

At the top right of the window:

☞ **Click** ⌄

The ribbon is displayed permanently:

You will see the options of the Home **tab:**

In this book the window of *File Explorer* will look like this with the ribbon fully visible:

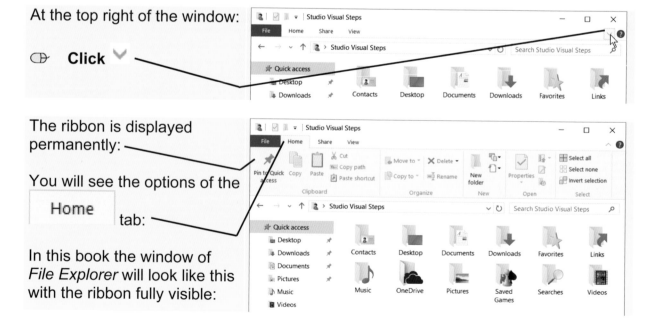

2.3 Changing the Display of the Window

There are several ways to view your folders in the window of *File Explorer*. Take a look at the display settings of your window:

Click the ⬚ View ⬚ tab

Place the pointer on ⊞ List

You will immediately see an example of this display:

Click ⊞ List

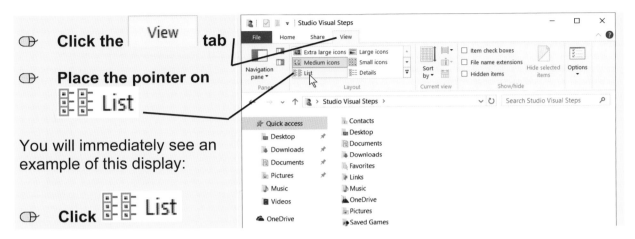

The display for this window is set to List. A blue frame appears around the option ⊞ List. This means that this option is active.

Just take a look at another view:

Click ▦ Large icons

Now the icons are displayed in a larger size:

Change the display back to medium icons:

Click ▦ Medium icons

Now the icons are displayed once again in a medium size:

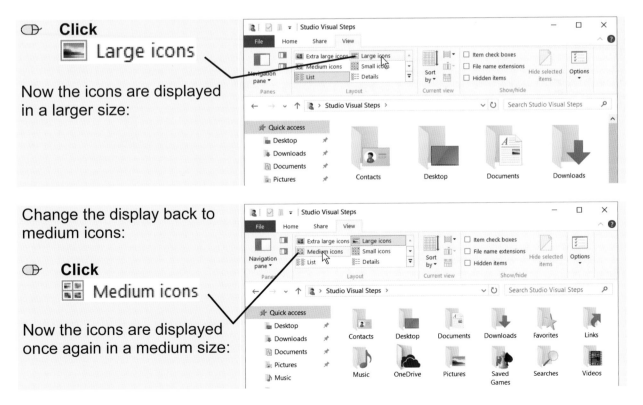

There are more options you can use to change the display of the folder. With

(Preview pane) and   (Details pane) you can add a preview pane or details pane to the window. Take a look at what happens when you add the details pane:

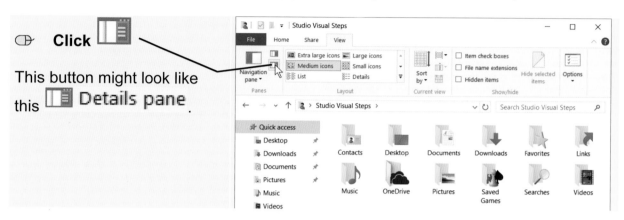

☞ **Click**

This button might look like

this   **Details pane** .

The details pane will appear on the right-hand side of the window. A blue frame

appears around the option   . This means that this option is active.

The details pane: ⎯⎯⎯⎯⎯⎯

When you select a file, you can see information about it in the details pane:

Now you can hide the details pane:

☞ **Click**

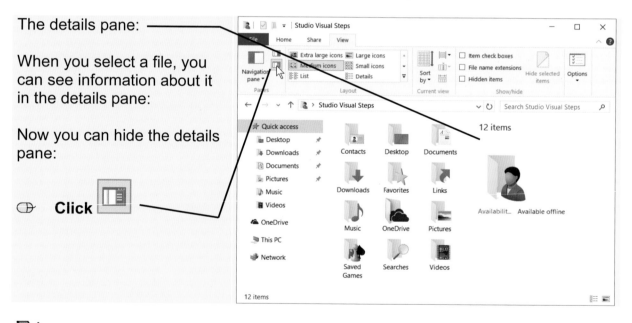

🢂 **Please note:**

Do not click   when there's no blue frame around this option. Click it only when

you see a blue frame   .

The window on your computer should look the same as the window below:

You are going to open a folder:

⊕ **Double-click**

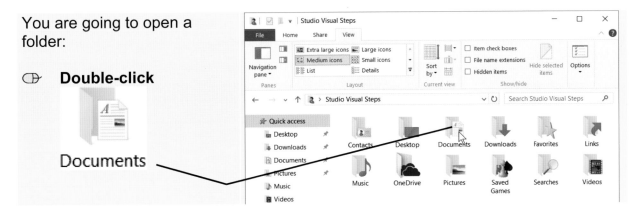

Documents

2.4 The Various Parts of the File Explorer Window

In addition to showing the contents of the folder, a window has specific areas that are designed to help you navigate to the files and folders on your computer and work with them more easily. Take a look now:

In the navigation pane you will see a number of folders that are present on your computer:

The Quick access list is a list of recent or frequently used folders. It is always visible: ✓

The address bar indicates which folder is open:

All the files in this folder are displayed in the file list:

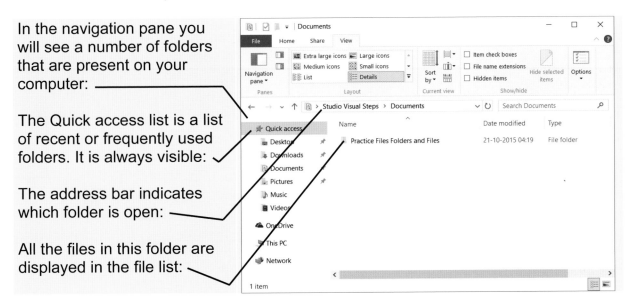

By using the navigation pane on the left side, you can quickly navigate to any folder on your computer. When you click an item or folder in the navigation pane, you will see the contents of that item or folder you clicked displayed in the file list, the main portion of the window.

In the previous section, you changed the display of your *Personal folder*. Now you have opened the *Documents* folder and you see that the contents are displayed differently. In *File Explorer*, you can change the view of how the files look in any window. For example, if you set the view to medium icons, your files will become more easily recognizable:

⊕ **Click**
     Medium icons

The display of the window will be changed:

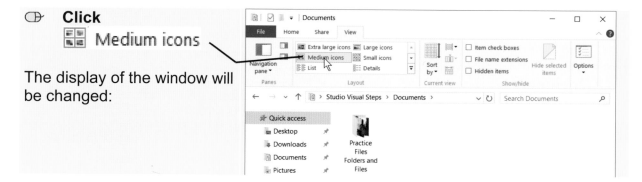

The *Documents* folder contains the *Practice Files Folders and Files* folder.

2.5 Navigating in the File Explorer Window

A folder window does not just show the content of a folder. It contains specific sections that will help you browse through the folders on your computer. For example, the navigation pane on the left-hand side will help you quickly navigate to certain folders on the computer. When you click a folder in the navigation pane, the content of the folder will be displayed in the file list, and some of the components of the window will change:

⊕ **By** **This PC**, **click**

⊕ **Click** **Documents**

Now you see the content of the *Documents* folder. The address bar has changed:

The toolbar at the top of the window has changed as well.

Please note: in your own window you may see different files here.

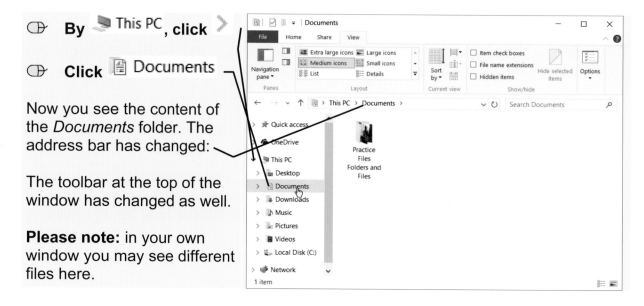

HELP! My view is different.

Are the files and folders not displayed as icons?

⊕ **Click**

Open the practice files folder:

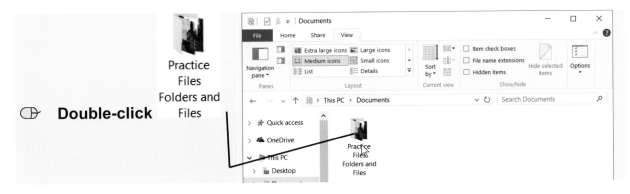

Practice
Files
Folders and
⊕ **Double-click** Files

You have opened the practice files folder. You can navigate between the folders you have previously opened. For this purpose, you will find two buttons in the upper left corner of the *File Explorer* window. To go back to the previous folder:

⊕ **Click** ←

You can also use ↑.

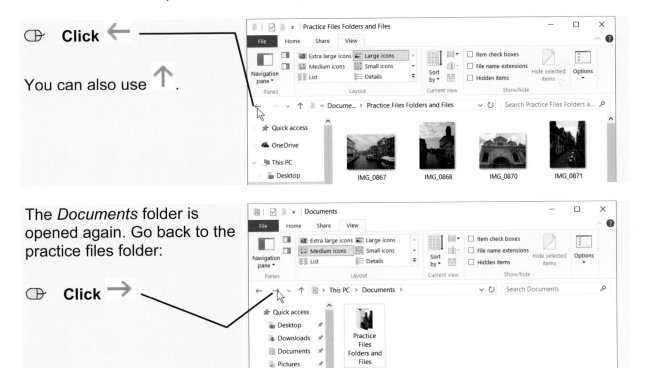

The *Documents* folder is opened again. Go back to the practice files folder:

⊕ **Click** →

2.6 Creating a New Folder

A folder is a container that helps you organize your files. Every file on your computer is stored in a folder, and folders can also hold other folders. Folders located inside other folders are often called *subfolders*. You can add new folders yourself. This can be handy for example if you want to separate the photos taken on different vacations.

With an eye towards maintaining order on your computer, in the following exercise you will be adding a new subfolder to the *Practice Files Folders and Files* folder. You may have already saved a number of documents on your computer in the *Documents* folder. After you have worked through this chapter, you will be able to arrange, sort and group these documents to your own liking.

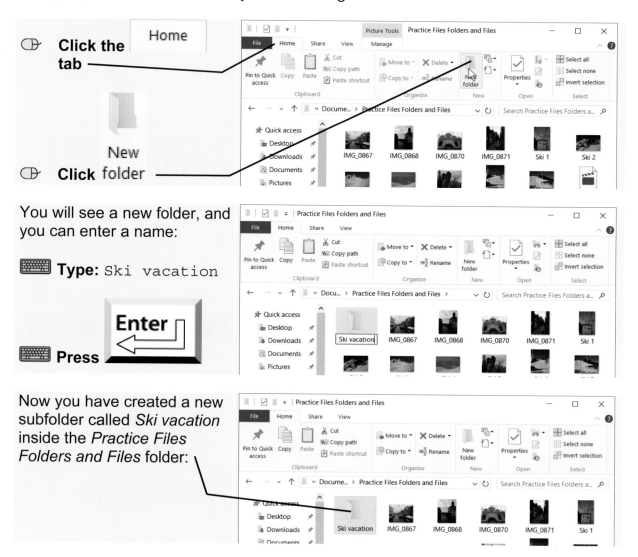

Click the tab

Click folder

You will see a new folder, and you can enter a name:

Type: Ski vacation

Press Enter

Now you have created a new subfolder called *Ski vacation* inside the *Practice Files Folders and Files* folder:

You can use this folder to save the photos and the video from the ski vacation.

2.7 Copying Folders and Files

You can easily copy files. For instance, when you want to edit a certain photo, it can be good practice to create a copy of the photo first. In the next step you will be copying a photo from the ski vacation. Remember the following rule: select first, act later. You can select a file by clicking the file's icon or its name.

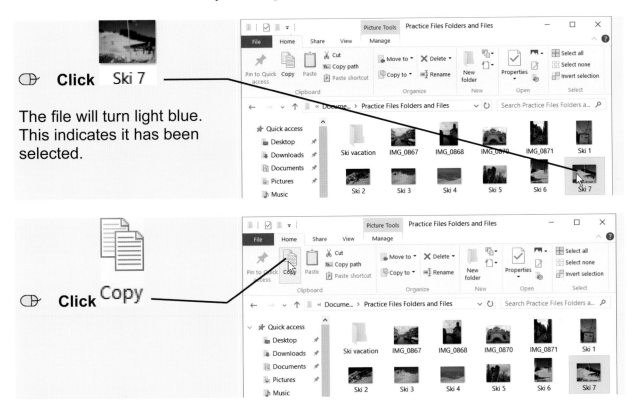

☞ **Click** Ski 7

The file will turn light blue. This indicates it has been selected.

☞ **Click** Copy

Now you have told *Windows* that you want to copy the file. The next step is pasting the copied file:

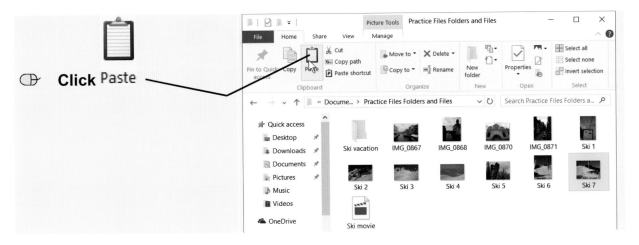

☞ **Click** Paste

The file has been copied:

Since you have not opened another folder, the file has been copied to the same folder.

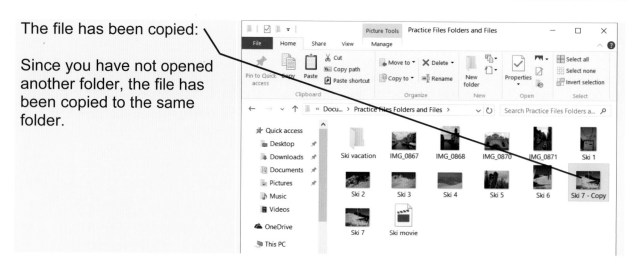

Now there is a copy of the file named Ski 7 - Copy in the same folder. Notice that the word 'Copy' has been automatically added to the name. This is because files with duplicate names are not allowed inside the same folder. Even though the content of the file is the same, the name of the file has to be different if it is located in the same folder.

💡 Tip

Another way of copying a file
You can also copy a file by right-clicking it.

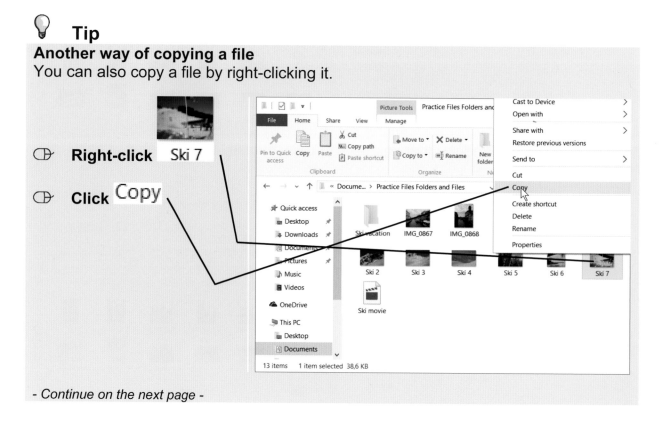

⊕ **Right-click** Ski 7

⊕ **Click** Copy

- Continue on the next page -

👉 **Right-click a blank section** ——

You will see a menu:

👉 **Click** Paste

The file has been copied.

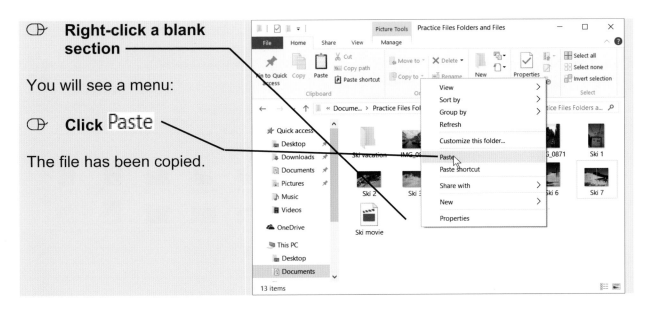

In this section you have learned how to copy a file. Copying a folder is done in the same way.

2.8 Moving Folders and Files

It is also possible to 'cut' a file or a folder, and paste it into a different folder. The file or folder is then moved to the other folder. In this section you can practice doing this by moving a file. The method for moving a folder is exactly the same.

👉 **Right-click** Ski 7 - Copy

You will see a menu:

👉 **Click** Cut

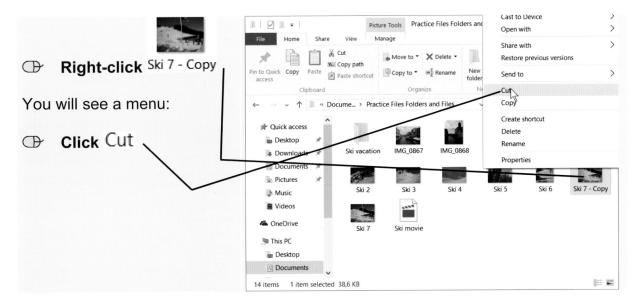

You can paste this file into the *Ski vacation* folder. First, open the *Ski vacation* folder:

Double-click

Ski vacation

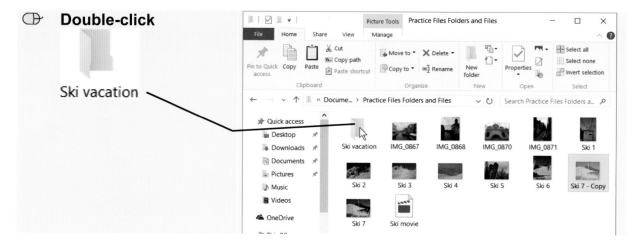

You will see the *Ski vacation* folder:

Right-click a blank section

You will see a menu:

Click Paste

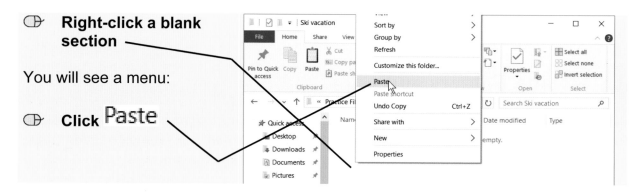

The file has been pasted into the folder. Now you can return to the *Practice Files Folders and Files* folder to see if the file has been moved out of this folder. You can do this in various ways. In this example you will be opening the folder from the address bar:

Click
Practice Files Folders and ...

The *Ski 7 - Copy* file has disappeared:

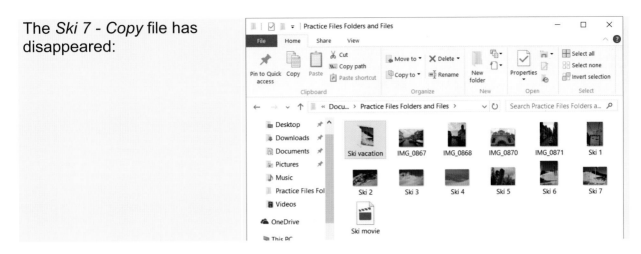

You can also move files and folders to a different folder by dragging them. Just give it a try:

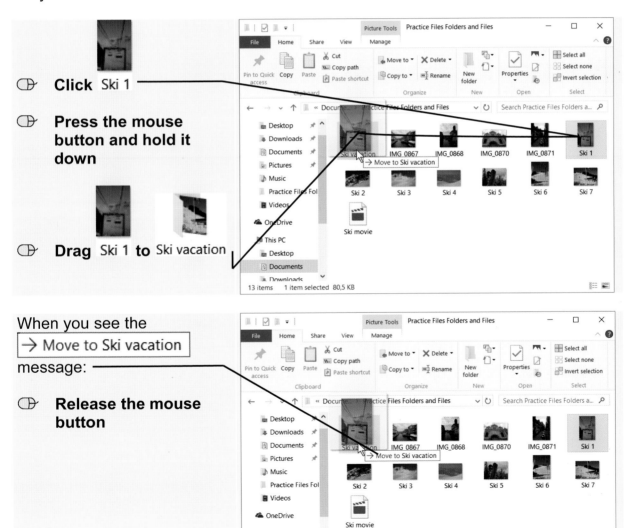

⊕ **Click** Ski 1

⊕ **Press the mouse button and hold it down**

⊕ **Drag** Ski 1 **to** Ski vacation

When you see the

→ Move to Ski vacation

message:

⊕ **Release the mouse button**

☞ **Open the *Ski vacation* folder** ✂4

You will see that the file has been pasted into the *Ski vacation* folder:

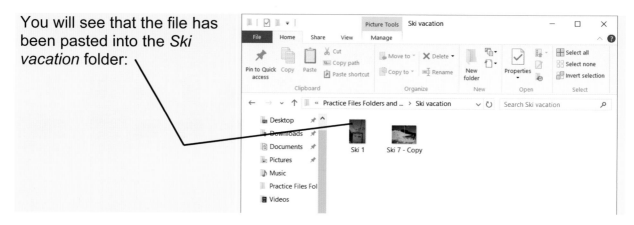

You can even move multiple files or folders all at once. You can try this with the video and another photo from the ski vacation. You can move them to the *Ski vacation* folder:

☞ **Open the *Practice Files Folders and Files* folder** ✂4

🖰 **Click**   Ski 2

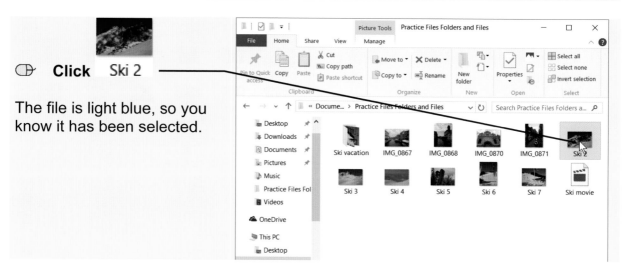

The file is light blue, so you know it has been selected.

By clicking you can only select one file at a time. But you can select multiple files or

folders by using the **Ctrl** key. This key is used together with the mouse. The

Ski 2   file is still selected.

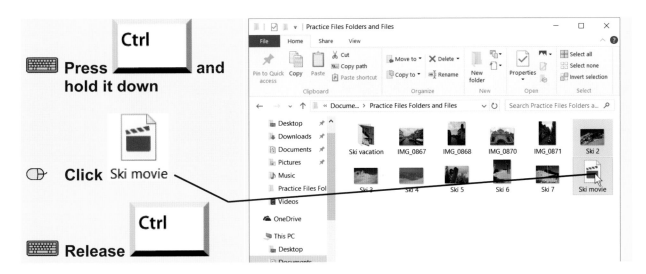

Now both the photo and the video have been selected:

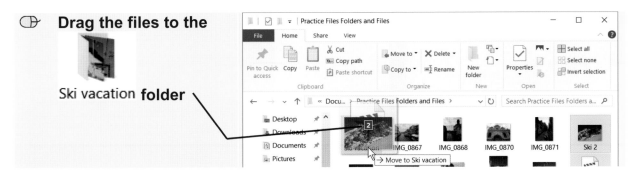

You can also select multiple files or folders that are adjacent to each other on the same row. You can do this with the last couple of photos from the ski vacation:

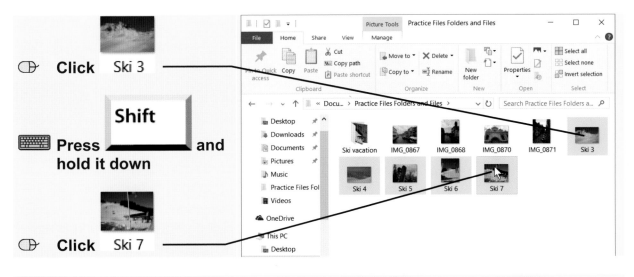

☞ **Move the photos to the *Ski vacation* folder** ✂️⁵

2.9 Creating and Saving a New File

If you would like to write something about the ski vacation, you can create a document and save it with the pictures. You can use *WordPad* for this, or a different text editing program. Since you will not need the *File Explorer* window for a while, you can minimize it:

Click —

Open *WordPad*:

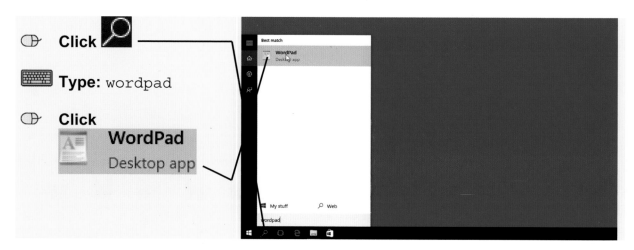

Click 🔍

Type: wordpad

Click

WordPad
Desktop app

If you are actually arranging your own vacation photos, you could write something about the places you went to, etcetera. In this example you can just type a short sentence.

Type: Our ski
vacation in
Austria

Save this document in the *Ski vacation* folder:

Click File

Click 💾 Save

You will see the *Save As* window. You want to save the document in the *Ski vacation* subfolder. You will need to open this subfolder first:

Double-click

Practice Files Folders and Files

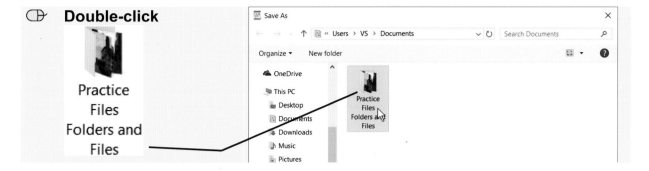

The folder with the practice files is opened:

Double-click

Ski vacation

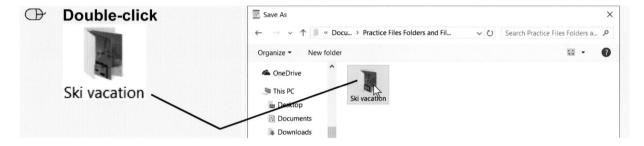

Now the *Ski vacation* folder will be opened. You will see the Ski vacation folder name in the address bar. At the bottom of the window you will see the file name. In this case the file is called *Document*. This is the default name entered by the program.

Here is how you change the name:

Click the box by File name:

Press Delete

Type: report

Click Save

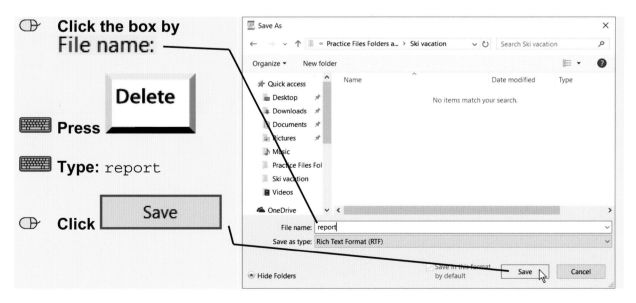

Now the file called *report* is saved in the *Ski vacation* folder. You can close *WordPad*:

Click ✕

Now you can open the window of the *Practice Files Folders and Files* folder on the taskbar again, and check to see if the file has been saved in this folder.

Click

Double-click

Ski vacation

In the address bar you will see that the *Ski vacation* folder is opened:

In the file list you will see your saved *WordPad* file, named

report:

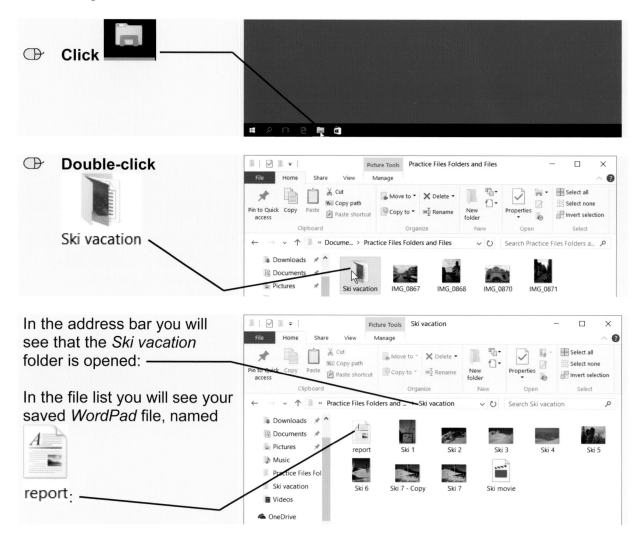

2.10 Changing Folder and File Names

Sometimes, you will want to rename a file or a folder. For example, you may want to rename the video from the ski vacation:

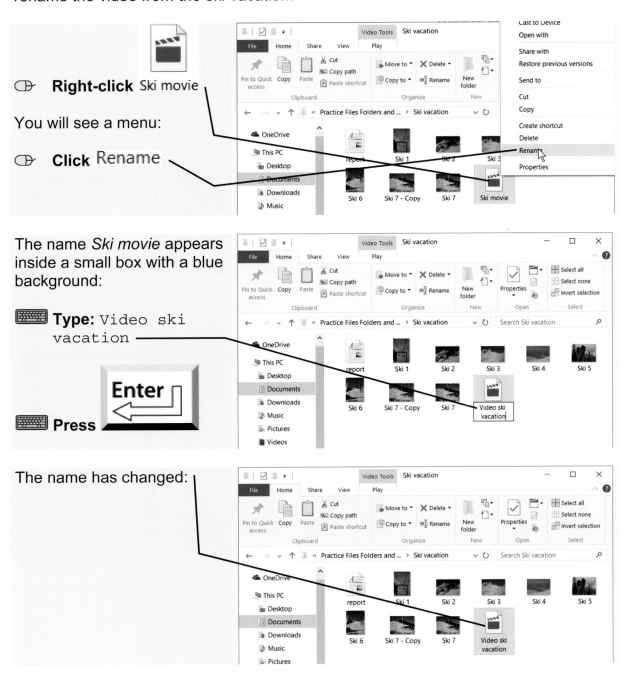

👉 **Right-click** Ski movie

You will see a menu:

👉 **Click** Rename

The name *Ski movie* appears inside a small box with a blue background:

⌨ **Type:** Video ski vacation

⌨ **Press** Enter

The name has changed:

You have just changed the name of a file. Changing the name of a folder is done in exactly the same way.

2.11 Deleting Folders and Files

It is better to delete superfluous files and folders. This will not only help to maintain order on your computer but makes it easier to glimpse through and find the files and folders you are looking for. You can practice deleting with the copy of the *Ski 7* photo in the *Ski vacation* folder:

⊕   **Click** Ski 7 - Copy

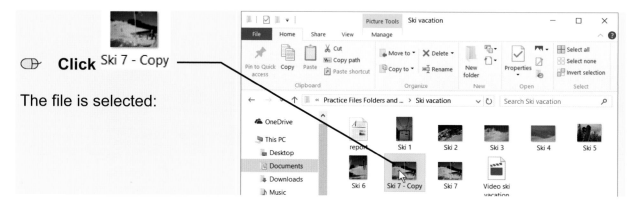

The file is selected:

Now you can delete the file.

⊕   **If necessary, click the**
    Home **tab**

⊕   **Click** ✖ Delete

You may see ✖.

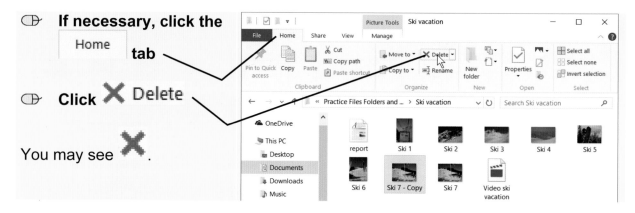

The file has disappeared from the *Ski vacation* folder. However, deleted files will not be completely deleted right away. As a safety measure, deleted files are moved to the *Recycle Bin* first. Only when you empty this bin, will the file be permanently removed. As long as a file is stored in the *Recycle Bin*, you can still retrieve it later on, if you wish. You will be doing that in the next section.

 Tip

Delete a folder
You can also delete a folder. First select the folder to be deleted by clicking it. Then you can delete the folder in the same way as the photo.

Please note:

Only delete your own files
Take care when deleting files. Only delete the files you have created yourself. If you have not created a file yourself, you may not even be able to delete it.
You cannot delete a file (or the folder that contains the file) if this file is still opened in a program. If you were to try this, you will see a warning message. Close the file first, and then try again.
Never delete files or folders belonging to programs you do not use. Deleting program files needs to be done in a different way.

2.12 Empty the Recycle Bin

All the files you delete from your computer are moved to the *Recycle Bin*. You can open this bin and view its content.

☞ **Minimize the *File Explorer* window** ^{6}

On the desktop:

👆 **Double-click** Recycle Bin

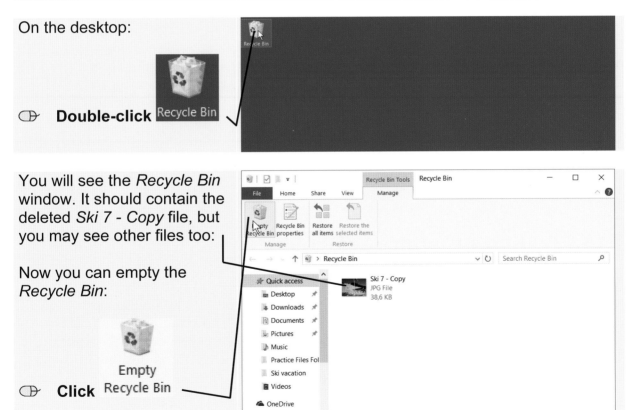

You will see the *Recycle Bin* window. It should contain the deleted *Ski 7 - Copy* file, but you may see other files too:

Now you can empty the *Recycle Bin*:

👆 **Click** Empty Recycle Bin

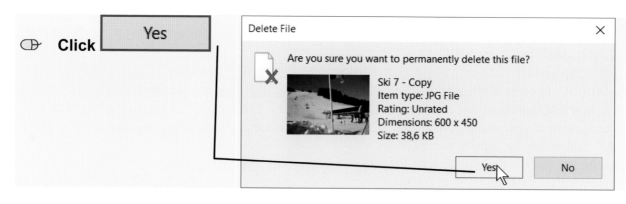

Click Yes

Delete File   ×

Are you sure you want to permanently delete this file?

Ski 7 - Copy
Item type: JPG File
Rating: Unrated
Dimensions: 600 x 450
Size: 38,6 KB

Yes   No

Now the file has been permanently deleted and can no longer be restored.

☞ **Close the *Recycle Bin* window** 1

💡 **Tip**

Restore an item from the Recycle Bin
Did you perhaps delete the wrong file, or on second thought want to restore a

deleted item? To restore all items all at once, you can use this button: Restore all items .
If you would like to restore one or more selected items, you will need to select it and

use this button: Restore the selected items . The file will be restored to the folder where it was removed.

2.13 Creating a Compressed Folder

Some files take up a lot of space on your computer. For example, certain types of photo files, such as BMP files. But audio files can also take up lots of space, especially WAV files, which can be just as large as illustrated documents. In these cases, you may want to create a compressed folder. Compressing means pressing the file into a smaller space, and is also called 'zipping'. This name derives from the .zip extension that is added to a compressed folder.

When you use a compressed folder, a folder is created in which you can place files. The size of the separate files you place there will be reduced. A compressed folder always needs to be extracted first, before you can open the files in this folder.

You have already become acquainted with this procedure when you copied the practice files. First, you open the *File Explorer* window on the taskbar:

☞ **Open the *Ski vacation* folder on the taskbar** 𝒝𝒝7

☞ **Open the *Practice Files Folders and Files* folder** 𝒝𝒝4

There are four photos in this folder from a vacation in Venice. These are large photo files. It would take a lot of time to send these photos via email. It is a good idea to compress the photos first before sending them to someone. Here is how to do it:

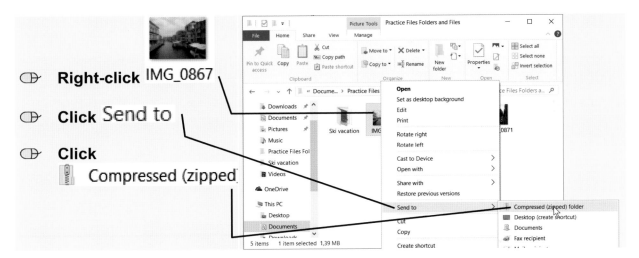

⊕ **Right-click** IMG_0867

⊕ **Click** Send to

⊕ **Click**
   Compressed (zipped)

Now the compressed folder will be created and placed in the folder with the practice

files. You will see a folder icon with a zipper   .

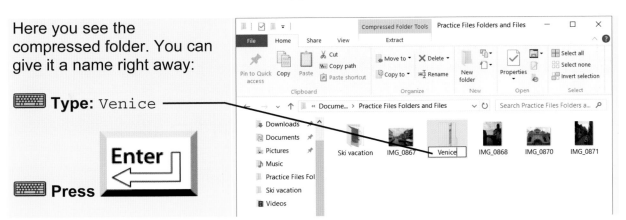

Here you see the compressed folder. You can give it a name right away:

⌨ **Type:** Venice

⌨ **Press** Enter

If you want to add other files to a compressed folder, you can do so easily by dragging a file or a folder to the compressed folder.

The file will then be automatically compressed. The original file will still be stored on the computer. In *section 2.7 Copying Folders and Files* you learned how to copy files to a folder.

☞ **Copy the photos *IMG_0868*, *IMG_0870* and *IMG_0871* to the compressed folder** 8

Now you have created a compressed folder. In the next section you will be copying this folder along with the *Ski vacation* folder to a USB stick or an external hard drive.

2.14 Copying to a USB Stick or External Hard Drive

If you want to copy a file to another computer, or save a backup copy of the file outside the computer, you can copy the file to a USB stick or an external hard drive. In this example you will be copying the *Venice* folder to a USB stick. If you are using an external hard drive, the steps you need to follow are identical. First you need to insert the USB stick into a USB port on your computer.

A USB port can be situated on the front or the back of the computer, or both. On a laptop, a USB port may also be located on one of its sides.

☞ **Find the USB port on your computer**

☞ **Insert the USB stick into the USB port and gently push it in**

Having trouble?

☞ **Then turn the stick over and try again**

When you insert a USB stick into the computer, you will probably see a message appear on your screen:

You can ignore it. It will disappear on its own.

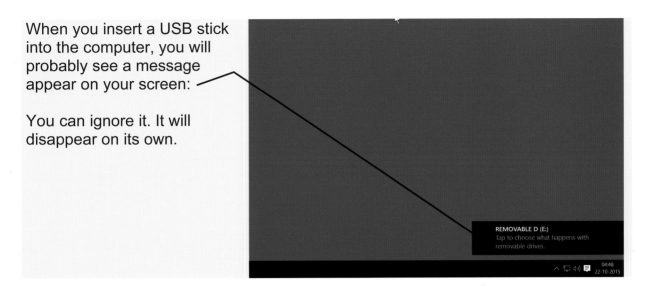

Open the folder on the USB stick in *File Explorer*:

☞ **If necessary, drag the scroll box downwards**

☞ **Click**
   REMOVABLE D

In this example, the USB stick is named Removable D. It may have a different name on your computer.

You will see the content of the USB stick. In this example, there are no files yet.

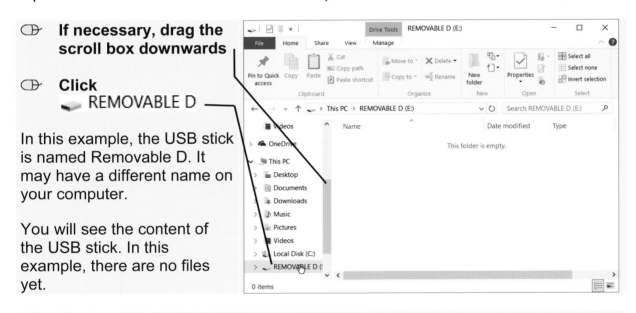

☞ **Open the *Practice Files Folders and Files* folder** 𝒪𝒪4

This is how you copy the *Venice* folder to the USB stick:

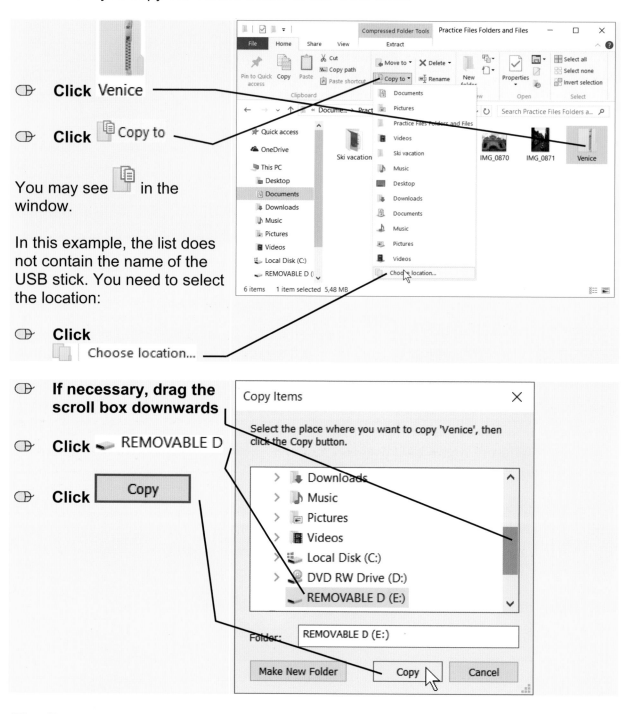

Click Venice

Click Copy to

You may see in the window.

In this example, the list does not contain the name of the USB stick. You need to select the location:

Click
Choose location...

If necessary, drag the scroll box downwards

Click REMOVABLE D

Click Copy

The file will now be copied to the USB stick. You may see a message indicating this. In general, a message will appear only with larger files.

Please note:

If multiple USB sticks are inserted, you will see the names of the other USB sticks. Then choose the one at the bottom. That will be the device you connected last.

Now you can check to see if the folder has been added to the USB stick. You can do this in the navigation pane on the left-side of the window:

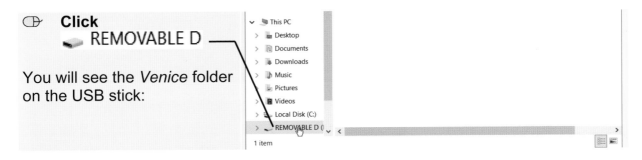

⊕ **Click**
   REMOVABLE D

You will see the *Venice* folder on the USB stick:

☞ **Close the window** ⏐⏐ᵍ¹

In the next section you will learn how to safely remove the USB stick from your computer.

2.15 Safely Remove a USB Stick or External Hard Drive

Before removing storage devices, such as USB sticks, you need to make sure that the computer has finished saving any information to the device. If the device has an activity light flashing, wait for a few seconds until the light has finished flashing before removing it. You also need to do the following.

If you click ⋀ in the lower right corner of your screen, you will see 🖫. You can use this button to safely remove the USB stick:

In the system tray, on the right-hand side of the taskbar:

⊕ **Click** ⋀

⊕ **Click** 🖫

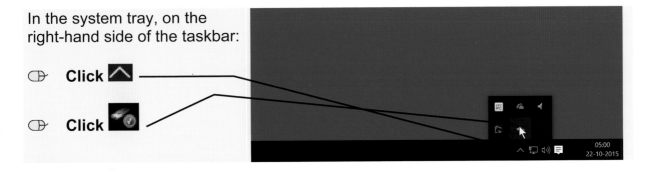

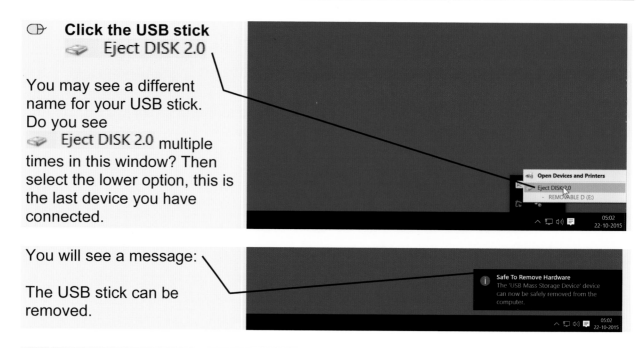

☞ **Click the USB stick**
     Eject DISK 2.0

You may see a different
name for your USB stick.
Do you see
     Eject DISK 2.0 multiple
times in this window? Then
select the lower option, this is
the last device you have
connected.

You will see a message:

The USB stick can be
removed.

☞ **Remove the USB stick from the computer**

In the next section you will be working with libraries.

2.16 The Libraries

Along with folders, *Windows 10* also contains libraries. Libraries make it easier to find
and manage files. A library looks a lot like a folder, but the main difference is, that a
folder contains the actual files. A library only contains references (links) to folders.
There are no files stored in a library. A library displays files that are physically located
in multiple locations on your computer. Instead of clicking through various folders and
subfolders to find a file or folder you need, you can find it quicker by including it in a
library.

The Libraries feature can offer quick and easy access to the files and folders you use
the most on your computer. By default, *Windows* has already created a few libraries.

In these libraries you can quickly and easily find your own files and folders. In the
Documents library you will find all the files from the *Documents* folder from your
Personal folder and from the *Shared Documents* folder. The *Shared Documents*
folder is a folder you share with other users on your computer.

Opening and saving files and folders in a library works the same way as with regular
folders. If you want to open and save a file in a program, such as *WordPad*, the first
things you often see are the libraries (the default setting).

☞ **Open *File Explorer*** 👣⁹

⊕ **Click** 〉

⊕ **Click** 🖫 **Libraries**

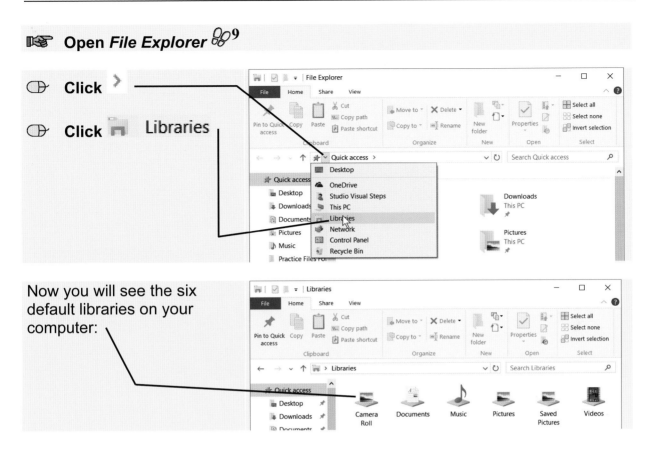

Now you will see the six default libraries on your computer:

2.17 Creating a New Library

In *Windows 10* you can also create a new library yourself, for example, to arrange certain folders on your computer. In this example you will be creating a library with the following folders:

- the *Ski vacation* folder;
- the *Pictures* folder, one of the default folders located on your computer.

By adding these folders to a library you can see how easy it is to collect files from different locations on your computer into a single library.

 Tip

Library with vacation photos and stories
You can create your own library, for example, to collect all your vacation photos and stories in one place.

To create a new library:

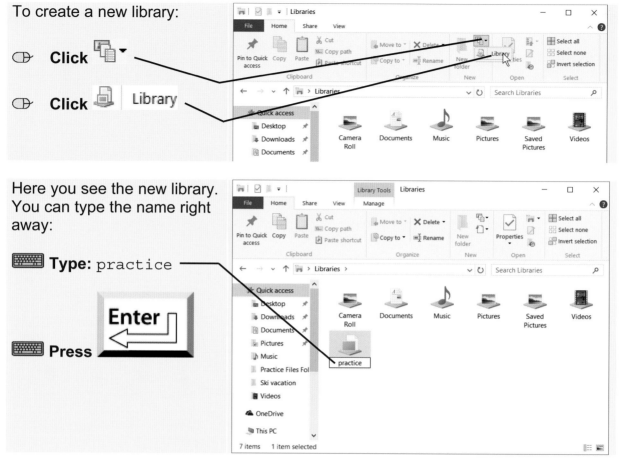

Click

Click Library

Here you see the new library.
You can type the name right
away:

Type: practice

Press Enter

You have created a new library. Right away, you can start adding folders to this
library:

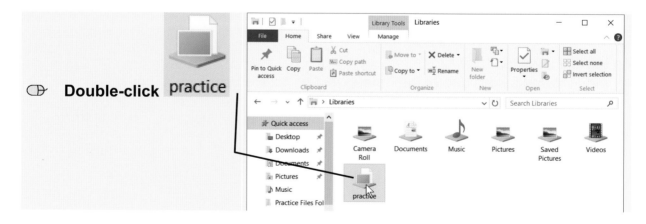

Double-click practice

You can see that this library is still empty. You can add a folder. This is called *including*:

☞ **Click**

Include a folder

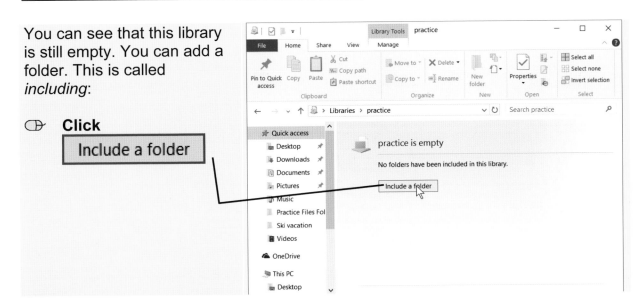

First, you are going to include the *Ski vacation* folder. For this you need to open the *Documents* folder:

☞ **Double-click** Documents

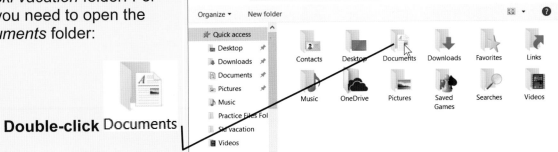

Practice Files Folders and Files

☞ **Click**

☞ **Click**

Include folder

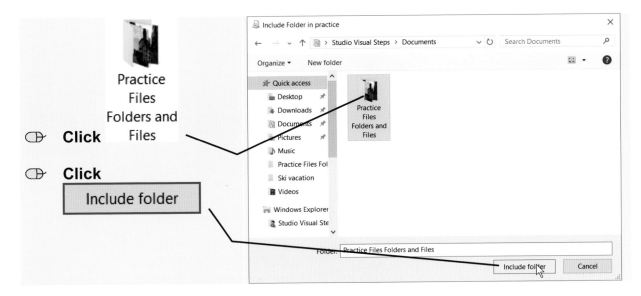

The folder is added to the library *practice*. You can add another folder:

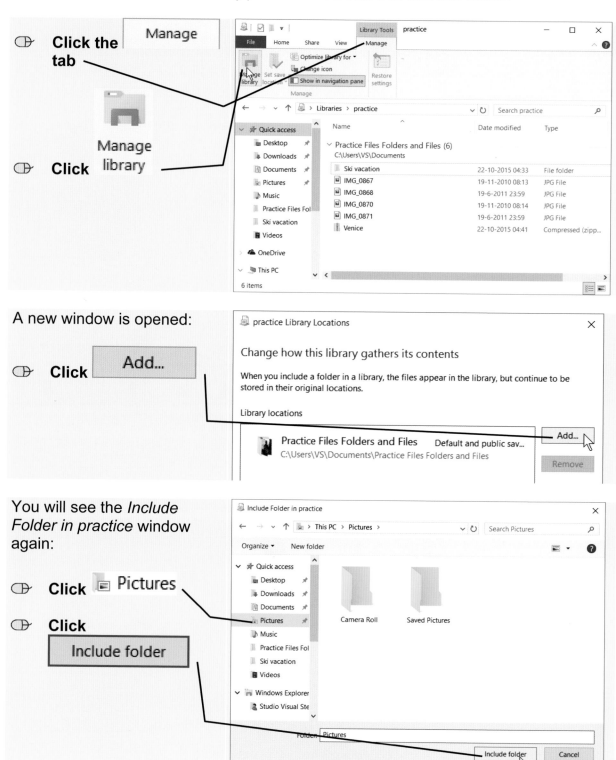

Click the Manage tab

Click Manage library

A new window is opened:

Click Add...

You will see the *Include Folder in practice* window again:

Click Pictures

Click Include folder

You will see both folders in this window:

At the bottom of the window:

☞ **Click** OK

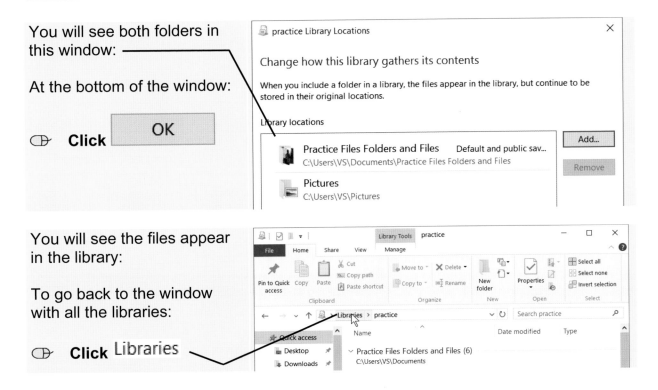

You will see the files appear in the library:

To go back to the window with all the libraries:

☞ **Click** Libraries

2.18 Deleting a Library

Now you can delete the *practice* library. This action means that you will only be deleting the library with its links (references) to the folders. The *Ski vacation* and *Pictures* folders are still stored in their original location on your computer.

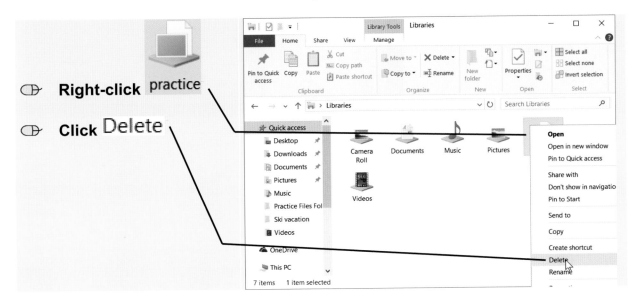

☞ **Right-click** practice

☞ **Click** Delete

Now the *practice* library has been deleted.

 **Close the *Libraries* window** ⚹¹

2.19 OneDrive

You can use *OneDrive* to save files online, on a secure server. This is also called 'in the cloud'. You can open these files again wherever you are in the world, provided you have an Internet connection, and share them on your cell phone, tablet, or even another computer. You have 15 GB of free storage space for each account.

 Please note:
If you want to use *OneDrive*, you will need to have a *Microsoft* account. This is a combination of an email address ending in hotmail.com or outlook.com, and a password. If you do not have a *Microsoft* account, you can create one on the web page signup.live.com.

Before you can use *OneDrive*, you will need to go through a short setup procedure. First, you open *OneDrive*:

👆 **Click** 🔍

⌨️ **Type:** onedrive

👆 **Click**

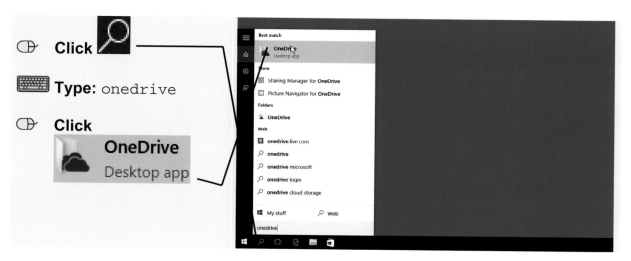

You will see this *Welcome* screen when you start up *OneDrive* for the first time:

In this window:

👆 **Click** Get started

You need to sign in with your *Microsoft* account:

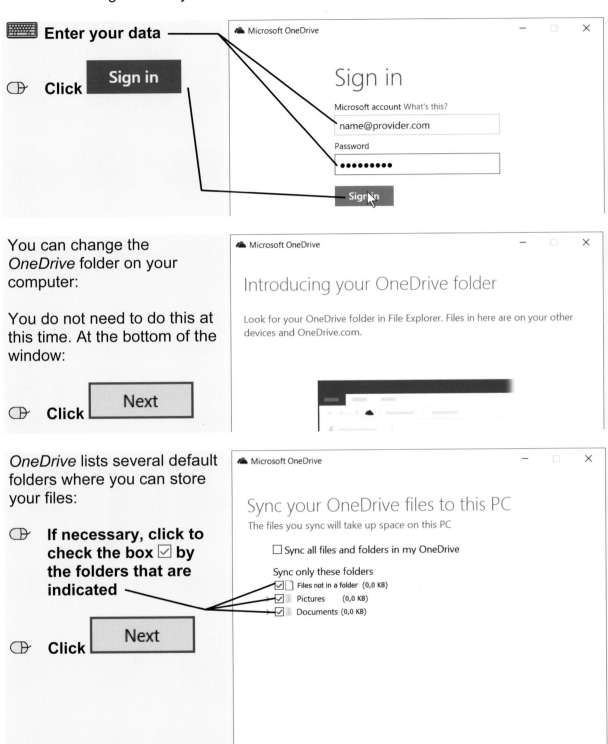

⌨ **Enter your data**

◐ **Click** Sign in

You can change the *OneDrive* folder on your computer:

You do not need to do this at this time. At the bottom of the window:

◐ **Click** Next

OneDrive lists several default folders where you can store your files:

◐ **If necessary, click to check the box ☑ by the folders that are indicated**

◐ **Click** Next

At the bottom of the window:

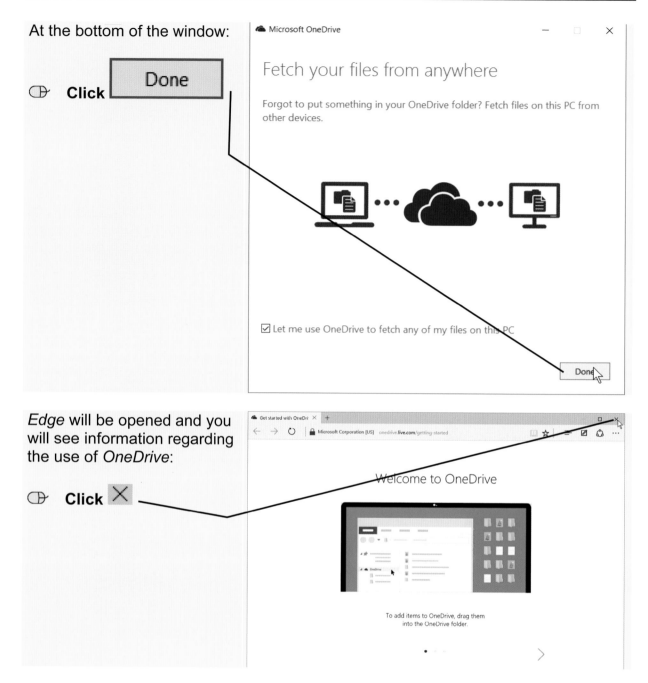

Click **Done**

Edge will be opened and you will see information regarding the use of *OneDrive*:

Click ✕

🖐 Please note:

If you want to use *OneDrive* you will need to take into account that information that is stored online is more vulnerable to hacking than data saved on your computer.

OneDrive will be opened in *File Explorer*.

You see two empty folders, *Pictures* and *Documents*:

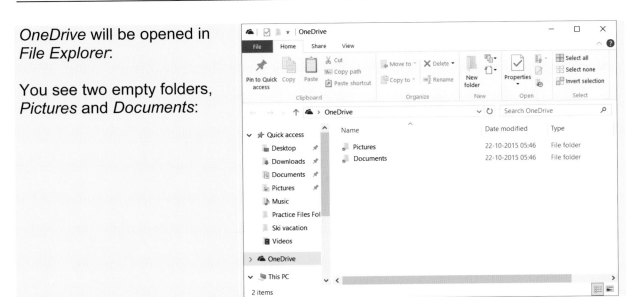

☞ **If necessary, change the view to Medium icons** 👣**11**

In this example you will be moving a photo from your computer to your *OneDrive* space. You do this by dragging the file from the folder:

☞ **Open the folder with the photo you want to move** 👣**4**

You move the photo:

⊕ **Drag the photo to**
☁ OneDrive

If necessary, drag another file to ☁ OneDrive.

If you see
→ Move to OneDrive , you can release the mouse button:

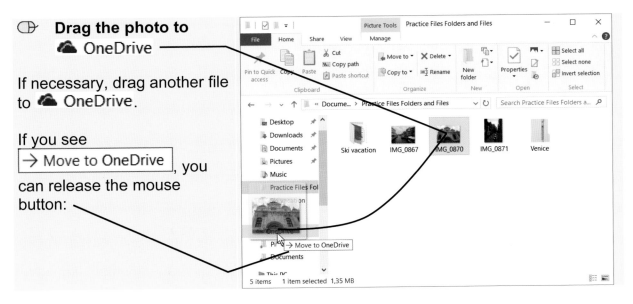

The photo has disappeared from the folder and is now stored in your *OneDrive* space:

☞　　**Click** ☁ OneDrive

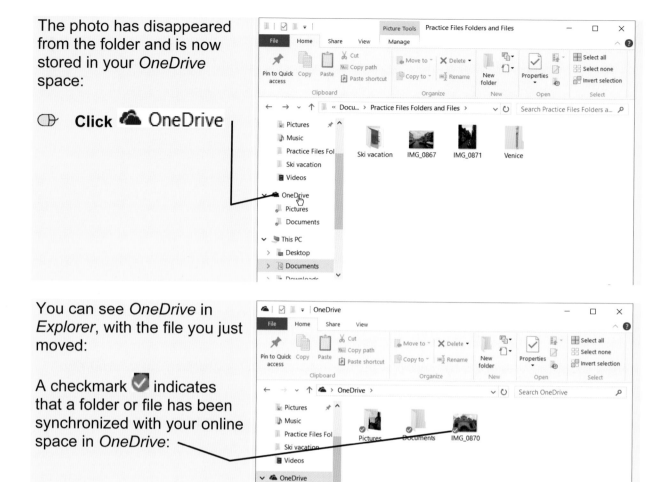

You can see *OneDrive* in *Explorer*, with the file you just moved:

A checkmark ✅ indicates that a folder or file has been synchronized with your online space in *OneDrive*:

This is how you move a file from *OneDrive* to your computer:

☞　　**Drag the photo to**
　　　📁 Pictures

If you see
→ Move to Pictures , you can release the mouse button:

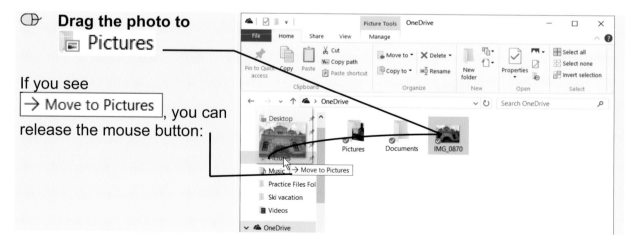

Now the photo has disappeared from *OneDrive* and is saved in Pictures:

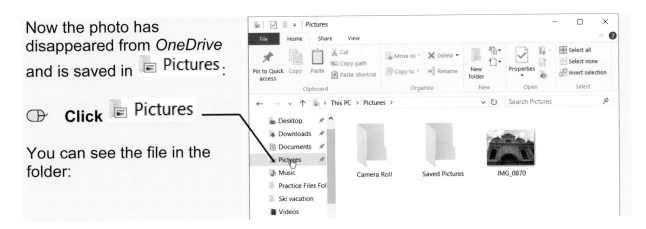

⊕ **Click** Pictures

You can see the file in the folder:

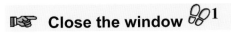

💡 **Tip**

Copy a file to OneDrive

You can also copy one or more files to your space in *OneDrive*. For example, this can be useful if you want to create a safe backup copy of a file outside of your

Ctrl

computer. In order to do this, you need to press ⎯⎯⎯⎯ and hold it down while you drag the file to 🌥 OneDrive.

☞ **Close the window** 👣¹

In this chapter you have learned how to use *File Explorer*. You have practiced moving, deleting and copying files, and you have seen how to drag files to a USB stick. You have also learned how to work with libraries and *OneDrive*.

2.20 Background Information

Dictionary

Address bar	The address bar appears at the top of every library or folder window and displays your current location as a series of links separated by arrows. By using the address bar, you can see which folder is opened.
Compress	Reduce the size of a file so it will occupy less space, which makes it easier to send the file by email. Compressed files often have the .zip file extension.
Compressed folder	In *Windows* you can compress files by copying them to a compressed folder. You can recognize the compressed folder by the zipper icon.
Details pane	A part of the *File Explorer* window that displays the properties of a selected file.
External hard drive	An external hard drive is also portable. It usually has a larger storage capacity than a USB stick.
Extract	Decompressing files that have been saved as compressed files. When you extract a file, a non-compressed version of the file is saved in the folder you indicate. The original file remains stored in the compressed folder.
File	The generic name for everything saved on the computer. A file can be a program, a data file with names, text you have written, a photo, a video or a piece of music. Actually, everything located on the hard drive of your computer is called a *file*.
File Explorer	The program that allows you to access, edit and manage your files and folders. You can open a file or launch a program, for example, with *File Explorer*.
File list	This is where the contents of the current library or folder are displayed.
Folder	A folder is a container that helps you organize your files. Every file on your computer is stored in a folder, and folders can also hold other folders.

- Continue on the next page -

Folder list	List of folders in the navigation pane. By using the folder list in the navigation pane, you can navigate directly to the folder or library you are interested in by clicking the folder.
Library	A library seems very similar to a folder. The difference is that the files you see in a folder are actually physically located there. The files and folders that you see in a library are not physically located there but are represented by links to other files and folders spread out over your computer. You can open files from and save files to a library. This is done in the same manner as working directly with a folder for example in *Documents*.
Navigation pane	Shows a list of folders and libraries that can be opened in the *File Explorer* window.
OneDrive	Through *OneDrive* you can save your files in the cloud, a storage space on the Internet. In this way you can easily access your files on other computers, as well as on your tablet or smartphone.
Personal folder	Your *Personal* folder is a folder that contains your *Documents*, *Pictures*, *Music* and *Videos* folders, as well as other folders. The *Personal* folder is labeled with the name you use to log on to your computer.
Preview pane	Part of the *File Explorer* window, where you can view the details of the file you have selected.
Quick access	A list of folders displayed in the upper left corner of *File Explorer*. If you often use a specific folder, it can be useful to add this folder to the Quick access list.
Recent files	Through Quick access you can access your recent files directly. You can use these in order to quickly resume working with a file you frequently use, for example.
Recycle Bin	When you delete a file or folder, it goes to the *Recycle Bin*. You can restore a file from the *Recycle Bin*. But if you empty the *Recycle Bin*, all of its contents will be permanently gone.
Subfolder	A folder within a folder.
USB stick	A small portable device, to store files and folders. Plugs into a computer's USB port. *Windows* will show a USB stick as a removable disk.

Source: Windows Help

2.21 Tips

 Tip

Quickly copy a file to a USB stick

If you know which drive letter is used to indicate the USB stick on your computer, you can quickly copy a file or folder to it directly from the folder window. You do that like this:

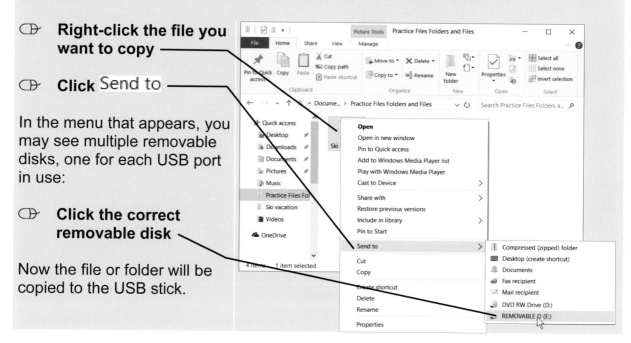

☞ **Right-click the file you want to copy** ─────

☞ **Click** Send to ─────

In the menu that appears, you may see multiple removable disks, one for each USB port in use:

☞ **Click the correct removable disk** ─────

Now the file or folder will be copied to the USB stick.

 Tip

Quick navigation

If you have opened multiple folders, one after the other, you can use the buttons to switch between the folders. But you can also jump directly to a previously visited folder:

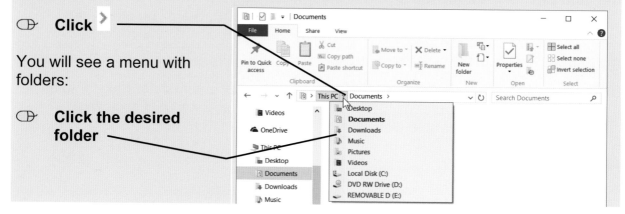

☞ **Click** ❯ ─────

You will see a menu with folders:

☞ **Click the desired folder** ─────

💡 Tip

Extract a compressed folder

In *section 2.13 Creating a Compressed Folder* you have learned how to compress or zip a folder. This is how you extract or unzip such a folder:

☞ **Right-click the folder**

☞ **Click** Extract All...

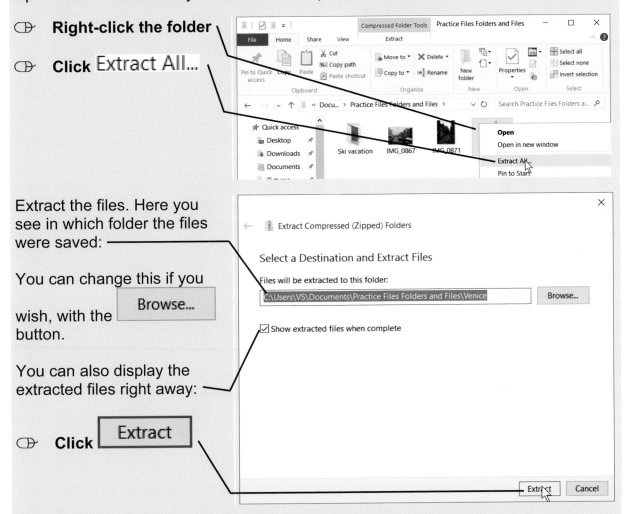

Extract the files. Here you see in which folder the files were saved: ————

You can change this if you wish, with the Browse... button.

You can also display the extracted files right away:

☞ **Click** Extract

The files will be extracted. You may briefly see a message window.

Once the files have been extracted, you will see them in a new window:

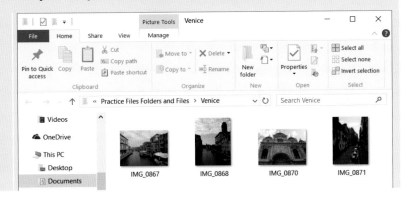

Tip

Quick access

One of the new functions in *File Explorer* is called *Quick access*. This is a list of frequently used folders. By default, this list contains the *Desktop*, *Downloads*, *Documents*, *Pictures* folders, and often the *Music*, and *Videos* folders as well. This list can be supplemented with the folders you use the most. If you often use a specific folder, it can be handy to add it to Quick access. Here is how you do that:

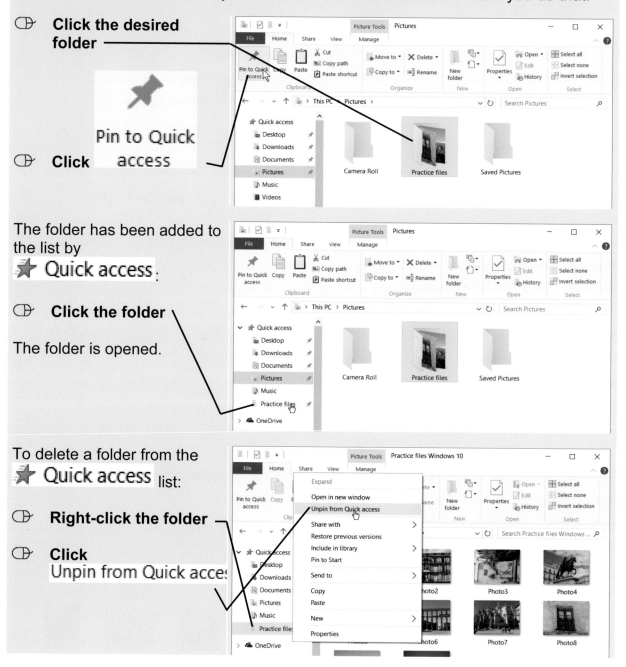

Click the desired folder

Pin to Quick access

Click

The folder has been added to the list by

⭐ **Quick access**:

Click the folder

The folder is opened.

To delete a folder from the ⭐ **Quick access** list:

Right-click the folder

Click Unpin from Quick acces

Tip

Recent files and frequent folders

Another function in *File Explorer* is the ability to display recently used files and folders. You can use this function to quickly resume working on a frequently used file:

If you want to view the frequently used folders and recent files, click
⭐ Quick access:

Frequent folders:

You will probably see more or different folders.

The recently opened files:

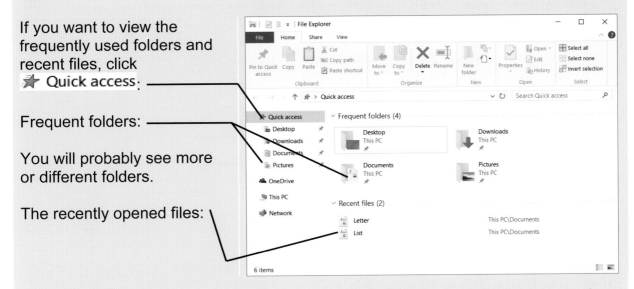

If you prefer, you can also disable the view of recent files and frequent folders. You do that like this:

👉 **Click** [File], ☑ Change folder and search options

At the bottom of the *General* tab you will see these options:

Uncheck the boxes if you do not want to display the files or folders anymore:

You can also simply clear the current history of recent files and frequent folders:

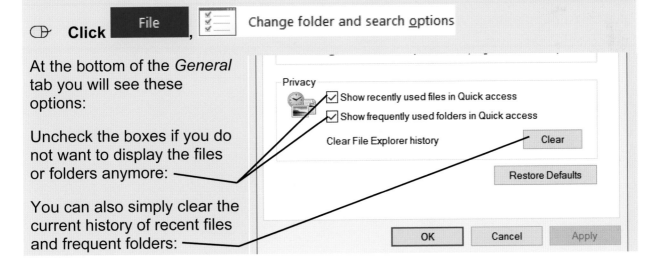

Tip

Searching files in a folder
There are many ways to find your files on your computer. Most of the time, you will start by using the search box that is available within any *File Explorer* window.

☞ **Click in the search box**

⌨ **Start typing**

As you type, search results will appear:

Just click a file name to open it.

If there are no search results, you will see this window. Now you can choose where you would like to continue searching, for instance your entire computer:

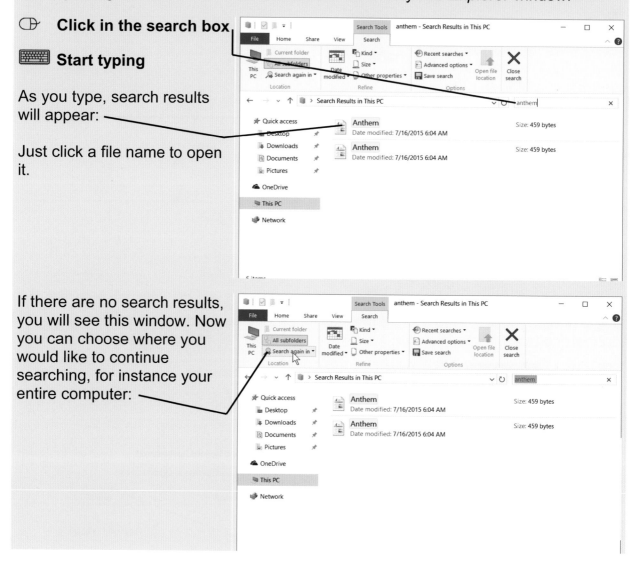

3. Making Useful Settings

You can edit various settings on a *Windows 10* computer. There are many components on your computer that can be adjusted to suit your own needs and preferences. For example, you can check whether there are options available that will make certain elements easier to work with on the computer.

Choosing the right settings for your computer is not just worthwhile because it makes complicated operations easier, but it also prevents you from experiencing negative consequences in the long run. For example, you can set up the mouse in such a way that it is easier to use. This can help prevent your hand or wrist from being overburdened.

In this chapter you will also read how to adjust the Start menu, the image of the lock screen, and the desktop background to suit your own taste.

You can just go ahead and experiment with different settings and find out for yourself whether they are an improvement. It is a good thing to know that you can always restore any setting you adjust back to its default state.

In this chapter you will learn how to:

- how to add program and app tiles to the Start menu;
- how to change the size of the Start menu;
- how to move tiles and create groups in the Start menu;
- about *Settings*;
- how to change the image of the lock screen and desktop background;
- how to set up the mouse;
- how to change the size of letters and icons;
- adjust the screensaver, the sound, and the energy saving settings.

3.1 Adding Program or App Tiles to the Start Menu

You can use the tiles in the Start menu to open a program or app. It is very easy; you just need to click the desired tile. You can also change the order of the tiles in the Start menu to suit your own preferences. As you work with your computer for a while longer, you may find that you use some programs and apps more frequently than others. You may have also installed a new program or app on your computer. These programs and apps are sometimes placed in the Start menu right away, but sometimes they are not.

You can easily add tiles for programs and apps that are not displayed in the Start menu yourself. One example of such a program is *WordPad*. You can practice adding a new tile to the Start menu for that program. Here is how you do that:

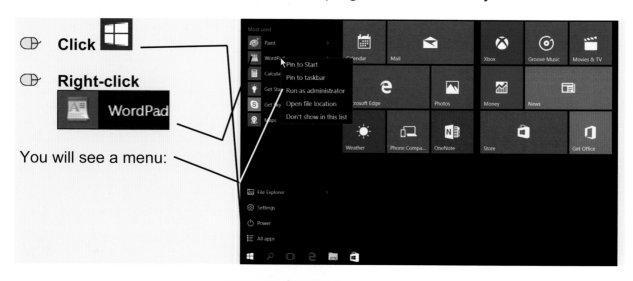

HELP! I do not see .

If you do not see the *WordPad* button, this is how to find it:

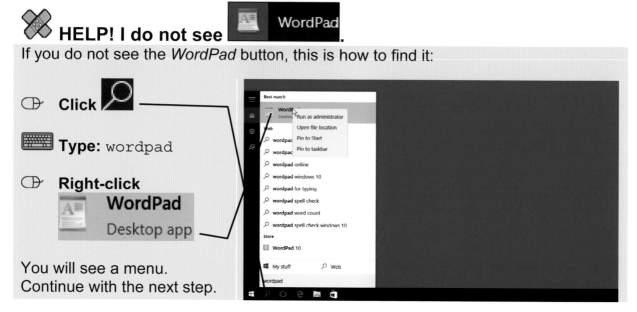

Add *WordPad* to the Start menu:

☞ **Click** Pin to Start

Notice that you can also attach the program or app to the taskbar.

This way, you can easily and quickly open frequently used programs and apps right from the taskbar.

WordPad has now been added to the Start menu as a new tile. From now on you can open this program right away, by clicking the tile:

3.2 Changing the Size of the Start Menu

If you have just started using *Windows 10*, the Start menu will not be very extensive. In due time, you will probably have more programs and apps. Some of these programs and apps will appear in the Start menu and the number of tiles will gradually increase. You can easily enlarge the Start menu to view more programs and apps at once. You do that like this:

Place the pointer on the top edge of the Start menu

The pointer turns into ↕:

Drag the pointer upwards

The Start menu will increase in height:

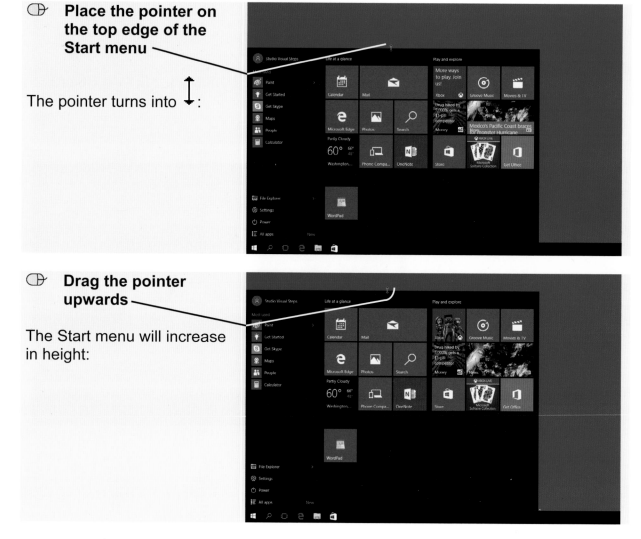

You can also make the Start menu wider or smaller, if you wish. To do that, place the pointer on the right edge of the Start menu and then drag the pointer to the right or left.

3.3 Moving Tiles and Creating Groups in the Start Menu

You can change the order of the tiles, if you wish, or arrange the tiles in various groups. In the following exercise you will be creating a new group for the *WordPad* and *Mail* tiles:

Drag the *Mail* tile

to

the right-hand side of the *WordPad* tile

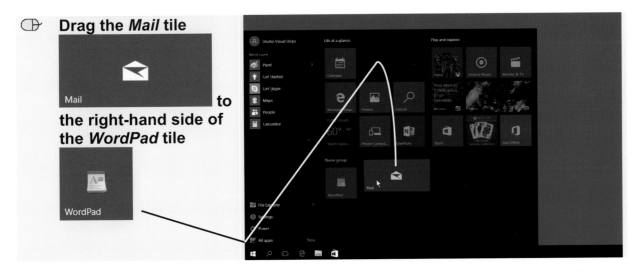

Now these two tiles are joined in a group. You can name this group. In this example, we will call it *Exercise*. You can also choose another name for the group, if you wish. And you do not need to use the same tiles as in this example; you can also add other tiles to the group.

Click above the two tiles

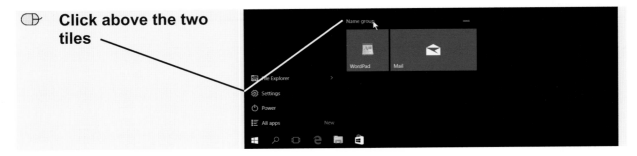

Name the new group, call it *Exercise*:

Type: Exercise

Press Enter

You will see the name appear above the group:

If you want to remove the tiles from the group, you can just drag them out of the group. When all the tiles have been removed from the group, the group name will disappear automatically.

3.4 Creating Multiple Desktops

In *Windows 10* there is a option for creating multiple desktops. In this way you can arrange *Windows* in an orderly manner, for example, by creating separate desktops for private matters and work-related tasks. You can also use a program or app on one of the desktops and it will not be opened on the other desktop. This way, you can perform tasks separately. Just take a look a closer look at how this works:

☞ **Open *WordPad*** ✔️⁹⁰¹⁰

The *WordPad* window is opened on the desktop. You can create a new desktop:

In the bottom left corner of the taskbar:

⊕ **Click** 🔲

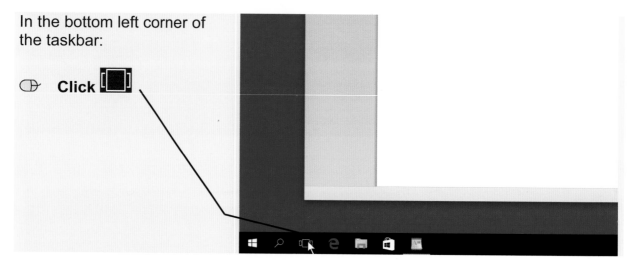

You will see the Task View. Here you can create a new desktop:

In the bottom right corner of the screen:

Click **New desktop**

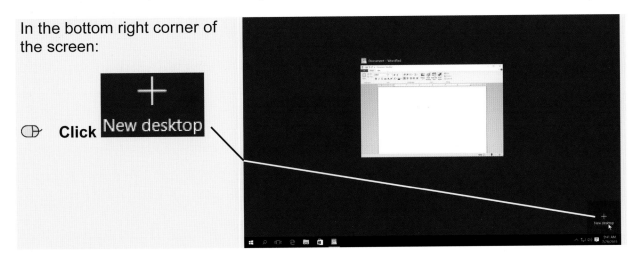

Now there are two desktops:

Click

Desktop 2

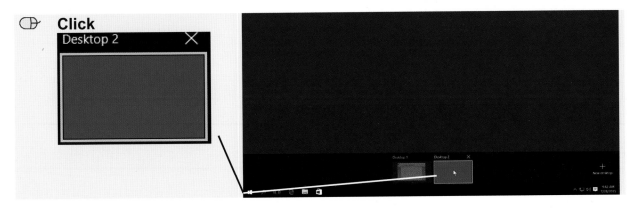

The *WordPad* program is not opened on the second desktop. If you want, you can open a second version of *WordPad* here, and work on another document.

For now, you can simply close the second desktop:

Click

You will see the Task View and you can close the second desktop:

Click

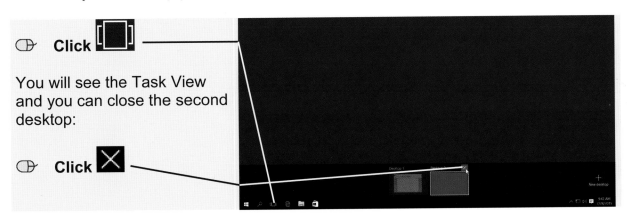

You will see the Task View:

Click the *WordPad* window

Close *WordPad* ✌1

3.5 Settings

If you would like to change any of the desktop or system settings in *Windows 10*, you need to use the *Settings* app. You can open the *Settings* app from the Start menu:

Click

Click

The *Settings* window will be opened:

The window is filled with all sorts of subjects, arranged by category:

Each category is indicated by an icon:

In *section 1.5 Adjusting Settings* you can read more about the different categories.

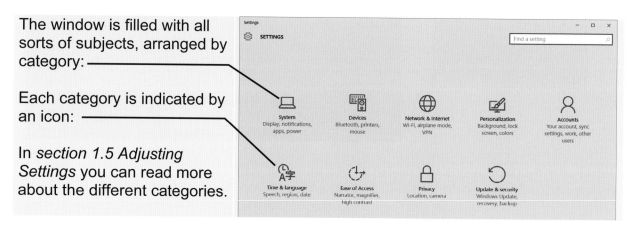

You can open the window for a particular category by clicking its icon. In the next section you will be taking a look at changing the image of the lock screen.

3.6 Changing the Image of the Lock Screen

You can change the image of the lock screen as well:

If necessary, open *Settings* ✌12

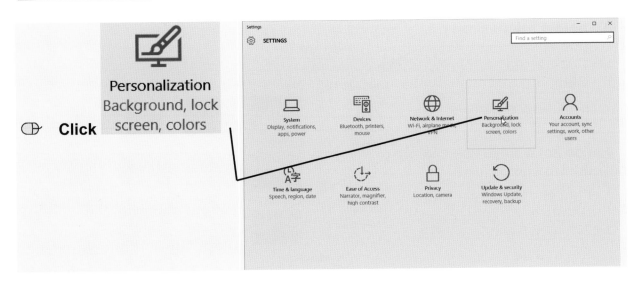

Personalization
Background, lock
screen, colors

⊕ **Click**

You will see the *Personal Settings* window. Here you can change the image on the lock screen:

On the left-hand side of the window:

⊕ **Click** Lock screen

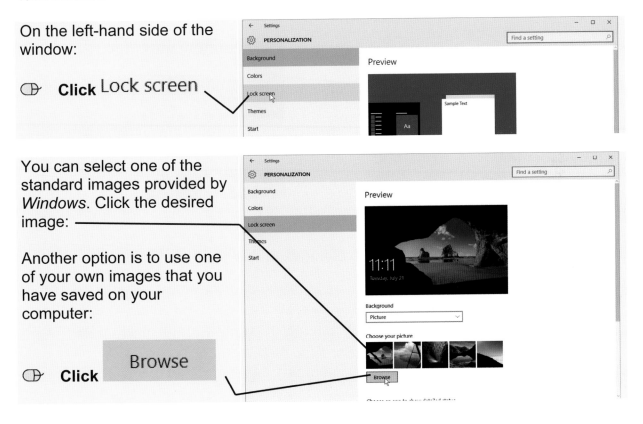

You can select one of the standard images provided by *Windows*. Click the desired image: ———

Another option is to use one of your own images that you have saved on your computer:

⊕ **Click** Browse

☞ **Select the desired**
   photo

⊕ **Click**

   Choose picture

If you do not want to use one
of your own photos, click

   Cancel

.

You will see the *Personal*
Settings window with the new
image of the lock screen:

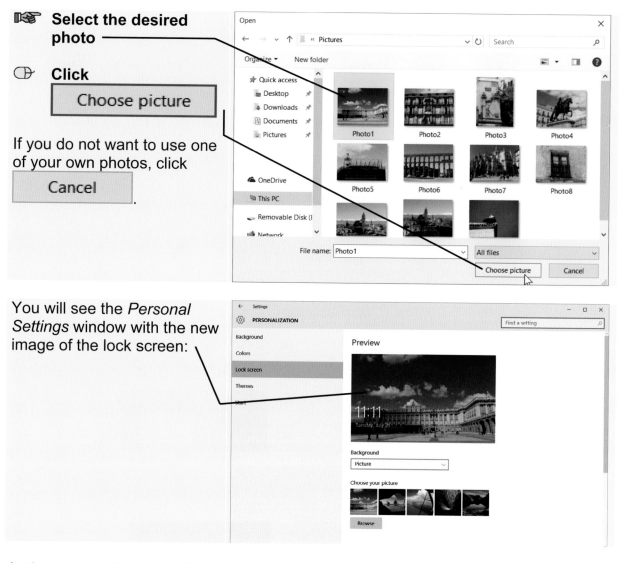

In the next section you will learn how to change the desktop background.

3.7 Changing the Desktop Background

Many people like to use a calm background (also called wallpaper) when they are working on their computer. But if you think your own background is rather dull and want to see something livelier, or you just want something else for a change, you can set a new background. Selecting a different background is very easy. You can change the desktop background by selecting an image or color yourself:

If you want to use an image that comes with the *Windows* system:

In the upper left corner of the window:

☞ **Click** Background

If necessary:

☞ **By** Background, **click** ⌄

☞ **Click** Picture

Note that you can also display a slideshow with multiple photos.

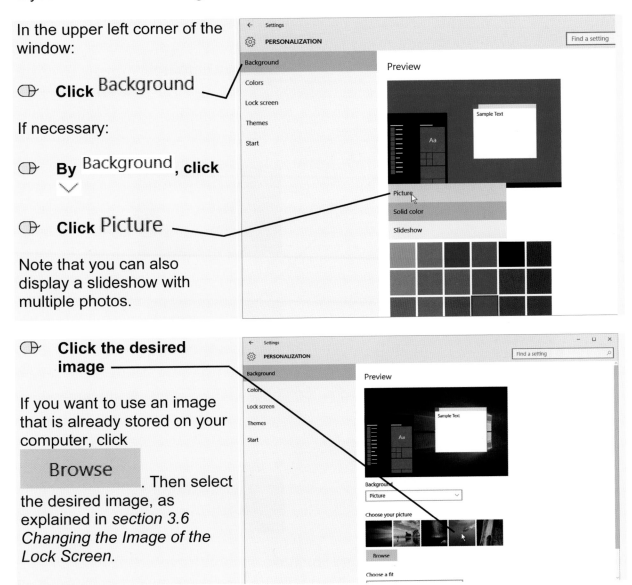

☞ **Click the desired image**

If you want to use an image that is already stored on your computer, click

Browse . Then select the desired image, as explained in *section 3.6 Changing the Image of the Lock Screen*.

If you prefer not to use an image, but a specific color instead:

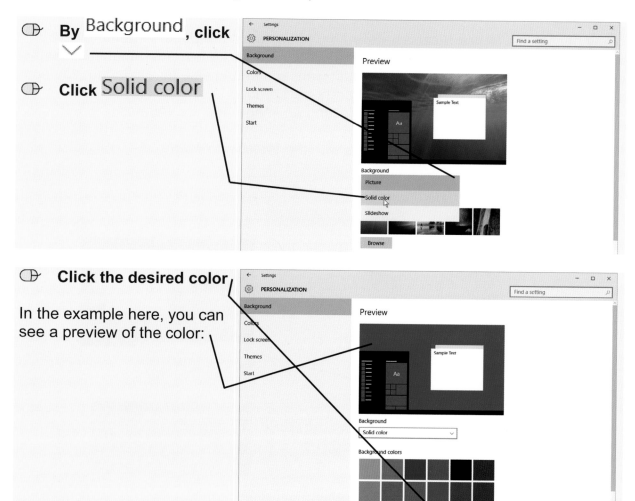

⊕ **By** Background **, click**

⊕ **Click** Solid color

⊕ **Click the desired color,**

In the example here, you can see a preview of the color:

In order to save the desktop background and go back to the *Settings* home screen:

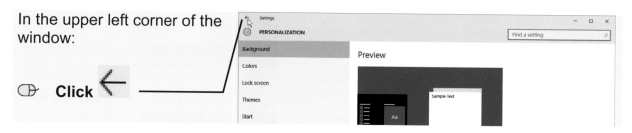

In the upper left corner of the window:

⊕ **Click** ←

You will see the new desktop background you have chosen. If on second thought you are not satisfied with the background, you can repeat the actions in this section.

3.8 Setting Up the Mouse

There are various ways to adjust the settings for your mouse. You can set:

- the speed;
- the double-click speed;
- the buttons for left-handed users;
- the mouse pointer.

You can take a look at the various options:

The mouse is located in the category *Devices*:

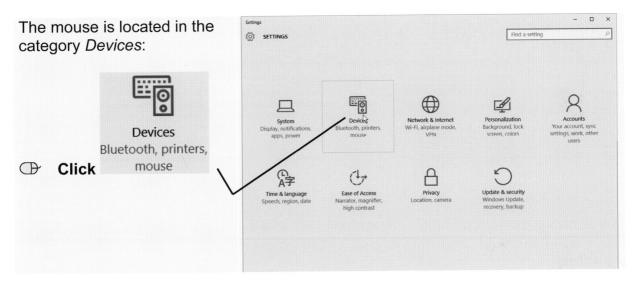

Click Devices
Bluetooth, printers, mouse

You will see the *Devices* window:

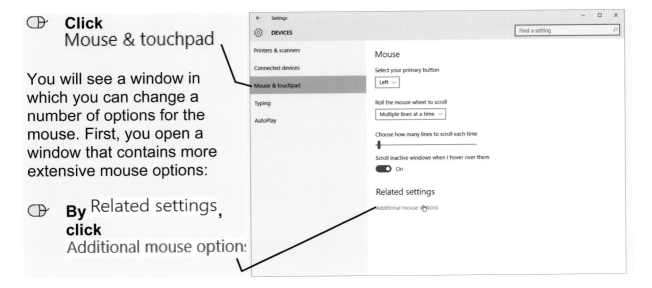

Click
Mouse & touchpad

You will see a window in which you can change a number of options for the mouse. First, you open a window that contains more extensive mouse options:

By Related settings,
click
Additional mouse options

You now see the *Mouse Properties* window:

Please note: This window may have a different appearance on your screen. Mouse manufacturers sometimes make a modified version of this window for their own products.

But the options shown will be comparable to the options in this example.

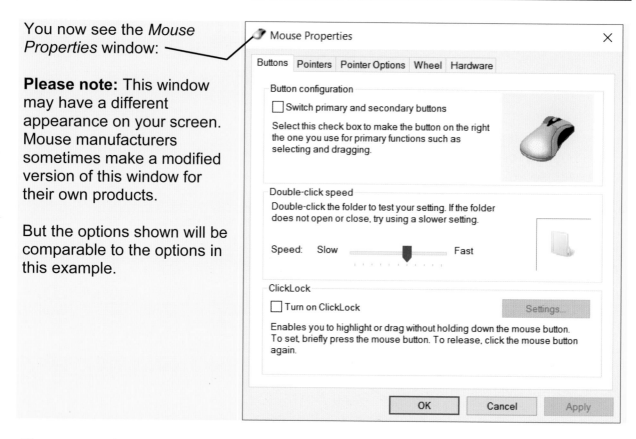

The speed of the mouse pointer determines the relationship between a movement made with the mouse over the tabletop and the movement of the mouse pointer on the screen.

- If the pointer speed is *too fast*, when you move the mouse only slightly on the tabletop the *movement on the screen is too large*.
- If the pointer speed is *too slow*, when you move the mouse a long way on the tabletop the *movement on the screen is only slight*.

For most people, the pointer speed is correct if a movement with the mouse on the tabletop surface or mousepad within the size of a CD box (this is approximately a 5 inch square) moves the mouse pointer from one corner of the screen to another corner.

If you still think your mouse pointer is too slow or too fast after you have practiced with it, you can try adjusting the speed. You do that like this:

☞ **Click the**

Pointer Options **tab**

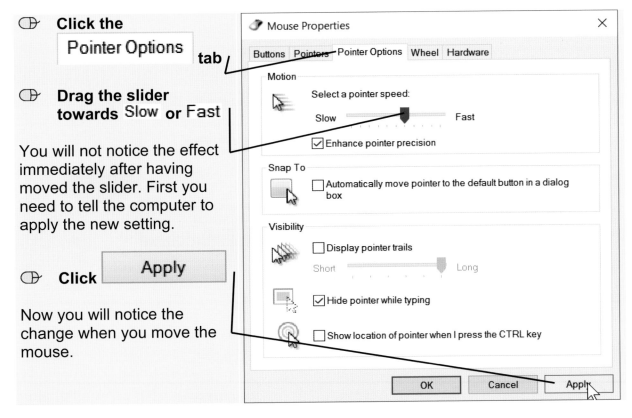

☞ **Drag the slider towards** Slow **or** Fast

You will not notice the effect immediately after having moved the slider. First you need to tell the computer to apply the new setting.

☞ **Click** **Apply**

Now you will notice the change when you move the mouse.

You can keep changing the position of the slider until you have found the setting that works best for you. Do not forget to click **Apply** to apply the new setting.

💡 **Tip**

Visibility of the pointer
Many computer beginners complain that they regularly lose track of the mouse pointer on the screen. It is very easy to add an effect to the mouse pointer to make it more visible. One of the things you can do is to give the mouse pointer a *tail* or a *pointer trail*. On the Pointer Options tab in the *Mouse Properties* window:

☞ **Click a checkmark** ✔ **by** Display pointer trails

Or:

☞ **Click a checkmark** ✔ **by** Show location of pointer when I press the CTRL key

You can also make the mouse pointer more visible by making it larger. This is done with a different tab:

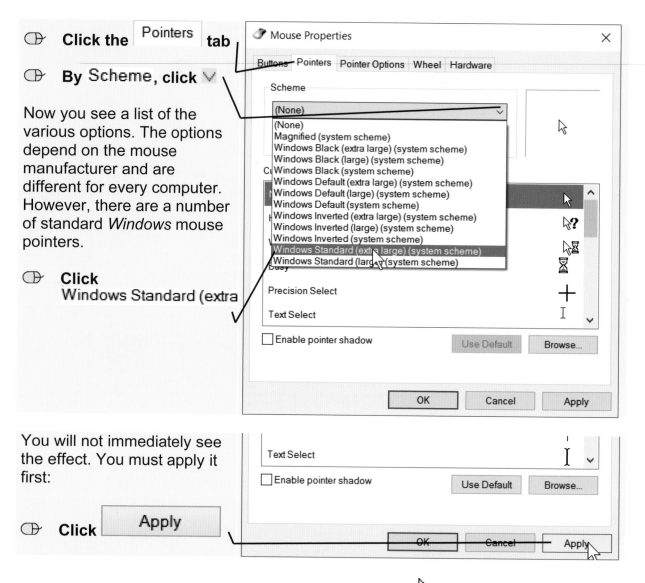

⊕ **Click the** Pointers **tab**

⊕ **By Scheme, click** ∨

Now you see a list of the various options. The options depend on the mouse manufacturer and are different for every computer. However, there are a number of standard *Windows* mouse pointers.

⊕ **Click**
   Windows Standard (extra

You will not immediately see the effect. You must apply it first:

⊕ **Click** Apply

Now you see that you have a very large mouse pointer: . If you like it, you can leave the setting as it is. If not, you can select the regular scheme Windows Standard (large) (system scheme) ∨ or you can try one of the other options.

You will also a see a number of options in the list to make the *mouse pointer turn black*: . For some people, the black version is easier to follow on the screen.

The double-click speed can also be adjusted. If you do not double-click fast enough, *Windows* does not recognize your two clicks as a double-click. Perhaps changing the setting will make it easier for you to double-click.

- Make the setting *slower* if you have trouble double-clicking.
- You can make the double-click speed *faster* once you have mastered the technique of clicking in rapid succession.

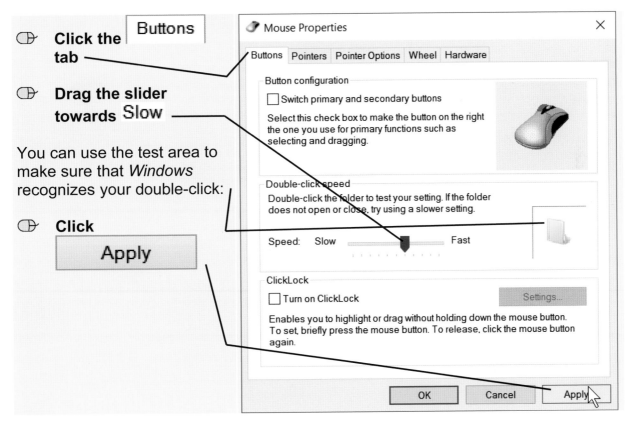

☞ **Click the** Buttons **tab**

☞ **Drag the slider towards** Slow

You can use the test area to make sure that *Windows* recognizes your double-click:

☞ **Click** Apply

HELP! I am having trouble with double-clicking.

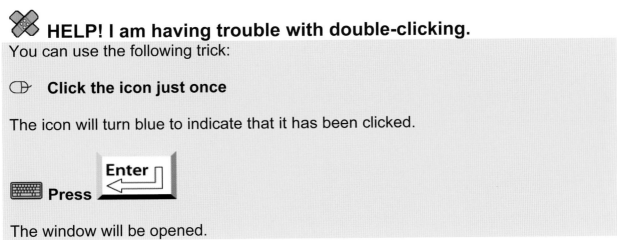

You can use the following trick:

☞ **Click the icon just once**

The icon will turn blue to indicate that it has been clicked.

⌨ **Press** Enter

The window will be opened.

If you are left-handed, you should also customize the mouse so that you can use it in your left hand.

 Please note:

If you are right-handed, you do not need to change anything.

 Check the box ☑ **next to**
Switch primary and second

Now the functions of the mouse buttons have been switched.

From now on you use the *right mouse button* where the instruction is to *Click*:

Click Apply

After you have finished adjusting the mouse settings:

Click OK

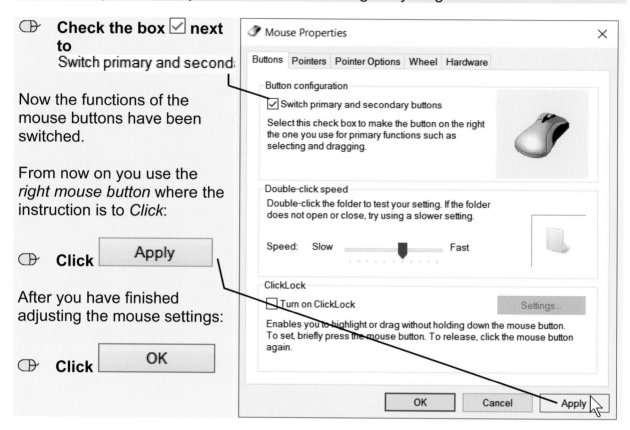

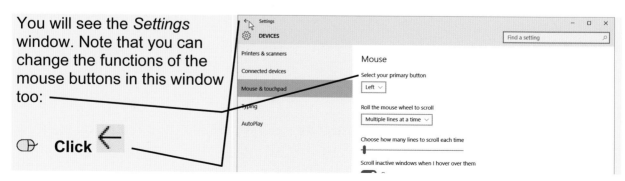

 Please note:

If you just switched the functions of the mouse buttons, from now on you will need to use the *left mouse button* when you are instructed to *Right-click*.

All the settings you have changed have been saved.

You will see the *Settings* window. Note that you can change the functions of the mouse buttons in this window too: ——

Click ←

3.9 Changing the Size of Letters and Icons

If you find it difficult to read letters and icons, you can display them in a larger size. The *Settings* window is still open:

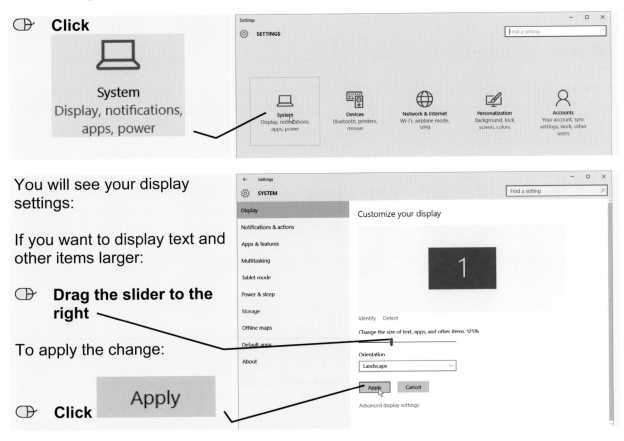

Click

System
Display, notifications, apps, power

You will see your display settings:

If you want to display text and other items larger:

Drag the slider to the right

To apply the change:

Click   Apply

If you want to permanently change the font size, you need to sign off:

Click   Sign out now

Sign in again for the best experience

Sign in again for the best experience
Some apps will look their best after you've signed out of Windows and signed in again.

Sign out now   Sign out later

You will be logged off.

Sign on 13

Notice that the size of the text and other items on the desktop have been adjusted.

3.10 Setting Up a Screen Saver

If you have not used your computer for a while, you may see an animated image on your screen. This is known as a *screen saver*. You can set up your own screen saver.

☞ **If necessary, open *Settings* 👣 12**

If certain topics are not displayed in the *Settings* window, you can find them easily by using the search box in the *Settings* window. Search for a screen saver:

In the upper right corner of the window:

🖱 **Click the search box**

⌨ **Type:** screen saver

You will see the search results:

🖱 **Click**

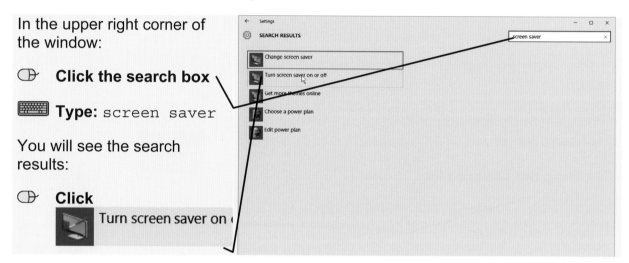

Turn screen saver on

💡 **Tip**

The search box in Settings
If you want to know more about a specific setting, or want to change a setting, but cannot find it in *Settings*, try entering the search terms in the search box shown in the upper right corner of the window.

A new window is opened. To set up a screen saver:

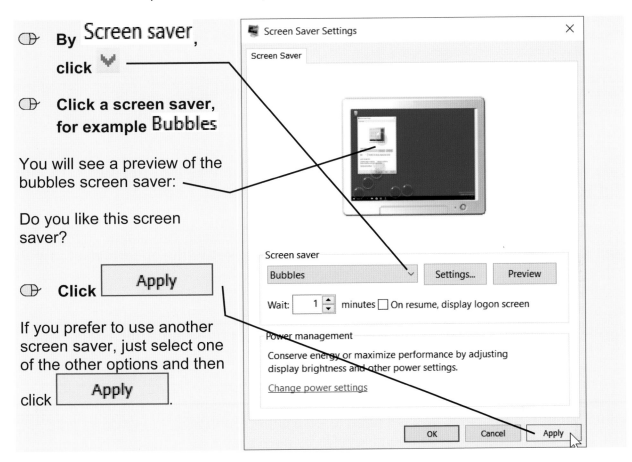

☞ **By** Screen saver,
   click ∨

☞ **Click a screen saver,**
   for example Bubbles

You will see a preview of the
bubbles screen saver:

Do you like this screen
saver?

☞ **Click** [Apply]

If you prefer to use another
screen saver, just select one
of the other options and then
click [Apply].

 HELP! I do not see a new window.
If you do not see the window with the screen saver setup right away, it may have
opened in the background. You can use the taskbar to open the window:

☞ **Click**  **in the taskbar**

When you are completely finished:

☞ **Click** [OK]

 Tip
Set a waiting period
If you have selected a screen saver, you can also set the inactivity period:

 . Change the inactivity period by clicking the arrow buttons ⏶⏷.

Tip

Screen saver with photos

If you have some nice pictures on your computer, you can use them as a screen saver. By Screen saver, select the Photos option. Next, click Settings... . Now you can choose the desired settings in the window that appears. In this case, you are actually using the screen saver as a slideshow. The slideshow will start after a period of time of inactivity.

3.11 Setting the Sound

If you are using a program or an app in which sound fragments are played, it may sometimes be necessary to adjust the sound level. These are the options you have:

- set the sound level in *Windows* itself;
- set the sound level in the program or app you are using;
- set the sound level with the volume button on your computer, on the speakers, or on your screen.

These three options are related. If the sound level in *Windows* is very low or muted, for example, then you will not hear anything when you turn up the volume on your computer. If this happens, you will need to adjust the sound level in *Windows* first. The best way of adjusting the sound level is by playing music on your computer.

On the far right of the taskbar you will see the speaker icon 🔊. By clicking this icon you can adjust the sound level in *Windows*.

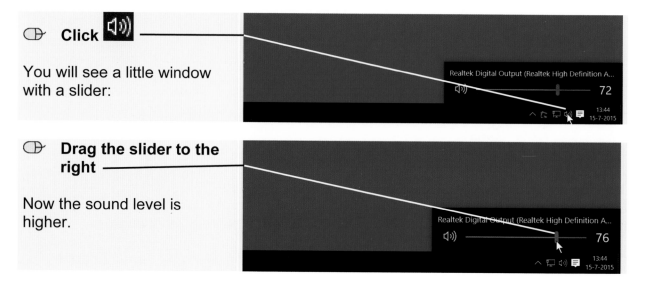

☞ **Click** 🔊 ─────

You will see a little window with a slider:

Realtek Digital Output (Realtek High Definition A...

72

☞ **Drag the slider to the right** ─────

Now the sound level is higher.

Realtek Digital Output (Realtek High Definition A...

76

Most computers have a button somewhere that lets you turn the sound on or off, or adjust the sound level.

On some computers, such as notebooks, the buttons are located on the computer itself. On other computers, these buttons may be placed on the speakers. If the speakers are built into the screen the buttons will be located on the monitor.

 Set the volume with these buttons

Now you should be able to clearly hear the sound.

HELP! I still do not hear any sound.

Do you still not hear any sound?

 Check if the speakers are properly connected

Still no sound?

 Consult the manual that came with your devices

You may find some clues that will help you.

Still no sound?

 Contact your supplier

3.12 Adjusting the Power Scheme

The *Windows* power scheme is a collection of settings that manage the energy usage of your computer. Sometimes it can be useful to take a closer look at the power scheme. For example, if you think your screen turns dark too soon or if you have a laptop that goes into sleep mode when left idle for just a few seconds.

Take a brief look at the power scheme of your computer.

Click

You will see the *System* window:

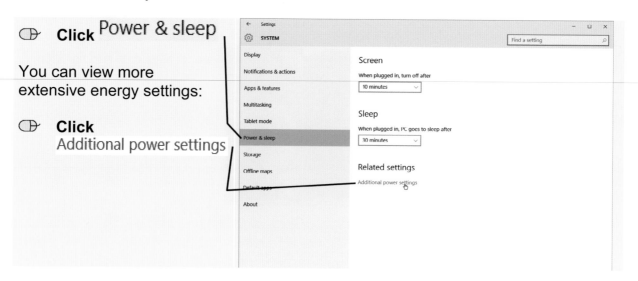

⊕ **Click** Power & sleep

You can view more
extensive energy settings:

⊕ **Click**
     Additional power settings

Windows contains the following default power schemes that will help you manage the energy usage of your computer:

- **Balanced (recommended)** : This scheme ensures full performance when necessary, and saves energy when the computer is not used for a while.
- Power saver : This scheme saves more energy, compared to the option above. The computer and the monitor can be disabled or switched to sleep mode earlier.
- High performance: This scheme ensures optimum performance. Laptop users will notice that their battery depletes faster if they use this scheme.

Your own computer may have other schemes available that have been given by the computer manufacturer.

⊕ **By**
     Balanced (recomme
     click
     Change plan settings

If the performance of your desktop computer or laptop is satisfactory, you do not need to change these settings. In that case, you can just read through this section. But if you are not satisfied, for instance, because your screen turns dark too soon, or your laptop goes into sleep mode too quickly, you can adjust the settings. Desktop computer users will see the following settings.

You can change the settings by selecting a different period of time by Turn off the display: and Put the computer to sleep:.

When you have finished changing the settings:

 Click Save changes

If you do not want to change anything, click Cancel .

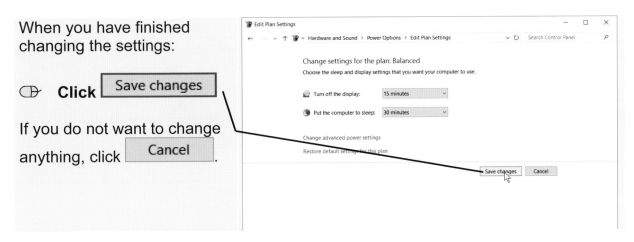

Laptop users will also see settings for On battery and Plugged in . You can change these too, if you wish.

HELP! I cannot change the power scheme.

If your computer is part of a company or organizational network, such as a school or a business, the systems administrator may have disabled or even removed some components. In that case, you may not be able to adjust the power scheme.

☞ **Close the *Power Options* window** ✂1

☞ **Close *Settings*** ✂1

Tip

How do I wake up my computer from sleep mode?
The sleep mode saves energy. Before the computer goes into sleep mode, all the open documents, programs and apps are saved. The computer can be taken out of sleep mode very quickly (usually within a few seconds) and you can resume working. Enabling the sleep mode can be compared to the pause play function on a DVD player. The computer immediately stops all operations and starts them up again so you can continue working where you left off.

Most computers can be woken up from sleep mode by pressing the power switch of the device. However, computers may differ in this respect. You might also need to press a key, click the mouse, or open the cover of a laptop or notebook, in order to disable the sleep mode.

☞ **Read the documentation or manual that came with your computer**

There you will find more information on this subject.

In this section you have learned how to customize the settings of your computer's *Power Plan*. Not satisfied about a particular setting? You can always go back to the original settings. Just follow this section and restore the default settings.

3.13 Background Information

Dictionary

Desktop	The work area on a computer screen, comparable to an actual desktop. When you open a program it appears on the desktop.
Desktop background	The desktop background is the area you work in on your computer. You can select one of the backgrounds that come with *Windows*, use a digital photo from your own collection, or set a plain, single-color background.
Power scheme	A power scheme or plan is a group of hardware and system settings that are used to manage the power usage of your computer. Power plans can help you save energy, enhance system performance or maintain a balance between these two functions.
Screen saver	Moving pictures or patterns that may appear on your screen when the computer has gone idle. This occurs after a certain amount of time when no user activity is detected with the mouse or keyboard.
Sleep mode	The sleep mode is intended to save energy. Before the sleep mode is enabled, all open documents, programs and apps are saved. The computer can restore itself quickly (waking out of sleep mode usually takes just a few seconds) so you can resume working.

Source: Windows Help

3.14 Tips

 Tip

Search for settings using the search function on the taskbar
You can very easily find settings by using the search function on the taskbar. Just give it a try:

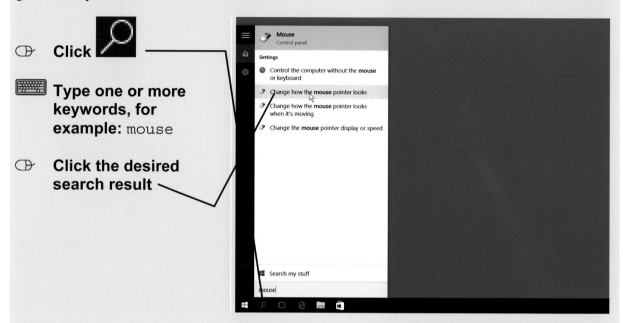

⊕ **Click**

⌨ **Type one or more keywords, for example:** mouse

⊕ **Click the desired search result**

The corresponding window will be opened.

 Tip

Setting up an accent color
You can define which *accent color* is used for various components in *Windows*. The accent color is used in windows and the Start menu, among others:

☞ **Open** *Settings*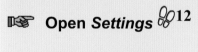

Personalization
Background, lock
⊕ **Click**   screen, colors

⊕ **Click** Colors

- Continue on the next page -

☞ **Click a color, for**

example

You can see the change immediately in the preview and in the left-side of the window:

☞ **Drag the scroll box downwards**

You can define whether the color needs to be visible on the taskbar and in the entire Start menu:

☞ **If necessary, drag the slider ⬤ by**
Show color on Start, taskb
to On

Here too, you can turn the transparency on or off for the Start menu, the taskbar, and the Action Center:

☞ **Click** 🪟

You will see the change immediately on the screen and in the Start menu:

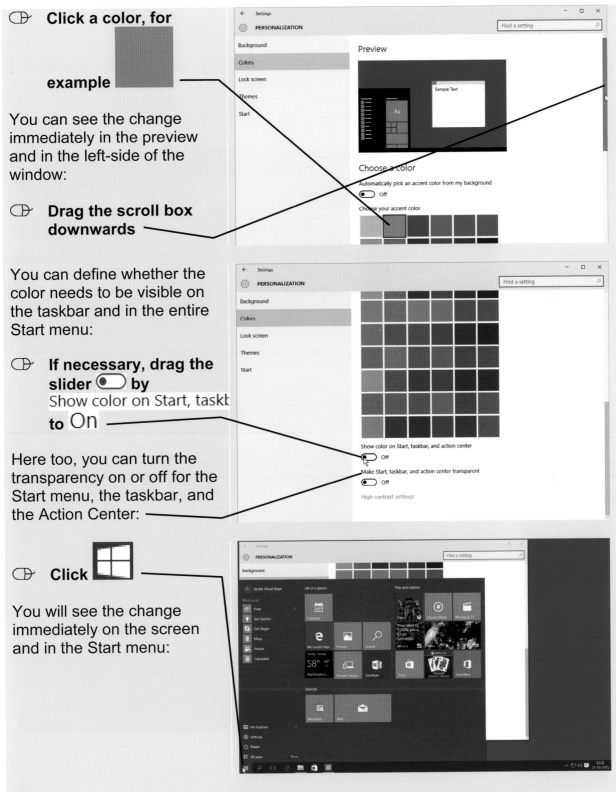

☞ **Set the desired accent color and the matching settings**

Tip

Turn live tiles on or off
In the Start menu you will see some tiles with an image that keeps changing all the time. These are the so-called live tiles that display current information, for example, the weather or news. You can turn the information for these live tiles on and off. This is how you turn on a live tile:

☞ **Right-click a tile**

☞ **Click**
Turn live tile on

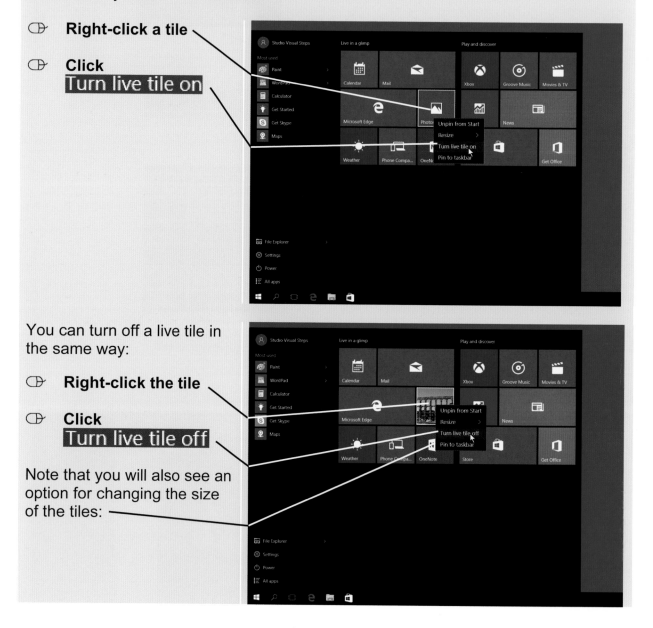

You can turn off a live tile in the same way:

☞ **Right-click the tile**

☞ **Click**
Turn live tile off

Note that you will also see an option for changing the size of the tiles:

4. Make Smart Use of the Internet

On the Internet you can find information on a wide variety of topics. You can manage your bank accounts, do some shopping, play games, or make video calls. Security is essential for computers that are connected to the Internet. There are a number of safety measures you can take yourself.

Edge allows you to set the safety settings by adjusting the security level for Internet access, for example. You can indicate which websites are trusted and which websites will get restricted access only. You can also ask *Edge* to block cookies, and use the SmartScreen filter.

In this chapter you will also read how to save and arrange favorite websites, and how to look up information on the Internet.

In this chapter you will learn how to:

- view the security and privacy settings in *Edge*;
- save and arrange favorite websites;
- search efficiently with *Google*;
- assess search results;
- search for information on a comparison website.

4.1 Security Settings in Edge

In *Edge* you can adjust several settings that will help you safely use the Internet. For example, you can set the security level for accessing the Internet. In this way you can determine how *Edge* should act regarding various websites. This setting can help prevent potentially malicious content such as viruses or malware from being downloaded to your computer without you knowing it. Malware is a collective term for malicious and harmful software.

☞ **Open *Edge*** 🦶²

To view the security settings:

In the upper right corner of the window:

⊕ **Click** ⁎ ⁎ ⁎

⊕ **Click** Settings

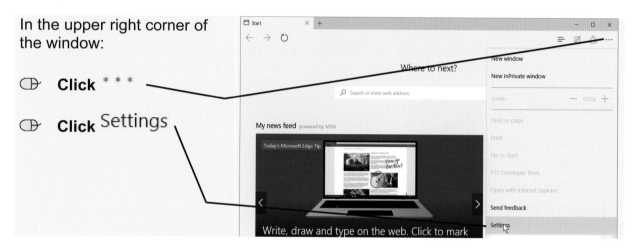

⊕ **Drag the scroll box downwards**

⊕ **Click**

　　View advanced settings

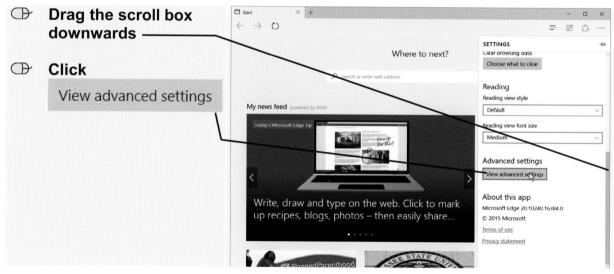

You will see the *Settings* window on the right-hand side:

 Drag the scroll box downwards ———

You will see that the setting for protection against malicious websites has been enabled: ———

You can read more about this later on in this chapter.

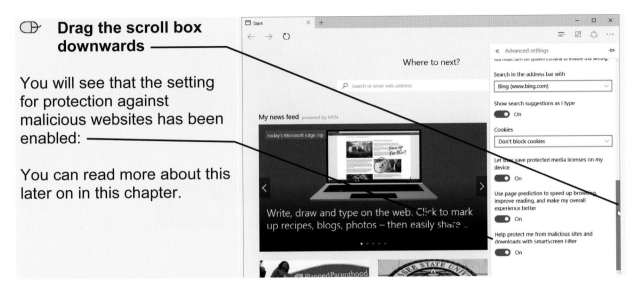

You may have heard of cookies. *Cookies* are small text files that are placed on your computer while you are surfing the Internet. These small files contain information about the things you have filled in on a web page in a form or in other ways.

For example, if you book a trip with an online travel agency, the website will create a cookie that contains the dates and cities you have filled in. Because of this, you can navigate forwards and backwards through the web pages, without having to fill in the data again on every page.

Note that these text files cannot 'run' on your computer (they are not programs), and their maximum size is quite small.

⤷ Please note:

Cookies are not dangerous. A website can only access the information you have provided yourself. Once a cookie has been saved to your computer, it can only be accessed by the website that has created the cookie.

One of the main provisions in the cookie law (adopted by all EU countries) is that consumers are entitled to know whether a website uses cookies. This law does not apply to all types of cookies. Cookies that are essential to the proper functioning of a website, such as filling a shopping cart, can be placed without your permission.

Asking for the visitor's permission is done in various ways. For example, a bar may be displayed above or below the window, as is seen in this example from the CNN website.

An example of a message
you can choose to ignore.
The rest of the page is visible:

There are also messages that
require you to accept the
information in the window, in
order to browse further on the
website.

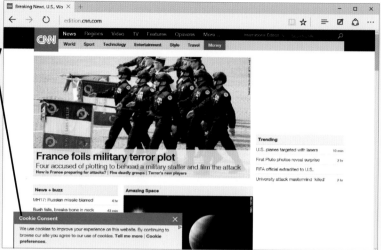

 Please note:

The cookie law only applies to websites in the European Union. If you visit a foreign
website outside the EU, you may not see any notifications regarding the use of
cookies, but most likely they will surely be used.

In *Edge* you can block cookies entirely, if you wish. But keep in mind that this may
restrict the functionality of a website.

By Cookies, **click**
Don't block cookie

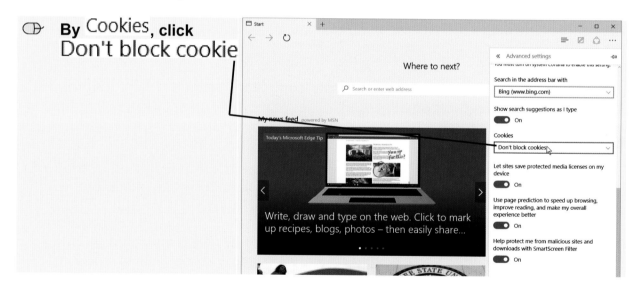

You will see three options:

Block all cookies: no cookie whatsoever will be accepted.

Block only third party cool
Third-party cookies originating from the ads on the websites you visit (such as *pop-ups* and *banners*).

Don't block cookies: cookies will be allowed automatically.

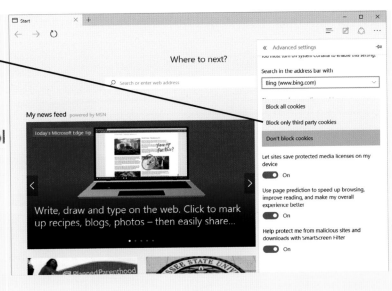

 Please note:

You may want to block all the cookies. But if you do this, there is always a chance of some websites not working properly. Of course you can experiment with different settings. If you do not like a setting, you can always select another one.

In this example we have not blocked any cookies:

Click
Don't block cookie

At the end of this chapter in the *Tips* you can read how to delete cookies in *Edge*.

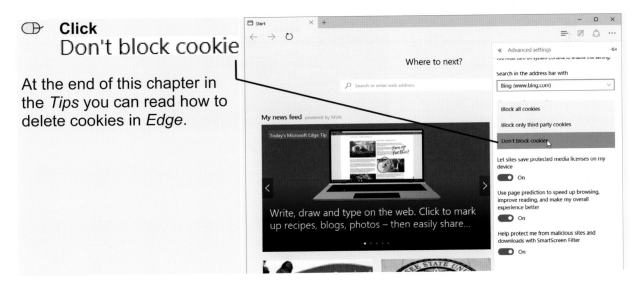

You can change even more settings in this window:

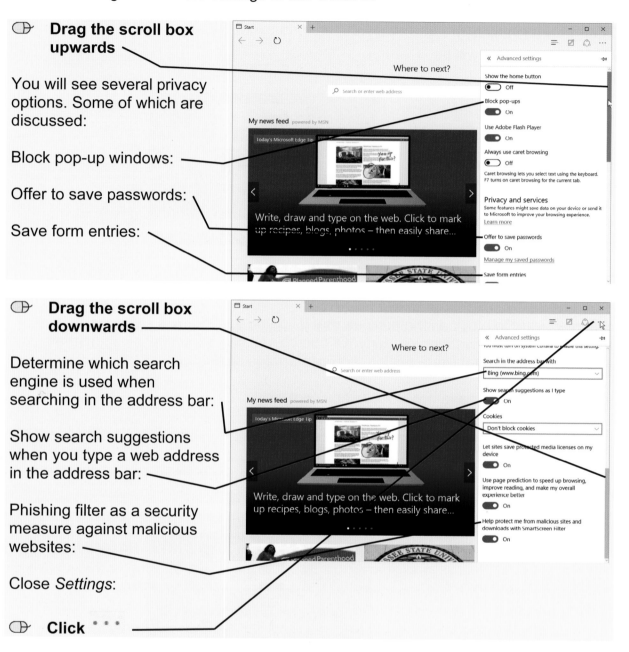

⮕ Drag the scroll box upwards

You will see several privacy options. Some of which are discussed:

Block pop-up windows:

Offer to save passwords:

Save form entries:

⮕ Drag the scroll box downwards

Determine which search engine is used when searching in the address bar:

Show search suggestions when you type a web address in the address bar:

Phishing filter as a security measure against malicious websites:

Close *Settings*:

⮕ Click • • •

Phishing is a method of persuading unsuspecting computer users to disclose their personal data or financial information by posing as a legitimate person or organization. In fact, phishing is a way of 'fishing' for information. In *section 5.1 Phishing* you can read more about this subject.

The *SmartScreen filter* in *Edge* will help to detect phishing websites. *SmartScreen* will also protect you from downloading or installing malware (harmful software). The *SmartScreen* filter uses three methods to protect you:

- The address of the website you visit is compared to a dynamic list of reported phishing websites and websites known to contain harmful software. If the website you are visiting is listed on this list of reported phishing websites, *Edge* will display a warning page and a warning in the address bar, telling you that this website is blocked in order to protect you.

- The websites you visit are analyzed, in order to find out whether they have any characteristics of a phishing website. If any suspect web pages are found, you will see a *SmartScreen* message that warns you about that. You can also give your feedback if desired.

- *SmartScreen* checks the files you want to download on the basis of a list of reported websites containing harmful software or other programs known to be unsafe. If any similarities are found, *SmartScreen* will display a warning message telling you that the download has been blocked for your own safety. *SmartScreen* also checks the files you download on the basis of a list of known files that are often downloaded by *Edge* users. If the file you are downloading, is not on this list, *SmartScreen* will display a warning message.

You can also let Microsoft check whether a specific web address is on the most recent list of phishing websites. And you can also report any suspicious websites.

In this section you have seen that these security settings are enabled by default in *Edge*.

4.2 Saving and Arranging Favorites

If you have found an interesting website, you can save its web address. Then you can quickly open the website without having to retype the web address again. Websites that are saved in this manner are called *favorites* in *Edge*. You can only save a web address as a favorite if the corresponding website is already opened. You can try this with the Visual Steps website:

☞ **Open the www.visualsteps.com web page** ✇²

In the upper right corner of the window:

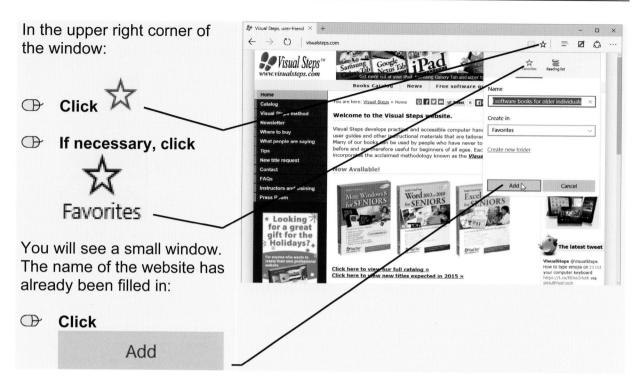

⊕ **Click** ☆

⊕ **If necessary, click**

☆
Favorites

You will see a small window. The name of the website has already been filled in:

⊕ **Click**

Add

The website has been added to your favorites. Now you can check and see how a favorite works. First, you need to open another website:

☞ **Open the web page www.cnn.com** 🐾²

You will see the news website cnn.com. Now you can quickly open one of your favorite websites:

In the upper right corner of the window:

⊕ **Click** ═

⊕ **If necessary, click**
☆

⊕ **Click a favorite, for example**
🐾 Visual Steps, user
http://www.visual

The favorite website you just saved will be displayed:

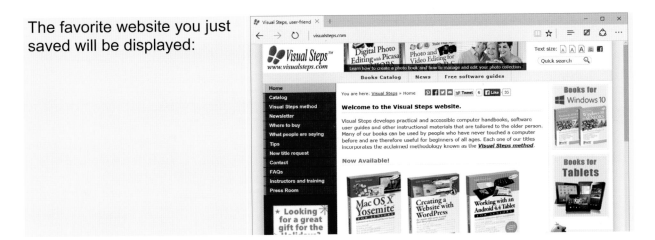

Edge remembers all your favorites, even after you have closed the program. You can collect a lot of your favorite websites in the same manner, and access them quickly at any given time.

You can assemble all your favorite websites in a single long list. But this is not very practical if you have a lot of favorites. It is better to arrange your favorites in separate folders. You can save the favorites ordered by subject, for example.
You can also use these folders to separate your own favorites from those of the other users on your computer.

To practice a little, you can create a folder for saving websites.

☞ **Open the web page www.seniornet.com** $\wp\wp$2

You will save this web page and create the folder all at once.

In the upper right corner of the window:

🖱 **Click** ☆

🖱 **Click Create new folder**

Add a name for the folder:

⊕ **Click the box by**
   Folder name

⌨ **Type:** Practice

⊕ **Click**
   Add

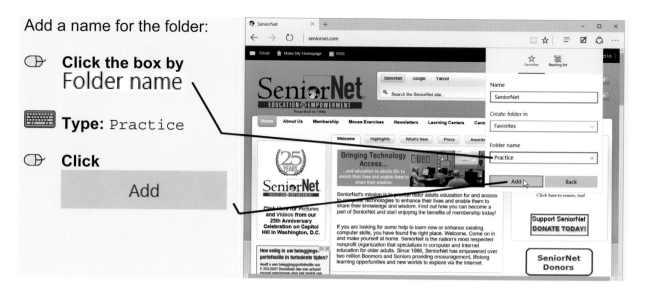

The folder has been created, and the web page has been added to the folder. You can check this right away:

⊕ **Click** ≡

In the favorites list, you see the ⬜ **Practice** folder:

⊕ **Click** ⬜ **Practice**

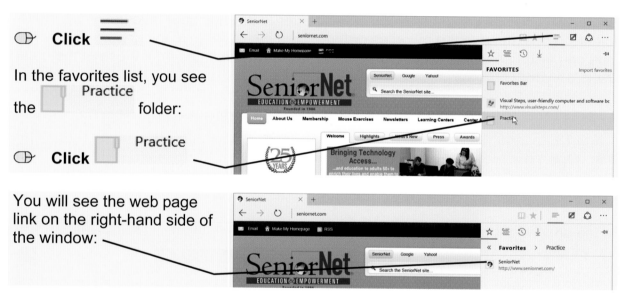

You will see the web page link on the right-hand side of the window:

It is very easy to save a web address in the new folder.

🖐 **Please note:**

You can only save a web address as a favorite, if the website in question is displayed in the *Edge* window.

 Open the web page www.wikipedia.com 𝒪𝒪²

You will save this website in the new *Practice* folder. Here is how you do that:

Click ☆

By Create in, **click** ⌄

Select the folder you have just created:

Click Practice

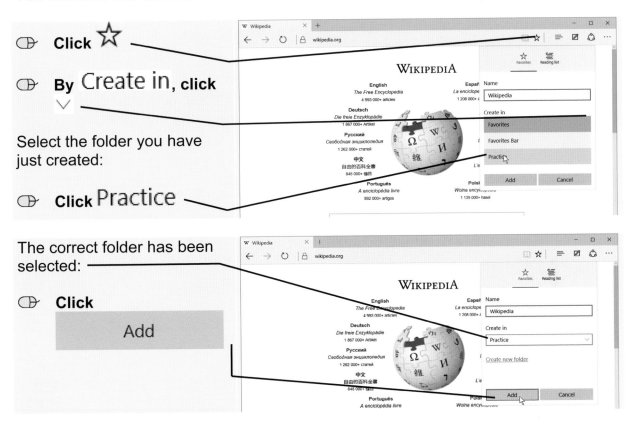

The correct folder has been selected:

Click

Add

Now you can check to see if the favorite has been saved in the correct folder. First you need to open another website, for example, the BBC website:

☞ **Open the web page www.bbc.com** 👣²

You will see the BBC home page:

Click ≡

The *Practice* folder is still open, and the Wikipedia favorite has been added:

Click W Wikipedia https://www.wikipedia.

Now you will see the
Wikipedia web page again:

If you have found an interesting website, you can save its web address. Then you can quickly open the website without having to retype the web address again.

4.3 Searching with Google

Google is mainly known as a popular search engine on the Internet. In most cases it will help you find what you are looking for. If this does not work, or if, on the other hand, you get too many search results, you can try the advanced search functions in *Google*.

☞ **Open the web page www.google.com** ✿²

You see the *Google* home
page:

In this example you are going to look for information on Vincent van Gogh. You start like this:

In the search box:

⌨ **Type:** Vincent van Gogh

While you are typing, the search results begin to appear:

⌨ **Press** Enter

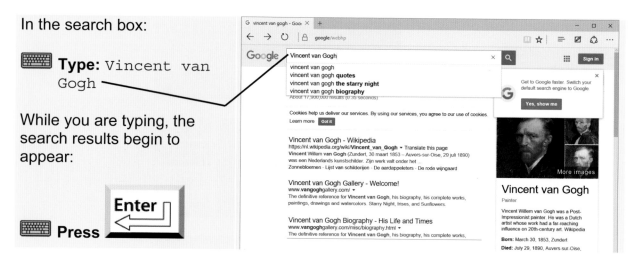

In this example, 17,900,000 pages have been found.

At the top you may see sponsored links. These are marked by the icon :

⏻ **Click the first search result**

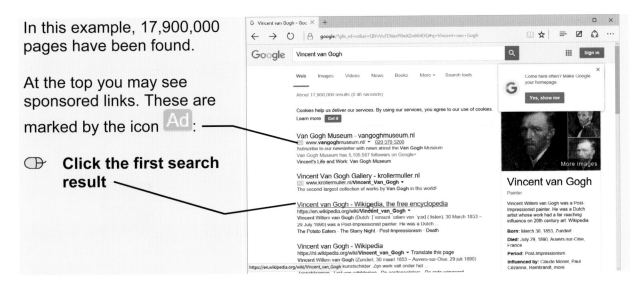

Please note:

The Internet is subject to constant changes. That is why the search results described in this book may have changed after this book was written. If you do not see the search result from the example above, just use one of the other search results.

You will see the *Wikipedia* page for Vincent van Gogh: You can read the information. But if you want to look at other search results:

You can go back again

 Click ⟵

The web page with the *Google* search results is displayed again.

Please note:

Wikipedia is a free encyclopedia, accessible to everyone on the Internet, and written by many volunteers. Every blue word in the text is a hyperlink to a new article regarding that word. *Wikipedia* has quickly become the largest reference book on the Internet. The *Wikipedia* website is regularly updated with new information. Qualified users are allowed to update pages whenever they want. That is why the window above may look different from the window on your screen.

A more specific search within the initial search results will usually get you closer to what you were looking for. However, if you know exactly what you are looking for, you can give the *Advanced search* option in *Google* a try:

⊕ **Click** ⚙

⊕ **Click**
Advanced search

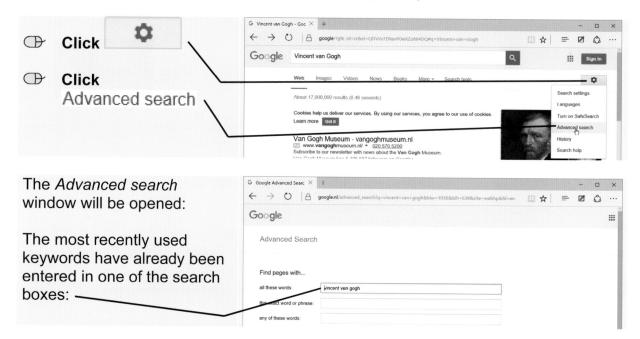

The *Advanced search* window will be opened:

The most recently used keywords have already been entered in one of the search boxes:

You are going to search all over again, so you can delete these keywords:

⊕ **Click the search box three times**

The words have been selected. Now you can delete them:

Delete

⌨ **Press**

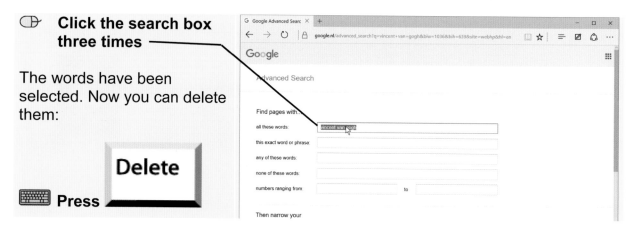

For example, you would like to know whether the Rijksmuseum in Amsterdam is open on weekends, and exactly what are the opening hours. First you fill in the name and location of the museum. The search box by **all these words:** will make sure the web pages containing both words will be found.

Although these words do not need to be entered in any specific order:

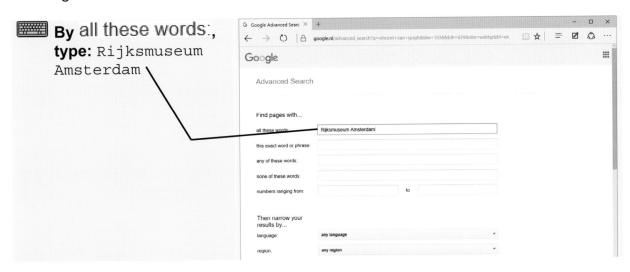

By all these words:,
type: Rijksmuseum Amsterdam

In the next search box, you can type additional keywords, for instance, part of a sentence, or a specific combination of words. Most search engines call this an 'exact word or phrase'.

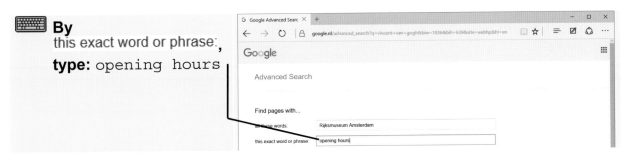

By
this exact word or phrase:,
type: opening hours

If necessary, you can enter more words by this exact word or phrase:. In that case *Google* will search for this exact phrase.

You can also type several words, of which at least one has to be found:

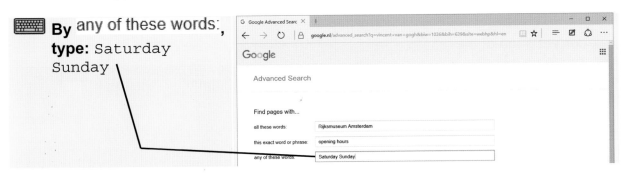

By any of these words:,
type: Saturday Sunday

You can enter even more conditions, but for now this will not be necessary. Start the search:

☞ **Drag the scroll box downwards** ——

☞ **Click**

Advanced Search

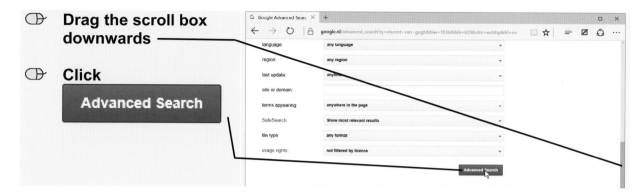

The search results will be displayed.

☞ **Click the first search result** ——

In this example, the first search result will lead you to the Rijksmuseum website, right away.

Please note: do not click an advertisement above the result.

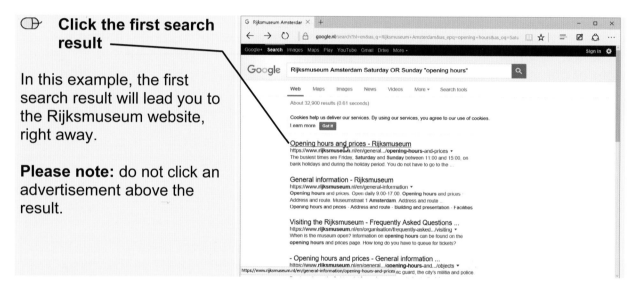

Since Internet is constantly changing, it is possible that the first search result does not lead you to the Rijksmuseum website. In that case you need to select the website that is most appropriate to your query.

The correct page of the Rijksmuseum website is displayed. That is to say, the page containing the information regarding the opening hours: ——

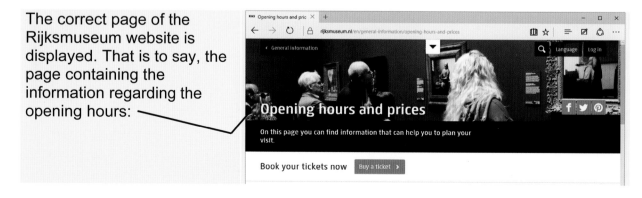

4.4 Interpreting Search Results

You can find a lot of information on the Internet on many different subjects. But the information you find is not always trustworthy or objective, as anyone can publish their own information. Many businesses will not publish negative comments about their own products. You could compare the information on a company website with what you read in advertisement leaflets. The facts on certain products will surely be accurate, but the products will also be more predominantly promoted.

There are many websites that offer reviews and opinions on products, such as www.pricegrabber.com. This is a website where products are compared and where consumers can post their reviews.
It can be useful to read other consumers' opinions, but keep in mind that these opinions are always highly individual. Reading a review on a subject is not enough to draw the right conclusion. Only when you can read multiple comments, preferably very extensive and supported by good arguments, will you be able to safely draw your own conclusion.

Even an online encyclopedia like *Wikipedia* is compiled by thousands of writers, who are often seduced into mentioning their own opinion on certain topics. Despite the checks performed by the editorial staff, some articles can be subjective, and therefore it is wise to check other sources as well.

In fact, on the Internet you should behave a bit like a journalist who is getting his information from different sources. If you want to get an idea of how trustworthy a website is, you should really check who has published the information on this website. You can often find a link called *About Us* or *Who we are* that provides information on the creators of the website and explains the reasons for making it.

4.5 Searching for Information on a Comparison Website

Comparison websites offer an overview of many different brands and products, without being associated with a specific manufacturer. This type of website is particularly useful if you are not yet sure what you want to purchase.

Well-known comparison websites are www.shopping.com, or www.kelkoo.com. Here you can read about the experiences of other buyers in order to find out if a certain web shop is reliable. These comparison websites also mention which web shops sell the same product too, and at what price. This way, it is easy to find out which web shop offers the best deal. Some web shops also use hallmarks or seals they have invented themselves. That is why it is recommended to thoroughly check out the web shops you want to do business with.

☞ **Open the web page www.shopping.com** ✐²

You will see the
Shopping.com website:

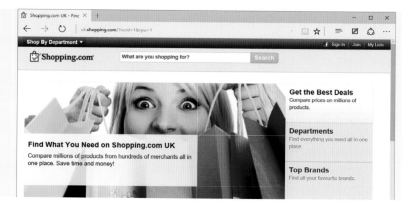

There are various ways of searching for a product on a comparison website. For example, you can search by using a small search engine. The search box is often placed on a fixed spot on the website. With this function you can search for a product name, a price, or a shop, for instance.

In the search box:

⌨ **Type:** `canon printer`

☞ **Click** **Search**

You will see all the Canon
printers on this website:

View the all-in-one printers:

☞ **If necessary, drag the
scroll box downwards**

☞ **By Printer Type, click ▶**

☞ **Click** All-in-One Printer

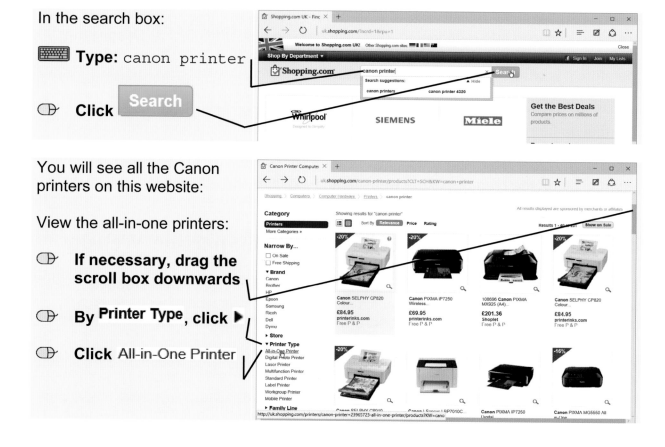

Now you will see all the Canon all-in-one printers together:

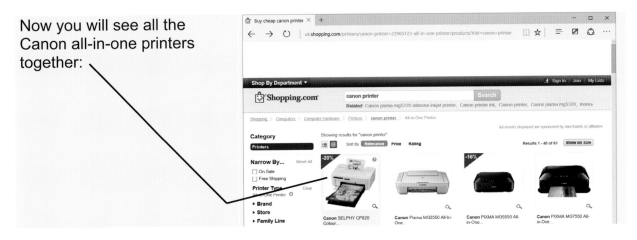

If you are not yet sure which brand you are looking for, you can also search in a different way. First, you open the printers page. You do this using the Computers category:

☞ **Click**

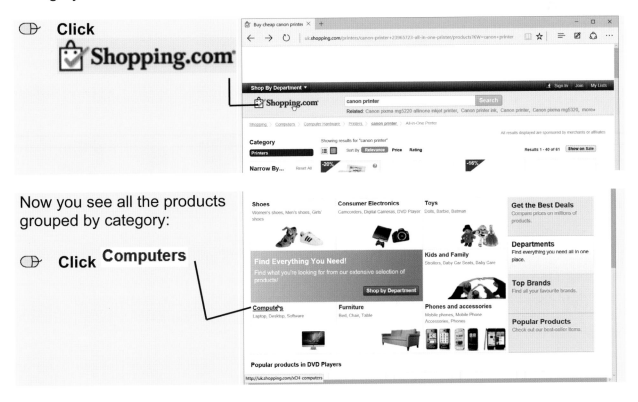

Now you see all the products grouped by category:

☞ **Click Computers**

 HELP! I do not see any categories.

The web page is constantly changing. Just wait until you see the category on your screen.

👉 **Drag the scroll box downwards** ───

👉 **By Computer Hardware, click Printers**

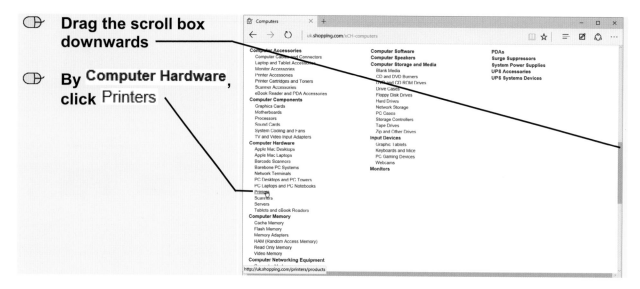

You will see the page with the printers:

You can browse through the printers:

You can quickly search by review and price:

You can also narrow your search with the options on the left-hand side of the window:

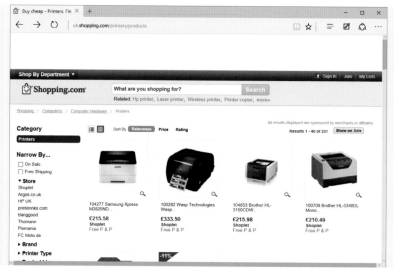

With the 'Narrow by' options you can search for almost all the product characteristics you might need. After you have selected these characteristics, the website will display the products that meet the criteria. For example, you can search for a Canon printer that will cost between 50 and 150 dollars:

👉 **If necessary, drag the scroll box downwards a little**

👉 **Click Price Range** ───

⌨ **Type in the boxes:** 50
    and 150

👆 **Click** [Update]

The search results will appear in the window:

👆 **Drag the scroll box downwards**

👆 **Click a printer**

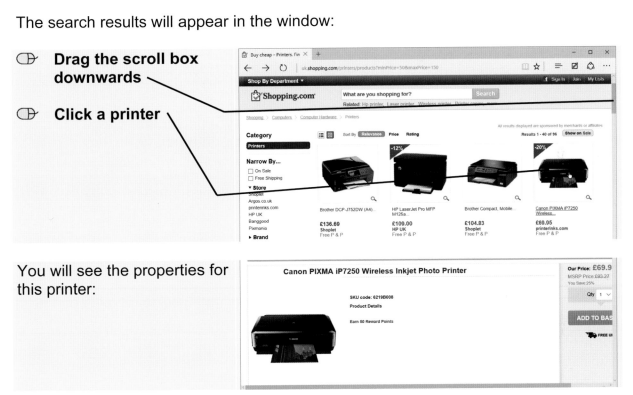

You will see the properties for this printer:

If you have found more information about printers, you can use this to decide whether you want to buy a certain brand of printer. On a comparison website, you can view the prices directly and other options from various shops. Once you have made a choice, you can access the web shop and order the printer right away, and have it delivered to your home address. You can read more information about safely purchasing on the Internet in *Chapter 5 Safely Using Email and Purchasing Items on the Internet.*

👉 **Close the windows** 👣¹

In this chapter you have received a few pointers for setting and checking your Internet security settings. You have also learned how to use the advanced search options in *Google*, and how to compare products and services on comparison websites.

4.6 Background Information

Dictionary

Advanced search	A separate search page in *Google* where you can enter very exact words or phrases for the search engine to find.
Comparison website	A website on which products and services are compared to each other regarding their characteristics, performance, and prices.
Cookies	Small text files that are placed on your computer by the websites you visit while you surf the Internet.
Exact phrase	Search terms that are treated as a unit. An option offered by *Google Advanced search*.
Favorites	Favorites are links to websites that you have added. By adding a website to your favorites list, you can go to that site by simply clicking its name, instead of having to type its address in the address bar.
First-party cookies	Cookies that come from the website you are viewing at that moment. They can be permanent or temporary. Websites can use these cookies to store information they can use when you visit the site the next time.
Google	A popular search engine.
Hyperlink, Link	A hyperlink or link is a navigational element in a web page that automatically displays the referred information when the user clicks the hyperlink.
Permanent cookies	Cookies that are stored on your computer which can be read by the website that created them when you visit that site again. These cookies will let you open the website much quicker, if you have visited it once before.

- Continue on the next page -

Search engine	A program that is constantly busy indexing web pages. *Google, DuckDuckGo* and *Bing* are search engines. You can use the search engine's web page to search for all the web pages that contain your search terms.
SmartScreen filter	The *SmartScreen* filter in *Edge* helps to protect you from phishing websites. If a website appears on the list of reported phishing websites, you will see a warning.
Temporary cookies	Cookies that are removed when *Edge* is closed. Also known as session cookies. Websites use these cookies to store temporary data. For example, the items you have put in your shopping basket in a web shop.
Third-party cookies	Indirect cookies that come from pop-up windows or banner ads on the website you are currently visiting.
Wikipedia	A multilingual, web-based, free content encyclopedia project. *Wikipedia* is written collaboratively by volunteers. The articles can be edited by anyone with access to the website.

Source: Windows Help, Wikipedia

4.7 Tips

 Tip

Safe surfing
In this chapter you have taken a look at various security settings in *Edge.* But remember, your own actions play a very large part in your security.

Here is a summary of things you can do to avoid mishaps:
- Always make sure that an antivirus and antispyware program is up-to-date and enabled.
- Always make sure that *Windows Firewall* or another good firewall is installed and enabled.
- Always make sure that *Windows* and the installed apps are up-to-date.
- Have *Windows Defender* or your other antivirus and antispyware programs scan your computer regularly.
- If something strange happens while you are surfing, break the connection immediately. If you do not need access to the Internet for a longer period of time, break your connection. This reduces the chance that others can break into your computer.
- Protect yourself from pop-ups, junk mail and phishing attempts by using the measures discussed in this chapter.
- Download files and programs from trustworthy websites only.
- Enter as little personal data as possible on websites.
- Do not click hyperlinks in emails and chat messages sent by strangers, and do not click suspicious links.
- Pay attention to the address and safety features of the website when you are doing your online banking or when you are buying something. The address (URL) should be exactly the name you expect and start with https://. Do not enter credit card or bank information, PIN codes or passwords unless you are absolutely sure you are on a secure website.
- Be careful when entering your email address on websites. Some websites try to gather email addresses to be able to flood them with spam later. It is a good idea to create an extra email account with a free provider like *Hotmail* or *Gmail* for use on the Internet. Use that email address to register on websites for example. If this address attracts a lot of spam you can always use a different address later on.

Tip

Delete browser history and cookies

While you are surfing the Internet, *Edge* stores information on the websites you visit. This is also called the *browser history*. The browser history consists of various parts, such as temporary Internet files, the history, passwords, small files stored on your computer by websites in order to save information about you and your preferences (cookies), and information you have filled in on forms on websites or in the address bar (such as your name, address, and email address). This is how you delete this data in *Edge*:

If you want to delete the history for an individual web page:

⊕   **Click** ☰

⊕   **Click** 🕘

⊕   **By the desired web page, click** ✕

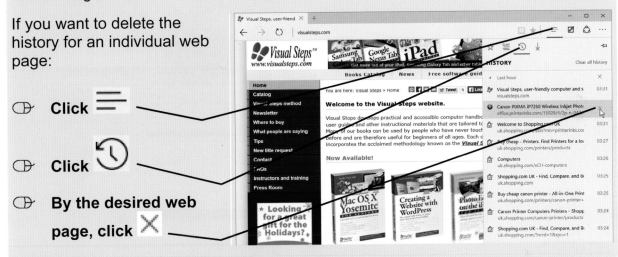

This is how you delete the entire browser history all at once:

⊕   **Click**
    Clear all history

You will see the components you can delete. In the dictionary shown earlier in this chapter you can read what each component is about.

⊕   **Check the box** ☑ **by the desired data**

⊕   **Klik op**
    Clear

The browser history will be deleted.

Tip

Reading list

You can also create a reading list in *Edge*. This list will contain links to web pages you want to read later on. You can read these pages even when you are offline and not connected to the Internet.

⊕ **Click** ☆

⊕ **Click** Reading list

You can type another name for this item, if you wish:

⊕ **Click** Add

The page will be added. This is how you view the content of the reading list:

⊕ **Click** ≡

⊕ **Click** ≣

You will see the reading list, including the web page you just saved.

In order to open a web page from the reading list:

⊕ **Click the desired web page**

5. Safely Using Email and Purchasing Items on the Internet

Are you receiving a lot of unwanted email every day? For example, phishing messages, spam, hoaxes, or chain letters. Nowadays, many of these types of messages will be blocked by your email service provider, but you can take steps yourself to prevent and delete unwanted email. In this chapter we provide some useful tips on how to do this.

You can order and pay for products and services online in a webshop. As you surf the Internet, it may seem amazing how easy it is to buy things right from your armchair, and in most cases, have them delivered to your front door.

There are various ways to pay for products and services you buy online. The seller determines the payment methods on offer. As a buyer, you need to agree to these methods. It is important to pay attention to the security issues regarding online payments, and you need to take the time to read the terms of delivery and warranty.

In this chapter you will learn more about the issues involved in making online purchases, such as recognizing a secure website and the payment methods being used. You can just read this information as a means to help you make informed decisions. Then you will know what to take into account when you purchase something yourself.

In this chapter you will get information on:

- phishing, spam, hoaxes, and chain letters;
- safe mail behavior;
- safe online shopping;
- payment methods on the Internet;
- identifying a secure website.

5.1 Phishing

Phishing is a method of persuading unsuspecting computer users to disclose their personal data or financial information by posing as a legitimate person or organization. In fact, phishing is a way of 'fishing' for information.

A familiar tactic in phishing is to send a fake email message that looks like a real message sent by a familiar, trusted source. This might be your bank, Credit Card Company, a web store, or another website you have previously visited. These fake messages are sent to thousands of email addresses.

In the email, the recipients are asked to check their bank data, for instance. The message contains a hyperlink for this purpose. If the link is clicked it may lead you to a website that may look like a bank's website. There you will be asked to enter personal information, such as name and address, bank account numbers, and PIN codes, supposedly to check if everything is OK.

An example of a phishing mail:

This email asks the clients from this bank to enter their personal information on a certain website. Criminals can then gain access to these accounts and empty them out.

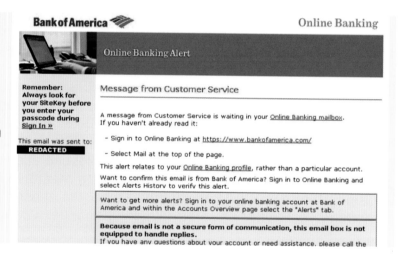

If you fall for this trick and enter your data, the information will be sent immediately to the criminals who have set the trap. Next, they may use your data to purchase items, open new credit card accounts in your name, or abuse your identity in other ways. These phishing mails and websites have a deceptively genuine look. They often use the bank's logo in the email, and the website may look like the legitimate website.

 Please note:

Nowadays, Internet criminals have thought of something new: contacting people by phone. One of the phony stories they use, is telling you there is something wrong with your computer. They tell you that the 'problem' can be solved if you enter various types of information (often personal data). This is also considered a kind of phishing.

5.2 Spam

By 'spam' we mean all those email messages containing unwanted and undesirable ads that seem to land in your inbox on a daily basis. These might be ads for ordering certain medication, online gambling, or shady dating websites.

Spam is intended to lure you to a certain website and get you to buy their products. The websites are usually run by swindlers who deliver worthless or illegal products, or simply do not deliver anything at all, once payment has been received.

Sometimes these messages may have originated from legal foreign companies, but since sending spam is prohibited in more and more countries, the odds of the companies concerned being trustworthy are very small. It is best never to react to this type of advertising email.

Here you see a few examples of spam:

From	Subject
Viagra Professional Store	The Highest Grade Meds And EXTRA LOW Price !
Be mail	Audi A4 quattro edition. Italia. Land of quattro®.
BM per Zurich Connect	RCA: Con Zurich Connect risparmi anche il 40%
alize5591148.77154@emailbasura.org	Do you desire to gratify your babe tonight?
Be mail	Approfitta in esclusiva della vendita evento DESIGUAL
Drugs-Store	SUMMER SALE SEASON STARTED! GRAB EXTRA 11% OFF!

Because there is always a small minority of computer users who react to spam, it is still worthwhile for the spammers to keep sending their spam mail. Sending an email does not cost them a lot of time or money. They often use a network of hacked computers. The computers themselves may have been taken over in an illegal manner and then are used remotely by criminals. This is often how email addresses are obtained.

The annoying thing about spam is that your mailbox can quickly be filled with useless email and it takes a lot of time to get rid of it. Without taking precautions, the amount of unwanted email can increase up to hundreds a day.
Nowadays, Internet service providers use spam filters that block a lot of spam from ever entering your inbox. Because of this you will already receive less spam on your computer. But it is still wise to take your own measures against spam on your own computer. There are antivirus programs that will protect you from spam. The *Mail* email program also has a spam filter option.

 Please note:

Not all advertising email is spam. If you have previously signed up with a company and entered your email address, you will most likely begin to receive email from them. If this is a respectable company, there will be an opt out link in the email message (often at the bottom) that will lead you to a web page where you can sign off from this service.

- Continue on the next page -

Keep in mind though, that even some spammers will offer to put a stop to their ads in their emails. They will ask you to click a hyperlink in the email in order to sign out and stop the ads. But instead of signing out, you have in fact sent a confirmation of your email address, which will lead to even more spam. Signing out in this way is only safe if you trust the company because you have previously purchased something with them, or have explicitly given them permission to use your email address.

5.3 Hoaxes and Chain Letters

A hoax is a deliberately fabricated falsehood made to masquerade as truth. The Internet is full of these hoaxes. When one is used in an email, it is often in the form of a chain letter.

For example, you receive an email message that tells you to forward this message to ten others as soon as possible. If you do not do this, something bad will happen to you or to your loved ones. This is the digital version of the classic chain letter. Other versions contain a sad story, for instance, about someone who is seriously ill, and can only pay for special treatment if the email is forwarded lots of times. Supposedly some kind philanthropist or corporation will then pay one cent for each email that is forwarded. This type of story is rubbish. The sick person does not exist and the photos in the message have probably been plucked from the Internet. If a company decides to help someone, they will never do it like this.

Sometimes these emails contain an 'urgent message' warning you about a dangerous virus on the Internet. They often try to induce you into removing a certain program from your computer. This is usually a program that is essential for the normal working of your computer. If you remove it, you will very likely experience problems with your computer.

If you receive this type of chain letter or hoax, do not forward it. The hoax is primarily intended to gather as many email addresses as possible to be sold or used in future spamming. Many hoaxes and chain letters are also distributed through *Facebook*.

A very well-known hoax is the message warning you against a new type of (fake) speed camera, used by the police. The recipients of this message are asked to 'behave socially' and share this message with as many others as possible. Many people will actually believe this.

New UK speedcamera scare story a HOAX

Pictures of a supposed new type of covert speed camera being tested in the UK is spreading through Facebook and email.

The picture of the 'camera' which is installed into the central barrier/armco is accompanied by a variety of information such as the claim that it is being trialled on the A52 in Nottingham and on the A1 in Lincolnshire.

The claims are entirely false. The images have been lifted from a Swiss Police PowerPoint presentation where this device is being trialled. The device is NOT a speed camera, it is a speed measurement instrument and it is deployed in conjunction with the standard speed camera on a pole.

It IS NOT a new form of covert speed camera and IT IS NOT being tested in the UK. Please spread the word to correct the misinformation being passed around.

If you would take the time to search text used in this message on *Google*, you would quickly discover that it is a hoax.

In this example of a phony message you have supposedly won a prize:

You can win this popular gadget by sharing a message and 'liking' a certain web page.

But if you carefully look at the web hyperlink or email address, you will see that this information is not the page or email address from a well-known, legitimate company.

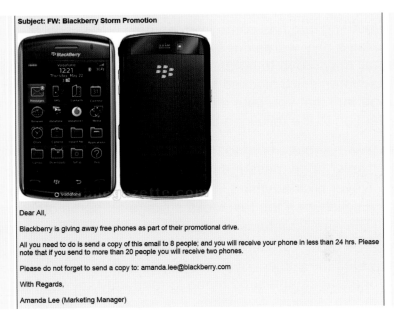

Subject: FW: Blackberry Storm Promotion

Dear All,

Blackberry is giving away free phones as part of their promotional drive.

All you need to do is send a copy of this email to 8 people; and you will receive your phone in less than 24 hrs. Please note that if you send to more than 20 people you will receive two phones.

Please do not forget to send a copy to: amanda.lee@blackberry.com

With Regards,

Amanda Lee (Marketing Manager)

This type of win-a-prize message is usually a scam. The purpose of the scam is to gather as many 'likes' as possible, then empty the page and sell it to others.

If you know what to look for, you can easily spot a fake 'you have won' message:

- the message is often in English with spelling mistakes;
- the message is not linked to the official website or the official *Facebook* page of the manufacturer;
- the *Facebook* page containing the fake message just contains a single message;
- if the offer appears to be too good to be true, it often is!

Another famous hoax features a picture of a wounded or sick child that is used to induce people to share the message with the claim that '*Facebook* will donate one dollar to a good cause for each shared message'… If *Facebook* intends to donate money they will not do it like this! Do not share these kinds of *Facebook* messages!

5.4 Safe Mail Behavior

There is a lot you can do yourself to prevent your computer from being infected by something that has come from an email message. A regular email message that contains only words does not pose a big threat. But an attachment included in an email may prove to be dangerous. Fortunately, various types of potentially harmful attachments are blocked by the security settings of your email program. But it still is important that you take a close look at your messages before you open them. Pay attention to the following things:

- Always make sure to use an up-to-date antivirus program.
- Never open messages from unknown senders. Delete them at once.
- Never click anything in an email containing text in a foreign language or in bad English, or if the text looks strange for some other reason.
- The email contains an attachment and you are asked to open this attachment.
- The email contains a link and you are asked to click it.
- Does the subject of a message seem familiar? Viruses sometimes use old messages and send these to randomly selected addresses of the contacts in an address book. If you think it is an older message, or a message that is not directed at you, then delete it at once. If the sender is really someone you know, you could always verify the email by calling this person first.
- Does the message contain an attachment with a strange name, or a strange file type? Do not be curious, delete it at once.
- The attachment is a program file, which you can tell by the extension .EXE, .COM, .PIF or .VBS. If you are in doubt about an attachment, then right-click the file. Next, you click *Save As*. Once this is done, you can select the desired folder on your computer and let your antivirus program scan this folder. Make sure not to open the file before you have scanned it.

Remember that deleted messages are stored in the *Junk* folder and that you regularly need to empty this folder as well.

5.5 Safe Online Shopping

You can buy all sorts of things on the Internet. Books, washing machines, bicycles cars, jewelry, computers, clothes, much more than we can list here. You can book your vacation or day trip, and pay for it on the Internet. You can even use the Internet to search for computer programs and purchase them online. Then later you can download and install them. All you need to do is enter your personal information on and the payment will be processed. In a short time, usually less than a day, you will be notified about your order. Then in just a few days it will be delivered to your door. There is no need for you to ever leave your home.

This is all very handy, but take care when you are shopping online. Take the same precautions as you do with online banking when you pay for your purchases.

The first thing to check is the reliability of the webshop you visit. Does the webshop actually deliver the goods you have purchased? A seal of approval, logo (or hallmark) is posted on many webshops to help you recognize this.

There are several seals in use, such as the Better Business Bureau and the Trust-e logo:

Some online shops such as L.L. Bean, for instance, have a sort of sticker that guarantees secure online shopping:

If a webshop has been awarded such a seal of approval, the webshop promises the customers to offer a certain degree of service when things go wrong while ordering or delivering goods.

In the United States, there are a variety of laws at both the federal and state levels that regulate consumer affairs. Among them are the federal Fair Debt Collection Practices Act, the Fair Credit Reporting Act, Truth in Lending Act, Fair Credit Billing Act, and the Gramm-Leach-Bliley Act. Federal consumer protection laws are mainly enforced by the Federal Trade Commission, the Consumer Financial Protection Bureau, and the U.S. Department of Justice.
The majority of states also have a Department of Consumer Affairs devoted to regulating certain industries and protecting consumers who use goods and services from those industries.

Many products and services have been reviewed by Consumer Reports, which gives you an idea of the reliability of online shops. Consumer Reports is not a national institution, you need to become a member to access and benefit from the information. They are a rating service that reviews anything from cars, appliances, electronics, home and garden, to financial services, and more. Their website is at www.ConsumerReports.org.

On a local level there is a popular alternative called Angie's List. This is handy when you need to find a local plumber, painter or other service in your local area.
Angie's List: http://www.angieslist.com/quick-tour.htm.

Many online shops offer information about their guarantee (usually 100% satisfaction guaranteed, or the like), safe online shopping, privacy and security measures and other legal information. You do sometimes have to look for it, though. Usually, there will be a help or support section with a lot of different topics.

On the http://www.bbb.org website you can search for businesses that are BBB accredited. In this way you can check whether the webshop you visit is trustworthy.

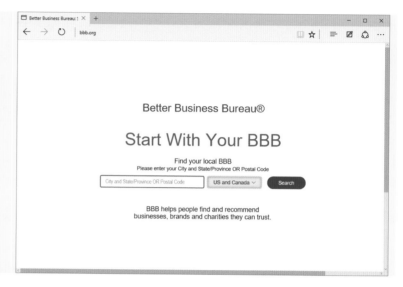

If the webshop does not have any seal of approval, you should carefully check out the business. The business name, address and phone number should be listed. You can use *Google Search* or the phone book to look up this information, but even if you do find something it does not guarantee that the business is 100% legitimate. Another idea is to visit comparison websites, such as www.shopping.com, or www.kelkoo.com, and read about the experiences of other buyers in order to find out if a certain webshop is reliable. These comparison websites also mention which webshops sell the same product too, and at what price. This way, it is easy to find out which webshop offers the best deal. Some webshops also use hallmarks or seals they have invented themselves. That is why it is recommended to thoroughly check out the webshops you want to do business with *before* you make a purchase.

When you choose a webshop, you can also pay attention to the shipping costs they charge. These may vary a lot, from one shop to another. And it is wise to check the options for returning goods and all the other general terms and conditions too. This information should be clearly mentioned on the site. This will save you from unpleasant surprises after ordering a product or other merchandise.

The next issue is the technical security of the webshop, although this is something that will be difficult to check. Is the system in which the webshop has been built, secure and protected from any unauthorized hacks by cybercriminals? If a webshop is awarded one of the legitimate seals of approval, they are usually required to carry out regular security checks and report their security status.

Along with the points described above, it is also very important that you keep your computer and browser software up-to-date by installing the most recent updates. Make sure your firewall is active and your antivirus program has been updated with the latest definitions. You should also be performing a virus scan at regular intervals.

Furthermore, it is recommended that you only use a Wi-Fi network that is secured with a password. This will prevent others from using your Wi-Fi connection. You should not use a computer you have borrowed or a public computer in an Internet café if you are sending personal or private information over the Internet. You usually have no idea what kind of security measures have been taken.

Many webshops require you to create an account when you want to purchase something for the first time.

You can often choose your own password for this account. Choose a unique, strong password and be sure not to use the same password for other services, such as your email service.

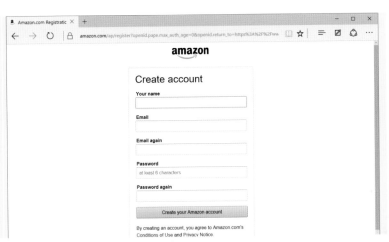

When you pay for purchases, more or less the same rules apply as for online banking. When you create a web account, make sure the web address starts with https://, and check if the padlock appears in the address bar:

In that case you can be sure the Internet connection to the web page is secure and encrypted and is therefore protected against unauthorized access.

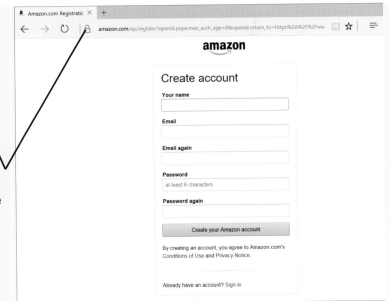

The last important issue is the safety of the payment method you use. Webshops usually offer a variety of payment methods. The most frequently used methods are payments through PayPal or various credit cards.

Each payment method works in a slightly different manner and will has its own unique set of risks or security measures, in case things go wrong.

When you go to check out, you can often choose between a variety of payment methods.

Many websites will offer information about the payment options on their website: ——

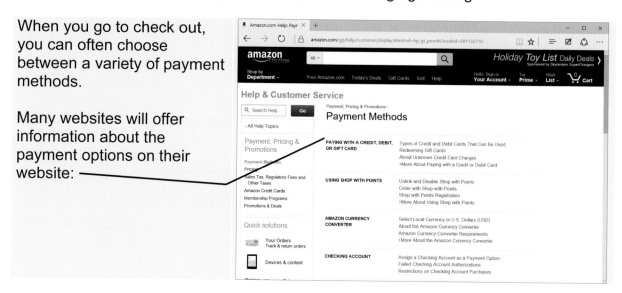

In the following section you can view a list of various payment methods and the pros and cons of each method.

5.6 Safe Online Payment Methods

There are various ways of paying for products and services on the Internet. The most frequently used payment methods are:

- bank transfer;
- one-time only payment authorization;
- credit card;
- PayPal;
- AfterPay;
- cash payments;
- gift card;
- prepaid credit cards.

There is a variety of payment methods used by online retailers from around the world to handle the purchases of goods and services. But what exactly are the advantages and disadvantages of each method? Here we briefly explain what the differences are.

Bank transfer

A bank transfer means you fill in a transaction form after you have received an invoice. You just follow the instructions on the invoice and decide when to pay the amount. The disadvantage of this method is that many webshops will only process the order after payment has been received and processed. This may cause the delivery time to be longer than with other payment methods.

One-time only payment authorization

This payment method means you give a one-time only authorization to a webshop or retailer to collect the amount due from your bank account for the purchased item. This authorization is only valid if a printed form has been signed and sent to the webshop in question. This takes quite a lot of time. The order is often only processed after the payment has been processed by the webshop's financial department. That is why very few webshops use this method.

Sometimes, you can authorize this type of a payment through the Internet. You will need to enter your bank account number on the web page which thereby authorizes the retailer to collect a certain amount from your account. This type of automatic payment collection is not legally valid. You will still need to sign and send the authorization form to the retailer to make the payment valid.

If an amount has been collected unjustly by means of a one-time only payment authorization, you can ask the webshop to withdraw the payment order. If the webshop does not comply, you can block all payments to this webshop through your bank account. Every new withdrawal by this webshop will then be blocked. You can reverse the payment of the amount that has already been withdrawn, usually within eight weeks.

Credit card

Paying online by credit card always poses a risk. You only need to fill in your sixteen-digit card number, the name on the card, the expiration date, and the security code (CVC/CID code) in order to pay. This information can be found on the card itself, and is easy to copy if someone gets a hold of it. That is why some companies such as *MasterCard* have added the *MasterCard SecureCode* as a means of extra security. This is a personal, secret code you need to enter when you want to pay online.

Credit cards are often used for online payments to foreign webshops. They may have a so-called chargeback policy. You can apply to use this policy if an order has not been delivered; a product appears to be damaged when you receive it; or if you have received the wrong product. The credit card company will claim the amount from the webshop and pay you back.

Both PayPal (see below) and the credit card companies lay the burden of proof with the webshop. If the retailer cannot prove he has delivered a certain product, for example, the consumer will always get his money back.
If you still want to pay by credit card, you could use a credit card with a low limit, or a prepaid credit card (see further on in this section).

PayPal

PayPal was established by the eBay online auction site. It offers consumers and companies an option for paying and receiving money online. It uses an email address associated with your PayPal account to transfer money. Businesses can also transfer money to you. The PayPal account is linked to your bank account or credit card.

A PayPal account provides you with a method for quickly transferring money online, free of charge. Many of the world's largest online retailers offer this payment method. In order to pay, you only need to know the recipient's email address. You just fill in the amount and click Send. The payment will be processed at once and your personal data is never disclosed to the online store.

PayPal also offers protection to its users. In that respect, the PayPal payment method is comparable to using a credit card. If you have purchased a product in an online store and paid for it with PayPal, but have not received the product, PayPal will make sure you get your money back.

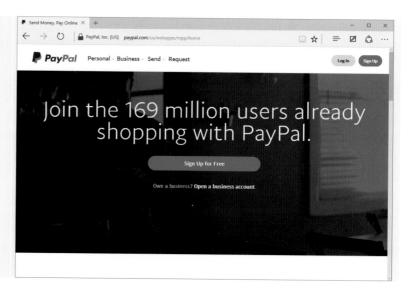

Purchases on eBay will also be reimbursed, usually for the full amount of the purchase. And if you purchase an item that does not match the listed description, you can often get your money back if you file a claim.

AfterPay

AfterPay allows you to pay for the goods after they have been delivered, through a bank authorization or your bank account, after you have been sent an invoice. More and more webshops are offering AfterPay as a payment method.
AfterPay does not interfere with the delivery process. The webshop itself bears the responsibility of getting their products to you so that they can be paid as quickly as possible. Some webshops charge a fee for using AfterPay.

They also may impose a limit to the amount for which you can order items. When you first purchase an item, you will be registered and a maximum amount will be set.

Cash payments

Another payment method becoming more popular by some webshops is the use of pick-up points, an address where the goods can be picked up and where you can pay for them in cash or pin with your bank card. Webshops that also have a 'real' shop often offer this possibility. If you buy items through second-hand sites or on eBay, you can also agree to pick up the goods in person and pay for them in cash.

Gift card

Paying with a gift card has also become increasingly popular in recent years. Nowadays, many (web) stores or services issue gift cards that can be bought in supermarkets, newspaper stands, and various other shops.

Examples of these gift cards are the *iTunes* gift cards, the Amazon gift card, and cards for various book and clothing shops. You can even buy gift cards for a visit to a beauty parlor, a restaurant and much more.

Paying with a gift card is safe, because you cannot spend more than the amount that is registered to the card. You do not need to spend the entire amount at once. But you should take into account that the card may be valid for a limited period of time. These cards often expire after a year or within a few years after the last purchase paid with the card.

Prepaid credit cards

Another safe payment method to use on the Internet is a prepaid credit card. With a prepaid credit card you cannot spend more money than is credited to the card. The card contains a sixteen-digit card number, just like other credit cards, an expiration date, and a security code on the back (CVC/CID code). You need to enter this information when you pay for an item online.

The best-known card is the 3V prepaid Visa card, but there are other cards available from other parties. PayPal even offers its own version: the PayPal Prepaid MasterCard®. You can buy the 3V prepaid Visa card in various supermarkets, newspaper stands, and gas stations for example in Canada and the United Kingdom.

In order to activate the card, you will need to create an account. Using the card is not free and there is often a minimum monthly fee required. There may also be additional fees for:

- adding or reloading funds to the card in a shop, or online;
- withdrawing cash with the card;
- payments outside your own country or outside the Eurozone;
- reversing an amount to your bank account;
- inactivity, if you do no use the card for longer than a certain period.

The Paysafe card is another type of prepaid credit card, with which you can pay online and remain anonymous. The card is available at several outlets, such as gas stations, newspaper stands, supermarkets, and tobacconists.
The Paysafe card is available in amounts of 10, 25, 50, or 100 euros or 10, 30, 50, or 100 dollars. You can combine up to ten cards, in order to pay larger amounts.

There are more than 4000 webshops that accept the Paysafe card as a payment method, and websites that offer items such as ringtones and games often accept this card too. The back of the Paysafe card contains a sixteen-digit PIN code, which will become visible if you scratch the surface of the card. You need to enter this code in the checkout section of the webshop.

When you create an account with My Paysafe card, you can load the PIN codes you have purchased. The total value of all the Paysafe card PIN codes you have loaded represents the amount of money you can use. If you use this method, you will no longer need to enter a sixteen-digit PIN code. You can use your user name and password for your My Paysafe card account instead.

5.7 After You Have Paid

After you have ordered and paid for your product, you will need to wait until it is delivered. Usually, you will receive an email message confirming your purchase order. You can also make a screen shot of the window with the payment data just in case you do not receive a confirmation email right away. To be on the safe side, you can also save a digital or paper copy of each order, order confirmation, and all the terms and conditions.

If you have paid using your online banking account, you will often receive an email confirming your payment. This email is usually sent within a few minutes of placing the order. You can also check your bank account after you have paid.

If there is something wrong with the payment or the receipt, you need to contact your bank, credit card company or webshop at once. If necessary, you can get your money back through chargeback (with a credit card), or a reverse entry (in the case that an automatic payment has been withdrawn from your bank account). The shop that delivers the product needs to be alerted about this as well.

If you have any complaints concerning the business or the products, the first thing to do is to contact the business in question. Be sure to save all your correspondence with the business. If you cannot reach an agreement, you can always contact the national Consumer Authority in your country (in the USA you need to contact the US Federal Trade Commission, in Australia the ACCC) and lodge a complaint against the webshop.

Another way of handling a complaint about an online retailer is by publishing your story or experiences on a consumer website, such as www.consumeraffairs.com:

If you publish a complaint on such a website, you need to take into account that these websites only mean to warn and inform the consumers. Publishing a complaint will not guarantee you that the webshop will take your complaint seriously.

In this chapter you have learned about various Internet payment methods and you have read about the various precautions you can take to protect personal information and stay safe when shopping online or using email.

5.8 Background Information

Dictionary

AfterPay	AfterPay allows you to pay for the goods after they have been delivered, through a bank authorization or your bank account. You will receive an invoice for the cost of the goods.
Hoax	A sting, swindle, deception, fake story, trick, con. Lots of hoaxes are spread through the Internet. If email is used, it is often in the form of a chain letter.
Https://	If you see this prefix in front of a web address, the Internet connection is secure (encrypted data traffic).
PayPal	PayPal is an online payment service with which you can quickly and safely pay for items in webshops that offer this payment method. PayPal is owned by the popular eBay auction website.
Phishing	A form of fraud in which the attacker tries to learn information such as login credentials or account information by masquerading as a reputable entity or person.
Spam	Unwanted, commercial email.
Spyware	A type of software that can display advertisements, such as pop-ups, collect personal information about you, or change your computer settings without asking permission.
Virus	A program that tries to distribute itself and spreads from one computer to another, thereby causing damage by deleting or corrupting data, or that annoys users by displaying messages or changing the information that is displayed on the screen.

Source: Windows Help, Wikipedia

6. Working with Facebook

Facebook is one of the most popular social networking sites on the Internet. Since its founding in 2004, there are now over a billion people worldwide using *Facebook* to keep in touch with friends, family and colleagues, and the number keeps growing. The name *Facebook* is derived from the 'face books' that appear on paper and are used by American universities to help new students and staff quickly get to know one another.

If you want to start using *Facebook* and get to know other members of this popular social network, you will need to sign up first for a free *account*. On *Facebook* this is called a *profile*. You can add personal information to your profile, such as your name, age, occupation, education, and hobbies.

Once you have created your own profile you can contact other members on *Facebook*. These may include friends and acquaintances, but also people you have never met before. In this way you can build your own 'social' network.

In this chapter you will learn how to register for a free *Facebook* account and enter the settings for your personal profile. You can read about the various privacy settings that can be applied so that you can manually control who is allowed to see your profile information.
You will also learn how to search for friends on *Facebook* and add messages and a photo album.

In this chapter you will learn how to:

- signing up with *Facebook*;
- fill in your profile;
- enter your privacy settings;
- enter your account settings;
- sign off from *Facebook*;
- sign in with *Facebook*;
- search for friends with the Find Friends function;
- search directly for friends and confirm friends;
- view the News Feed;
- post news messages;
- post a message on a friend's timeline;
- add a photo album;
- deactivate your account.

Please note:

The Internet is changing all the time and websites are frequently updated. As a result, the screen shots in this book may differ from the actual images on your own screen. This will usually not affect the operations described in this book. If you notice a change, try to look for a similar button or option available.

 Please note:

The costs of maintaining the *Facebook* network are covered by advertising. A new user will need to get accustomed to these ads appearing. As time goes by, you may soon learn that it is fairly easy to simply ignore them.

6.1 Signing Up with Facebook

In order to use the services offered by *Facebook*, you will need to register for a free *Facebook* account. This account will give you access to *Facebook*. Once you have an account, you can start building your own network of friends on *Facebook*.

The first thing you need to do is to visit the *Facebook* website:

☞ **Open the www.facebook.com website** 👣^{2}

You will see the *Facebook* Sign Up page:

In order to create an account, you will need to enter some basic information:

⌨ **By** First name, **type your first name** ⎯⎯⎯

⌨ **By** Last name, **type your last name** ⎯⎯⎯

⌨ **By** Email or mobile number **and** Re-enter email or mobile **type your email address** ⎯⎯⎯

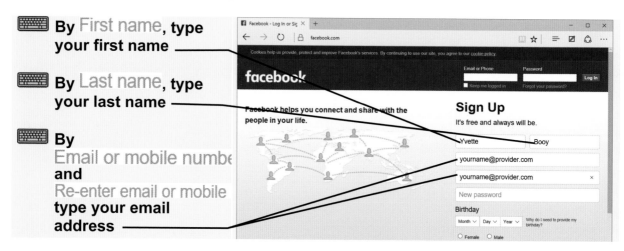

Tip

Use an alias
If you prefer not to use your full first and last name, you can also use an alias.

Please note:
Use a valid email address which you actually use to check your email. During the registration process you will receive an email message that will let you activate your account. This email address will also be used for password retrieval, in case you forget your password and want to receive a new one.
If you prefer not to use the email address from your Internet service provider, you can use an *Outlook.com* (*Hotmail*), *Yahoo!* or *Gmail* address instead. You will need to have an account with one of these web-based email services to do this. If you wish you can create this through the websites www.hotmail.com and www.gmail.com.

You can choose you own password. This password needs to consist of at least six characters, and can contain letters, numbers, and punctuation marks.

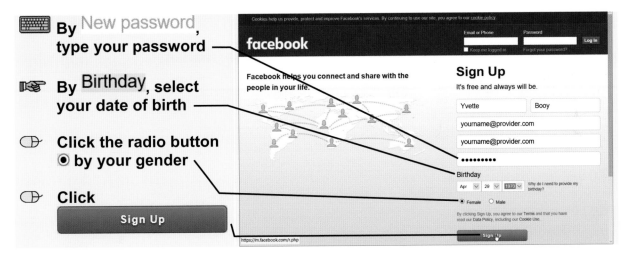

By New password,
type your password

By Birthday, select
your date of birth

Click the radio button
⦿ by your gender

Click

 Tip

Password
Make sure to pick a safe password that you can easily remember. For example, a combination of (capital) letters and digits.

You may see a bar at the bottom of the window, asking whether you want the program to remember your password. For security reasons, it is better to decline:

If necessary, click

No

You will see this window:

Facebook offers to help you
find friends by using your
email address book. For now,
this will not be necessary:

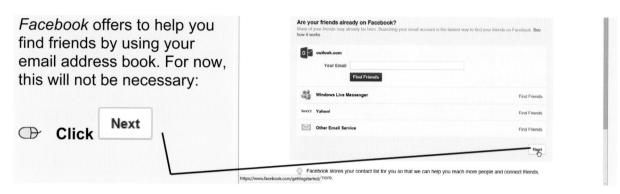

⬡ **Click** Next

In the next window you can add a photo to your profile. This will make it easier for
your friends to recognize you when they try to find you on *Facebook*. This does not
always need to be a photo of you, for that matter. Some people prefer to use a photo
of their favorite animal, hobby, or other subject.

This is how you add a photo
that is stored on your
computer:

⬡ **Drag the scroll box
downwards**

⬡ **Click** Add Picture

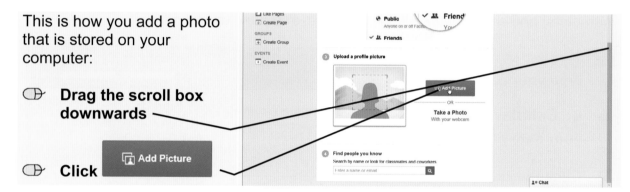

You will see this window:

☞ **Open the folder
containing the photos,
for example**
   Pictures

⬡ **Click the desired
photo**

⬡ **Click** Open

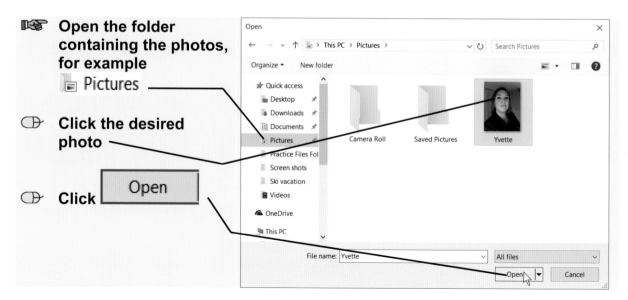

Now the photo will be uploaded to *Facebook*. After a few seconds, you will see this window:

The registration process is nearly completed. *Facebook* has sent you two email messages.

☞ **Close the *Facebook* window** 👣¹

☞ **Open your email program**

☞ **Open the email message from *Facebook* with the title *Just one more step to get started on Facebook***

In the email message:

☞ **Click**

Confirm Your Account

Please note: at the bottom of the message you will see a confirmation code. It is a good idea to keep this email. You may need this confirmation code later on.

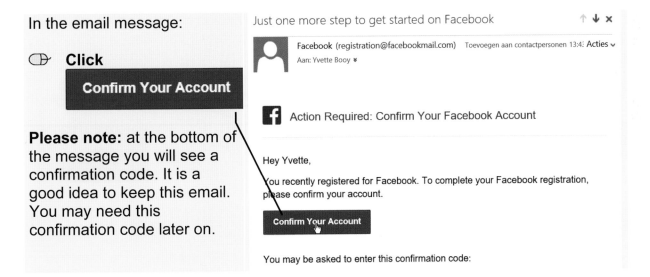

Facebook is opened again. You need to sign in:

⌨ **Type your email address**

⌨ **Type your password**

☞ **Click** **Log In**

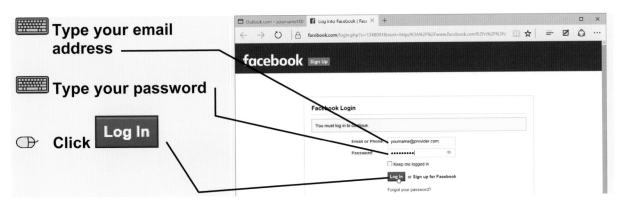

You will see a window notifying you that your account has been confirmed:

Now your registration is complete.

☞ **Close the window with the email message** 🦶¹

6.2 Filling In Your Profile

Your profile contains personal information that can be viewed by the people who visit your *Facebook* page. You can add more data to your profile, if you like:

In the upper right corner of the window:

☞ **Click your name, for**

example **Yvette**

🔽 **Please note:**

Be careful when adding personal information to your profile, such as your address and phone number. In most cases, it is not wise to publish this data on the Internet. If you decide to do this, you need to make sure you have set up the correct privacy settings. For more information, see *section 6.3 Viewing and Editing Your Privacy Settings*.

Add a college:

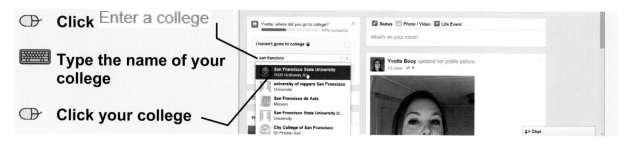

☞ **Click** Enter a college

⌨ **Type the name of your college**

☞ **Click your college**

Click Save

You can add your hometown:

In the left of the window:

By Enter a city **, type your hometown**

You will see one or more suggestions:

Click your hometown

Click Save

By Enter a high school**, type your high school**

You will see one or more suggestions:

Click your school

Click Save

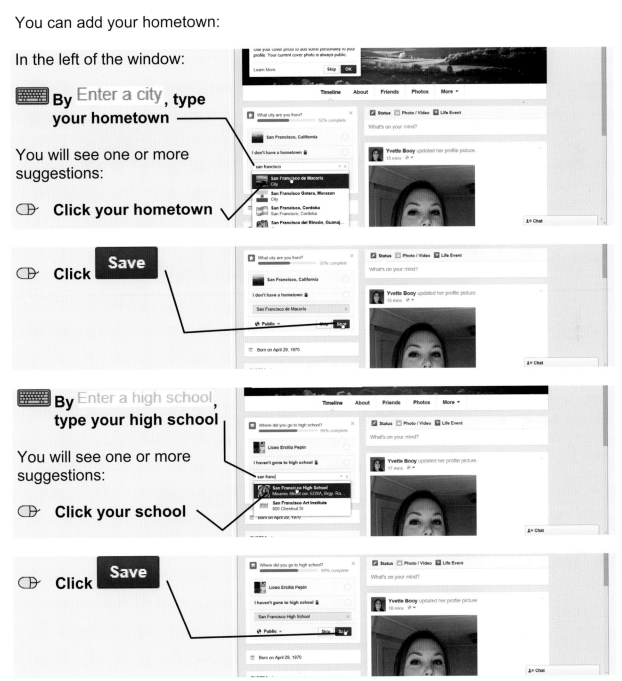

You will be asked for more information. It is up to you to decide how much data to fill in. You can always decide later to add this additional information. In this example we will skip this step:

You will be asked for your job location:

By Enter an employer, type the name of your employer

If necessary, click the name of your employer

Click **Save**

This information will help you later on, when you are searching for friends on *Facebook*. You can skip the information that does not apply to you, or that you do not wish to share with others. You can always add to, or modify this data later on.

You may see a small window in the upper left corner, where you are asked to post a status. You can skip this for now:

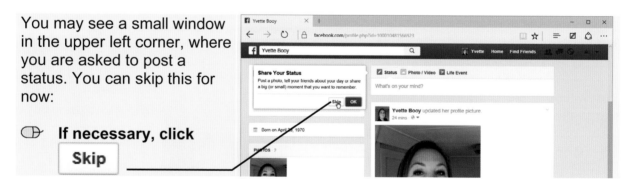

If necessary, click

Skip

☞ **Enter the other data, if you wish**

Or:

Click **Skip** until you see this message

View the data you have entered to your profile:

If necessary, drag the scroll box upwards

Click **About**

On the page containing your profile information you will see various categories. You can fill in the Family and Relationships category, if you want. In this category you can enter your current marital status, for example:

Click Family and Relationships

Click Add your relationship stat

By Relationship Status, click ⌄

Click the desired option, for example Married

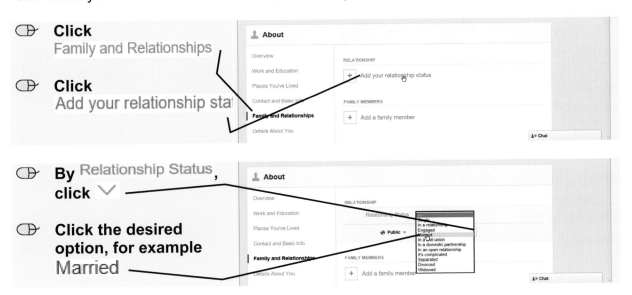

Click

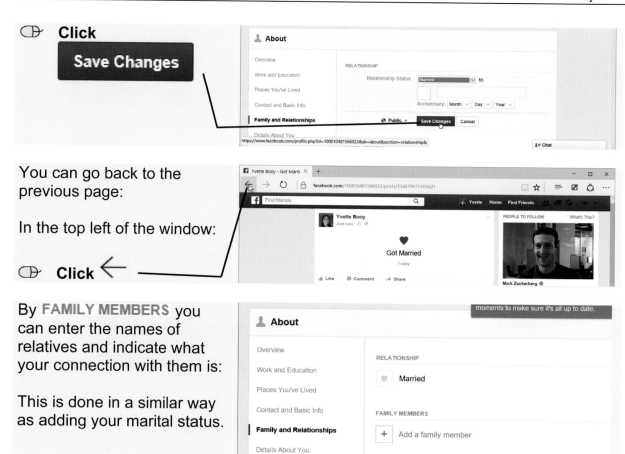

You can go back to the previous page:

In the top left of the window:

 Click ⟵

By **FAMILY MEMBERS** you can enter the names of relatives and indicate what your connection with them is:

This is done in a similar way as adding your marital status.

💡 **Tip**

Family members in your list of friends
If you have added any family members to your list of friends, you can select them in this window and enter the family relation. If your brother confirms that he is actually your brother, the family relation will be displayed in his profile too.

If you wish you can add more information to the categories listed below, for example:

Work and Education: here you can add information about your education and the places where you have worked.
Places Lived: here you can enter the places where you lived or your place of birth.
Relationship and **Family**: here you can add your current marital status. You can also add the names of family members and describe in which way they are related.
About You: here you can write something about yourself.
Contact and Basic Info: here you can add your address, phone number, website, language skills, religious beliefs, and political preference.
Life Events: here you can add events that happened in your life. For example a voyage you have made, or when you moved to another home.

It is completely up to you, which categories you do and do not want to use.

☞ Add information to the categories you want to use in your profile

When you have finished editing the data in a specific category:

⊕ **Click**

Now you can take a look at your timeline:

⊕ **Click your name, in this example**
Yvette Booy

Here you see your so-called timeline. To view your profile page:

⊕ **Click About**

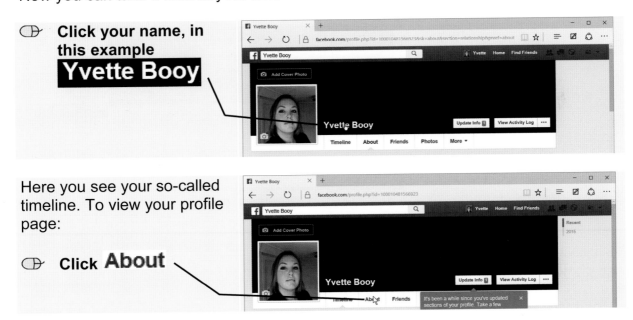

You will see how your profile is displayed to your friends:

Naturally, your own profile will look different than the one shown in this example.

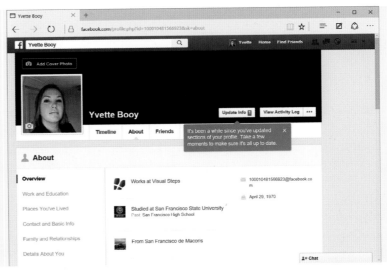

6.3 Viewing and Editing Your Privacy Settings

On the Internet, privacy is always an important issue. This is especially true for *Facebook*. In your profile's privacy settings, you can indicate exactly who is authorized to view the various types of information. You can also indicate who can view the information when you update or add new information to your profile.

First, take a look at the general privacy settings for your *Facebook* account:

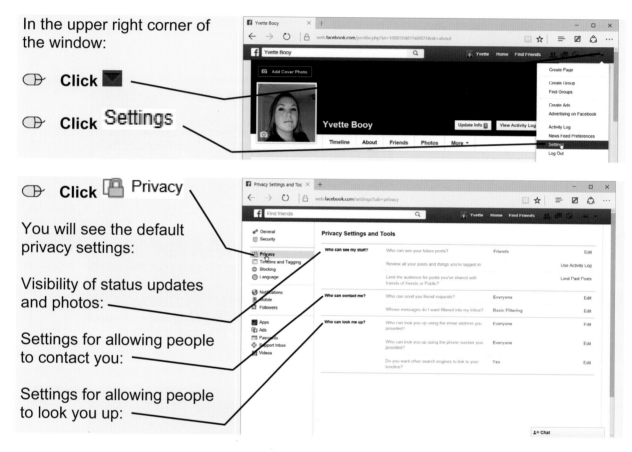

In the upper right corner of the window:

⊕ **Click** ▼

⊕ **Click** Settings

⊕ **Click** 🔒 Privacy

You will see the default privacy settings:

Visibility of status updates and photos:

Settings for allowing people to contact you:

Settings for allowing people to look you up:

The privacy settings let you indicate who is allowed to see multiple sections and activities. By default, most privacy settings in *Facebook* are set to *Everyone*. This means that everybody is allowed to see the relevant data. This will encourage people to contact others and create extensive social networks.

But you can also choose to allow a restricted group of people to view your information, such as *Friends*. These are people who have first applied to be your friend on *Facebook*, and who you have added as a friend.

For example, you can authorize only your friends to read your *status updates*. Status updates are brief messages you add to your profile. These may tell people what you are doing or where you have recently been.

If you only want your friends to be able to read your status updates:

 By
Who can see your future posts?

click Edit

 Click ▼

 Click 👥 **Friends**

In this window you can also set the privacy settings for other activities. Most sections will not yet be very clear to you, but you can always edit them later on.

The settings for making contact are an important item in this section. These settings determine who can search for you using your email address, and who can send you a friend request, among other things.

🢂 **Please note:**
If you place restrictions on the search options for your profile, your circle of friends will not extend and grow as quickly.

 If necessary, drag the scroll box downwards

 By
Who can look you up using provided?

click Edit

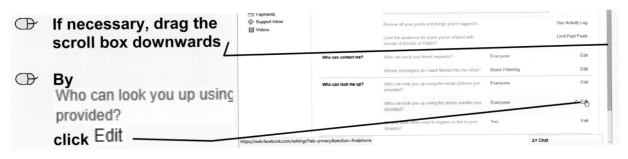

☞ **Click** ▼

☞ **Click the desired**
   option, for example
   🧍 **Friends**

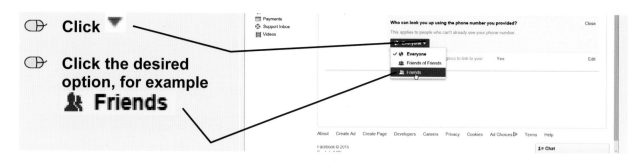

You can edit the other privacy settings in the same way.

☞ **Read the descriptions and edit the other privacy settings, if you wish**

This is how you view some additional settings:

☞ **Click**
   📄 **Timeline and Tagging**

You will see the settings for
the timeline and tagging:

Who can add content to your
timeline: ─────────────

Who can view the content on
your timeline: ───────────

Managing the settings for
tags (for more information on
tags, see *section 6.13 Adding
a Photo Album*): ───────

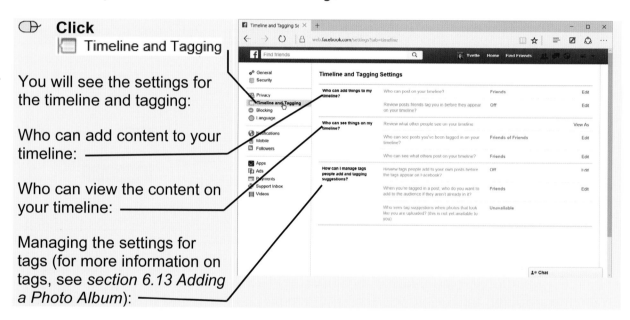

☞ **Read the descriptions and edit the other privacy settings, if you wish**

☞ **Click your name**

There are even more privacy settings. For example, you can determine who is
allowed to see the data in your profile when you edit it.

Here is how to view and change these settings:

⊕ **Click** | Update Info |

You will see this window about adding a cover photo. In the *Tips* at the end of this chapter you can read how to add a cover photo.

You can skip this step:

⊕ **Click** **Skip**

In the next window:

⊕ **Click** Add More Details

You will see the page with your profile data. If you want to edit the privacy setting for your work:

⊕ **Click**

Work and Education

When you place the pointer on an item, you will almost always see the privacy icon

🌐 (Everyone):

⊕ **Place the pointer on the name**

⊕ **Click** 🌐

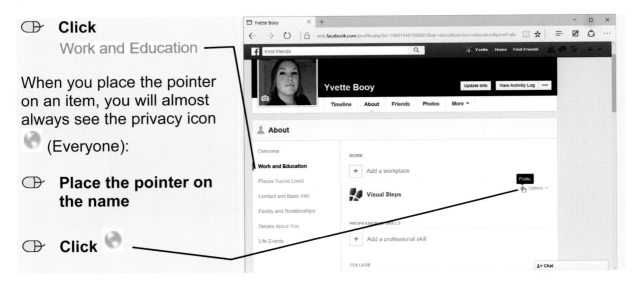

If necessary, drag the scroll box downwards

Click 🌐 **Public** ▼

Click the desired option, for example 👥 Friends

Click **Save Changes**

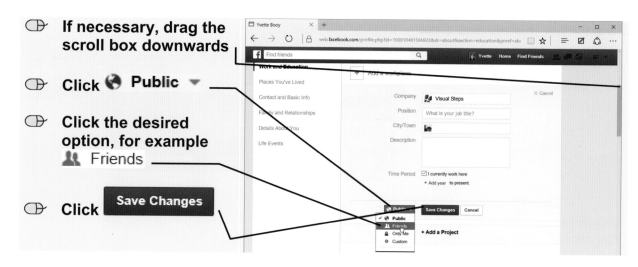

In this way you can determine exactly which information is accessible to the various visitors who want to view your profile. Now you can go back to your page:

Click your name, for example **Yvette**

6.4 Viewing and Editing Your Account Settings

You have already created an account with *Facebook*. There are various settings that are associated with this account. These include the data you have entered in order to sign up, such as your name and email address, but also settings regarding security, messages, and payments.

Here is how to view your current account settings:

In the upper right corner of the window:

Click ▼

Click **Settings**

You will see the settings for your account:

For example, if you want to change your password:

☞ By**Password** click
Edit

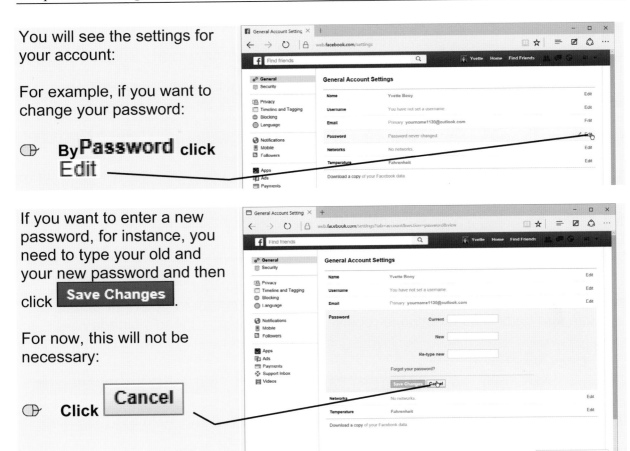

If you want to enter a new password, for instance, you need to type your old and your new password and then click **Save Changes**.

For now, this will not be necessary:

☞ **Click** **Cancel**

There are several setting categories for your account:

Security: here you can enter the security settings, such as safely navigating with *Facebook*, and receiving messages in case of new applications.

Privacy: here you indicate who is allowed to post and view messages on your timeline.

Timeline and Tagging: here you indicate who is allowed to post and view messages on your timeline.

Blocking: here you can manage your blocking settings.

Language: here you can set a different language.

Notifications: here you can determine for which *Facebook* events you want to receive a message, for example, when a friend sends you a message.

Mobile: here you can authorize *Facebook* to send messages to your cell phone as well.

Followers: allow followers. They will receive public messages and not be allowed as friends.

Apps: here you can state whether apps (programs) are allowed to communicate with your account.

Ads: here you can determine in which way you want to allow your data to be used for advertisements on *Facebook,* and how you want to view these advertisements.

Payments: here you can enter the settings for any payments through *Facebook*, for example, if you want to pay for certain services or games.

Support Inbox: here you see an overview of the status of the photos, timelines, and profiles on which you may have commented or posted a message.

Videos: here you can enter settings for videos, for example, the quality of the image.

In the following section, you can take a closer look at the **Notifications** category. Here you can indicate which activities you want to be kept up-to-date. For example, you can turn on or off the option to receive a notification of a friend's birthday.

Click **Notifications**

By **On Facebook**, click Edit

The notification is currently enabled. If you want to disable this option:

By **Birthdays**, click **On ▼**

Click **Off**

The notification setting has been changed. Now you can view the page with the settings for followers. Followers can see your posts in the news feed.
By default, friends will follow your posts, but they can also allow others (who are not your friends) to follow your posts.

You can change this setting:

Click  **Followers**

You will see the setting for the people who can follow you. By default, it is set to **Friends ▼** :

☞ **You can also view the other pages/categories, if you wish**

A number of the other options will probably not mean a lot to you at this point in time. But once you have a bit more experience using *Facebook*, and have worked through this chapter, you can go back and view your account settings later, and change them to suit your own needs and preferences.

You can close the settings:

Click your name, for example Yvette

6.5 Signing Off from Facebook

If you have finished working with *Facebook*, you can close the site. In order to do this, you will need to sign off. This is always the best thing to do, to ensure that other persons using your computer will not be able to use your *Facebook* account. Here is how to sign off:

In the upper right corner of the window:

Click ▼

Click Log Out

Now *Facebook* is closed. The next time you want to use your *Facebook* account, you will need to sign in again. In the next section you can read how to do this.

☞ **Close the *Facebook* window** ✍*1*

6.6 Signing In with Facebook

In order to use your *Facebook* account, you need to sign in first. This procedure prevents others from gaining unauthorized access to your account.
You can sign in like this:

☞ **Open the website on www.facebook.com** ✍*2*

You will see the *Facebook* Start page:

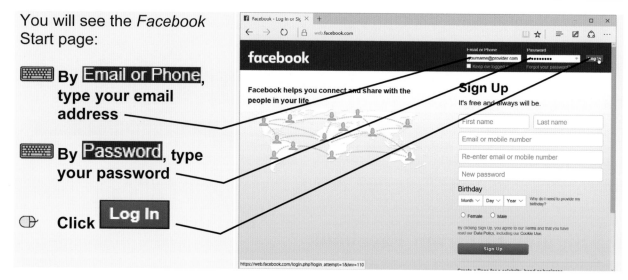

⌨ **By Email or Phone, type your email address** ⟶

⌨ **By Password, type your password** ⟶

☝ **Click Log In**

➥ **Please note:**

When you sign in, you will see the  option. If you check the box ☑ by this option, other persons using your computer will be able to use your *Facebook* account as well. We recommend leaving this option unchecked.

You will see the Home page of your account.

6.7 Searching for Friends with the Friend Finder

Facebook has a useful function that will let you check which contacts in your email address book are already active on *Facebook*. This function is called the Friend Finder. The Friend Finder can check the contacts belonging to your email account from a web-based service (*Gmail, Outlook, Yahoo!*), to see if they are active on *Facebook*:

In the upper right corner of the window:

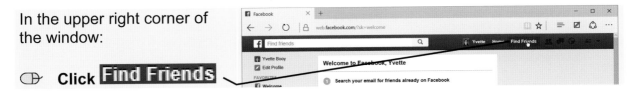

☞ **Click** `Find Friends`

 Please note:

Facebook will not use the contact data of your contacts without your permission.

In the following example we will search for contacts in a *Outlook.com* or *Hotmail.com* account. If you wish, you can search for contacts from your own email provider in a similar way, such as AOL, Verizon, icloud.com, yahoo.com, *Gmail*, or the *Skype* program. If you are using *Gmail*, you will need to download your address book first, and then upload it to *Facebook*. Follow the instructions in the windows that are shown, in order to do this.

Another easy way of finding friends, is by doing it manually. You only need to know the name or email address of the person you want to add. This way of finding friends is discussed a little further on in *section 6.8 Search Directly for Friends on Facebook*.

You will see various email services:

☞ **Click the desired email service**

If your email service is not listed, you click ✉. Like you do for *Gmail*.

⌨ **If necessary, type your email address**

☞ **Click** `Find Friends`

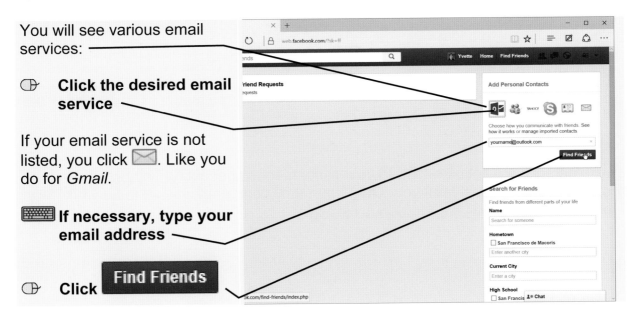

You may need to sign in:

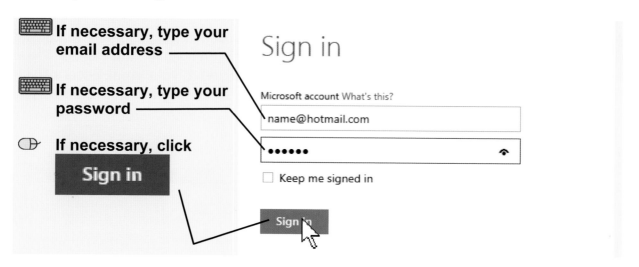

⌨ **If necessary, type your email address**

⌨ **If necessary, type your password**

☞ **If necessary, click**

Sign in

The system will search for friends.

If you use a different email provider, email program, or other email service, then click

the relevant service, type the email address, and click **Find Friends**. Follow the instructions in the next few windows.

In this example, there are a few contacts found who have a profile page set up on *Facebook.* This is how you add the contact you found as a friend:

☞ **Click** **Add Friends**

If you do not want to add a person you can uncheck the box ☑ by their name.

Please note:

These persons will not be added to your list of friends right away. They will first receive a friend request from you. Only when they confirm they want to be your friend, will they appear in your friends list.

Your address book may also contain a few people who do not yet have a *Facebook* account. You can invite these people through an email and ask if they want to create a *Facebook* account to keep in touch:

⊕ **Uncheck the box ☑ by the person(s) whom you do not want to invite**

⊕ **Click**

The invitation is sent.

This is an example of the invitation that is sent:

After the first invitation, two more reminders will be sent if the person does not answer.

6.8 Search directly for Friends on Facebook

You can also search directly for friends who already have a *Facebook* profile set up and send them a friend request:

In the search box:

⌨ **Type your friend's name**

⊕ **Click the account of your friend**

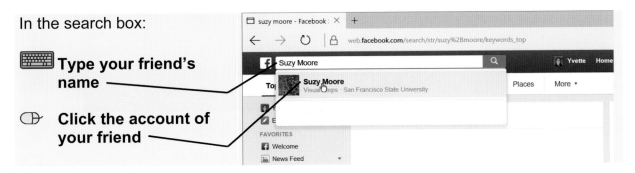

You will see the *Facebook* information about your friend. You can send him a friend request:

 Click   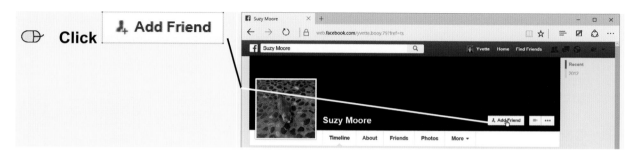

 **Tip**

Who am I looking for?
If you are not sure which person in the list is your friend, just click some of the names. You will see the information shared by these persons with others who try to find them on *Facebook*. This may help you to find the right person.

Please note:
You will be able to find lots of acquaintances through the search function in *Facebook*. However, some of your friends and acquaintances may be a member but they cannot be found by *Facebook*. This may be caused by the privacy settings of the person you are trying to find. Also, the *Facebook* search engine does not always perform at its best.
If you know that someone is already on *Facebook*, but you still cannot find him, you can try to send him an email and ask him to find you and send you a friend request. This may help.

You will see the confirmation **⅃₊ Friend Request Sent** .

In this way you can add more friends who have their own *Facebook* profile. After you have finished sending friend requests, you can go to your own *Facebook* profile:

 Click your name

6.9 Confirm Friends

The persons to whom you have sent a friend request will need to confirm that they actually are your friends. They can also decide to ignore your request.

You can do the same, if anybody tries to add you to their friends list. When this happens, you will see this icon 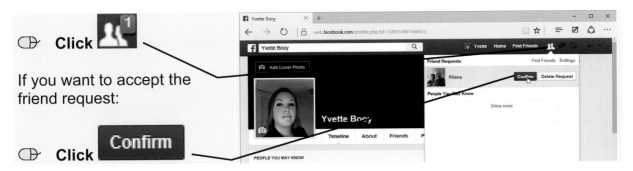 in the upper right corner of the window. If you have not yet received a friend request, you can just read through this section.

☞ **Click**

If you want to accept the friend request:

☞ **Click** Confirm

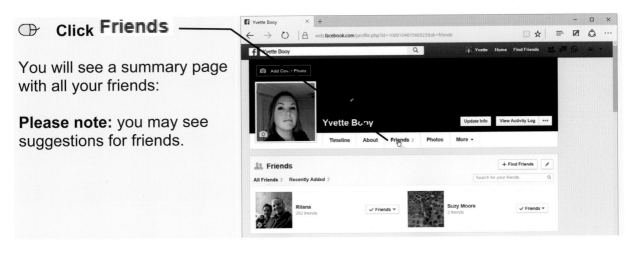

Of course you can also ignore the request by clicking Delete Request .

The friendship has been confirmed. Now you can take a look at your friends list. In the upper right corner of the window:

☞ **Click your name**

You will see your profile page. On this page your friends are also listed:

☞ **Click** Friends

You will see a summary page with all your friends:

Please note: you may see suggestions for friends.

Tip

Suggestions for friends
Facebook will continuously try to help you find your friends. You may notice from time to time, various types of suggestions given on different pages or while carrying out a specific action.

For instance, you will receive suggestions when you sign in with your account. In order to visit a person's profile page, click the person's name. In order to add

someone as a friend, click .

6.10 Viewing the News Feed on Facebook

The News Feed is a list of messages on your *Facebook* Home page. Here you see the messages regarding your own and your friends' activities on *Facebook*. The News Feed is continuously updated. For example, if one of your friends updates his profile or adds a new friend, you will see a message about this in your News Feed. The other way round, your friends will see the messages regarding your activities on *Facebook* too.

 Tip

Privacy
The News Feed will never contain any messages about the profiles or photos you view, which notes you read, which friend requests you have ignored, or which friends you have removed from your friends list. You can read more about privacy settings in *section 6.3 Viewing and Editing Your Privacy Settings*.

☞ **Click** ⬜f

☞ **Click** 🖻 **News Feed**

You will see the most important news messages:

News regarding an artist/celebrity or a company you are following:

News posted by a friend:

Options to react:

Please note: in this example you will see a news item posted by an artist. Of course, you will see different posts in your own news feed.

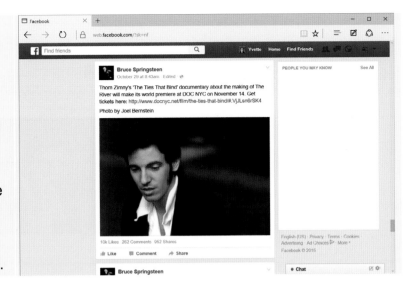

News messages can originate from various sources. Initially, they will come from friends, but also from the groups you have joined, official pages of which you are a fan, and the artists or other celebrities of whom you are a fan and who are mentioned in your profile.

Below each news message you will see a number of actions you can undertake. These can vary according to the type of news message:

If you like the news message:

☞ **Click** 👍 **Like**

You will see that your action is added to the number by the hand icon 👍 : ———

If you want to comment on a message, click 💬 **Comment** .———

If you want to share the news message with friends, or post it in your profile:

⊕ **Click** ➤ **Share** ———

⊕ **Click Share...** ———

You will see the window called *Share This*:

At the top of the window you can indicate where you want to place the message: ———

⌨ **Type a comment** ———

At the bottom you can indicate who is allowed to view this message: ———

⊕ **If necessary, drag the scroll box downwards**

⊕ **Click Share** ———

The message has been posted.

6.11 Posting News Messages

No matter how useful it may be to be automatically informed of your friends' actions, it is much more fun to post your own messages. You can do this by updating your *status*, in other words, by posting a *status message*.

Your status messages will appear in your own News Feed and also in your friends' News Feeds. You can enter your status message both on your profile page and on the News Feed page:

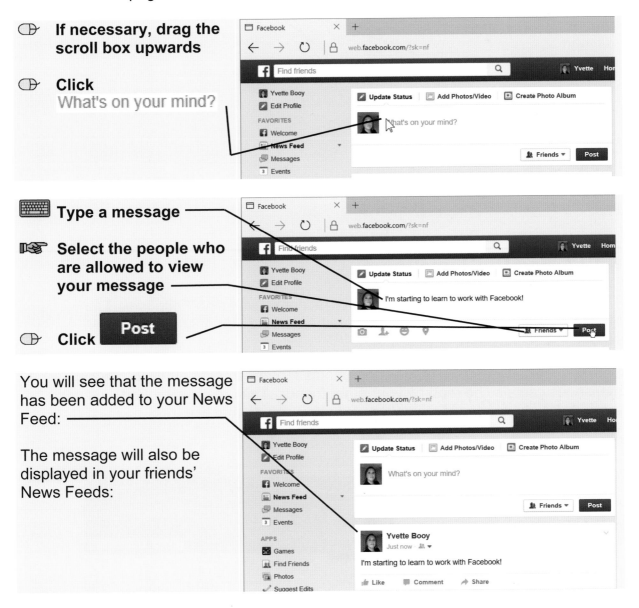

☞ **If necessary, drag the scroll box upwards**

☞ **Click**
What's on your mind?

⌨ **Type a message**

☞ **Select the people who are allowed to view your message**

☞ **Click** **Post**

You will see that the message has been added to your News Feed:

The message will also be displayed in your friends' News Feeds:

ᵠ **Tip**

Add more information to status messages
You can use the icons below the message box to add extra information to the status message:

Use **👥 Friends ▼** to determine who is allowed to view your message: ——

Use **👤⁺** to let others know who you are with at the moment: ——

Use **📍** to indicate where you are: ——

Use **📷** to add a photo: ——

Use **☺** to tell others what you are doing, or how you feel: ——

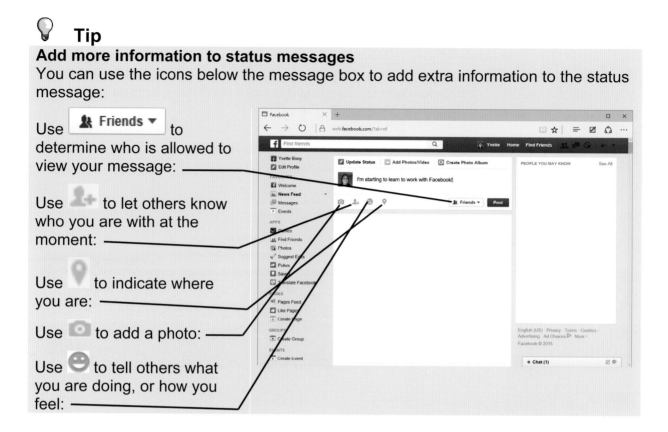

6.12 Using the Timeline

The timeline presents a summary of your recent activities on *Facebook*. The difference with the News Feed is, that on the timeline you only see your own activities, and not those of your friends.

Your friends can leave messages and photos for you on your timeline. These messages can also be read by your other friends. The other way round, you can place items on your friends' timelines too. You can do that like this:

☞ **Click your name, for example, Yvette**

On the timeline you see a summary of your recent *Facebook* activities: ——

Here you see the various components:

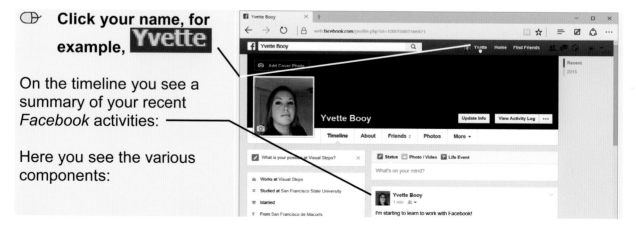

In order to post a message on a friend's timeline:

Click **Friends**

Click the name of a friend

Now your friend's profile is opened.

By ✎ **Post**, click *Write something...*

⌨ **Type a message**

Click **Post**

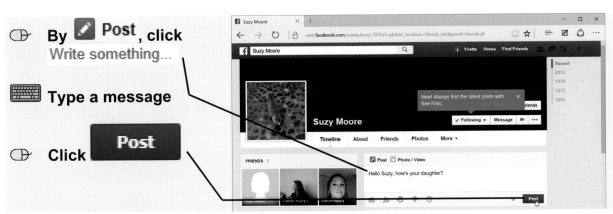

Now your message has been posted on your friend's timeline:

Mutual friends will see this message appear in their own News Feed.

If you want to delete the message, you use the ∨ and **Delete** button:

Please note: your friend can delete this message as well.

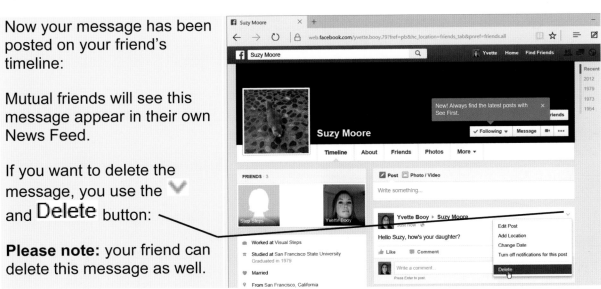

6.13 Adding a Photo Album

Another way of keeping your friends posted about your daily adventures is by posting photos on your *Facebook* page:

  👆 **Click your name**

  👆 **Click Photos**

  👆 **Click** + Create Album

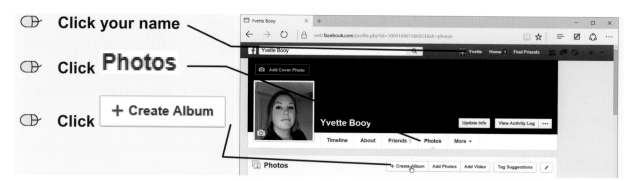

Open the folder that contains the photos you want to use. In this example, the photos are stored in the *Pictures* folder. Your own photos may be stored in a different folder.

  👉 **Select the desired folder**

  ⌨ **Press Ctrl and hold it down**

  👆 **Click the desired photos**

  ⌨ **Release Ctrl**

  👆 **Click** Open

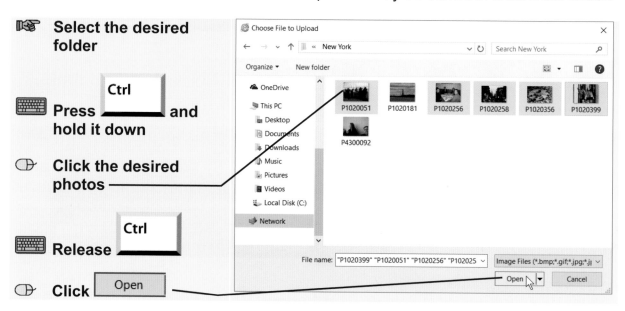

💡 **Tip**

Select all the photos
If you want to add all the photos in the folder, you need to select these by simultaneously pressing **Ctrl** and **A**.

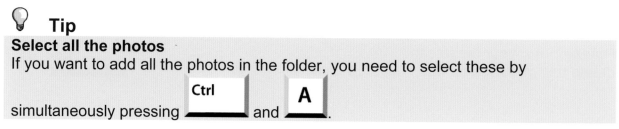

The photos will be uploaded. Meanwhile, you can type a name and a description for the album:

👆 **Click** **Untitled Album**

⌨ **Type a name**

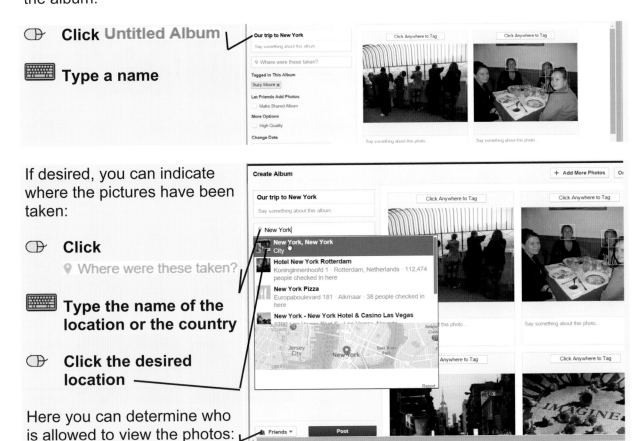

If desired, you can indicate where the pictures have been taken:

👆 **Click**

📍 Where were these taken?

⌨ **Type the name of the location or the country**

👆 **Click the desired location**

Here you can determine who is allowed to view the photos:

Facebook recognizes the faces on your album photos. If any of your friends are in the pictures, you can add a *tag* to their faces right away. Of course, you can also tag your own face, if you appear in a picture. This is how you add tags:

👆 **Click the face**

⌨ **Type the first letters of your friend's name, or of your own name**

👆 **Click your friend's name, or your own name**

The tag will be added.

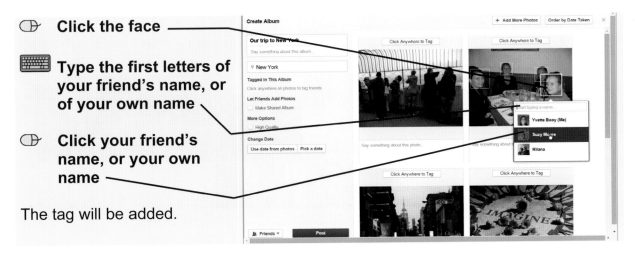

You can also skip the tagging action if you want, by clicking 'Skip Tagging Friends'. This is how you add a caption to a photo:

By the photo, click **Say something about this photo...**

Type a caption for this photo

If you wish, you can add captions to the other photos. Once you have finished you can post the photos:

In this example we have chosen to publish the photos in a standard quality. Publishing photos with a high resolution will take more time to upload:

In the bottom lift corner of the window:

Click **Post**

You can add friends to this album, as contributors. This means they can add photos and other contributors to the album:

For now you do not need to do this. If necessary, you can close the notification window:

If necessary, click **Okay**

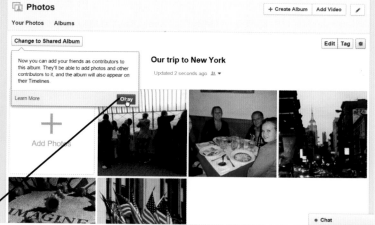

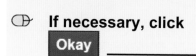

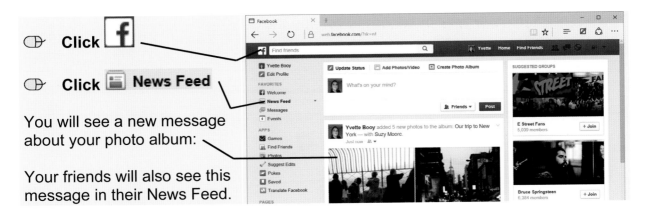

Click ![f]

Click 📰 **News Feed**

You will see a new message about your photo album:

Your friends will also see this message in their News Feed.

6.14 Deactivate Account

If you no longer want to use *Facebook*, you can deactivate your account. To do that:

☞ **Open the *Account Settings* window** 🐾**14**

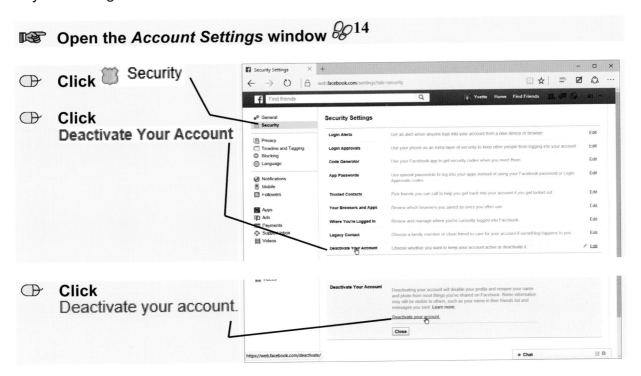

Click 🛡 **Security**

Click **Deactivate Your Account**

Click **Deactivate your account.**

You will need to enter your password to confirm the deactivation:

Facebook will ask you why you want to deactivate your account. Select a reason from the list shown:

Now your account has been deactivated and you will no longer receive any email messages from *Facebook*. Your profile and all your account information will no longer be accessible to other *Facebook* users. They will not be able to find you on *Facebook* anymore.

If you ever want to re-activate your *Facebook* account, you just need to log in again with your original email address and password.

In this way, the account is not permanently deleted. If you do want to log in again and you have lost your login information, click **Forgot your password?**. Then follow the instructions in the next few windows.

☞ **Close *Edge* 👣¹**

In this chapter you have learned about the main functions of *Facebook*.

6.15 Background Information

Dictionary

Account	An account gives a user access to a service provided. You need an email address and a password in order to use *Facebook*.
Deactivate	If you deactivate your account, your profile and all the information that goes with it, will no longer be accessible to other *Facebook* users. This means you will be removed from *Facebook*, but you will still be able to re-activate your account later on, if desired. With deactivation, the account is not permanently deleted.
Facebook	A free social networking site where you can easily communicate with friends and acquaintances, and get to know other people.
Friend finder	A component on *Facebook* that can be used to find friends in your email address book, or in other applications, such as *Skype* and *Hotmail*.
Friend request	A message you receive when another *Facebook* user wants to add you as a friend. You can accept this request or ignore it.
News Feed	Part of your *Facebook* profile. In the News Feed you can see the recent posts from your *Facebook* friends. If you are a fan of a page, or member of a group, you will also see their recent posts.
Profile	Your profile contains information about you that is visible to your friends. On the *Privacy Settings* page you can determine which group of *Facebook* users is allowed to view certain parts of your profile.
Status update	A component of your *Facebook* page with which you can let your friends know about something you did or are doing right now.
Tag	A keyword or a name you can add to a note, a photo, or a video.
Timeline	Part of your *Facebook* page. Here, you and your friends, fans, or members can post messages for others to read.

Bron: Facebook Help

6.16 Tips

 Tip

Become a fan of Visual Steps
You can search for groups and official pages in the same way as you search for friends. For this you use the search box. In this example we are searching for the Visual Steps page:

 Type: Visual Steps
Books

☞ **Click** 🔍

If you want to become a fan of this page, click 👍 Like .

 Tip

Add cover photo
You can personalize your timeline by adding a cover photo, like this:

☞ **Click** 📷 Add Cover Photo

☞ **Click** OK

☞ **Click** 🗐 Upload Photo...

👉 **Select the desired photo**

☞ **Click** Open

The photo has been added:

You can change the position of the photo by dragging it:

When you have finished:

☞ **Click**

Save Changes

7. Twitter

Twitter is a social networking service that centers on a single question: 'What are you doing at this moment?' *Twitter* users, also called Twitterers (or tweeters), write messages (tweets) and post updates on a wide variety of topics, some more interesting than others. In this way, it is quick and easy to share websites, tips, news and information. For example, people will often want to express their sympathy following an unfortunate news event.

You can easily keep in touch with your (grand)children, friends, and acquaintances and stay abreast of each other's activities. You will not need to keep everybody informed by calling them every time. A single message will spread the news among all your followers.

Also, you can use *Twitter* to quickly and easily react to current affairs, for instance, while you are watching a news show or entertainment show on TV. You can also react to things you hear on the radio, or read on a web page, or in a newspaper.

The goal of using *Twitter* is gathering a network of people who follow you, or whom you are following yourself.

In this chapter you will learn how to create an account, post tweets, and reply to tweets.

In this chapter you will learn:

- how to create an account;
- to sign in with your *Twitter* account;
- to search for other people with a *Twitter* account;
- to post messages (tweets);
- to reply to tweets;
- to react to a tweet with a mention;
- retweet messages;
- to delete tweets;
- adding pictures to a tweet.

Please note:

The Internet changes on a daily basis. For this reason, the images in this guide taken from the Internet at the time of writing may differ from those you see on your own computer. For most of the actions described in this chapter it should not make any difference. If you see any differences, just look for a similar button or option.

7.1 Create an Account

To be able to twitter (post messages) you will need to have an account. First, you go to the *Twitter* website, where you can create an account:

☞ **Go to the website www.twitter.com** 👣²

You will see the *Twitter* home page. To create your own account:

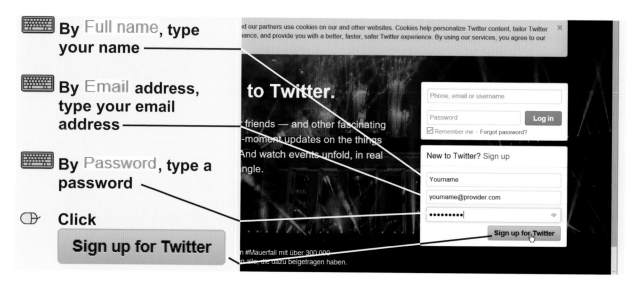

⌨ **By** Full name**, type your name**

⌨ **By** Email **address, type your email address**

⌨ **By** Password**, type a password**

⊕ **Click**

Sign up for Twitter

You may be asked whether you want *Edge* to remember the password. In this example we will choose not to let the program store the password. In this way you can make sure that other users of your computer cannot use your *Twitter* account:

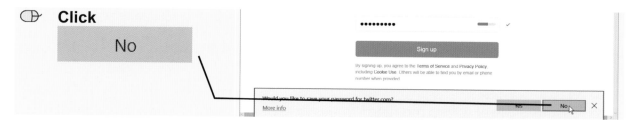

⊕ **Click**

No

In the next window you will see the information you have just entered:

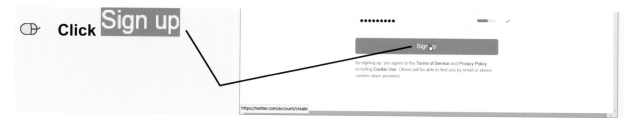

⊕ **Click** Sign up

You will be asked to enter your phone number. You can skip this step:

 Click Skip

In the next window:

 **By** Username, **type your user name**

 Click Next

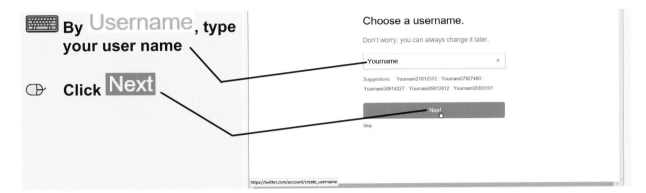

 **HELP! User name already exists.**
If the user name you have chosen is already in use, you will see the following message ✖ This username is already taken!. Then you will need to choose a different user name.
⌨ **Type a different user name**
Or:
☞ **Choose a user name by the suggestions**

☞ **Write down your user name and password on paper and store it in a safe place**

You will see the home page:

 Click Let's go!

In the next window you can indicate the things that interest you. *Twitter* will display some suggestions regarding *Twitter* accounts that may interest you. For now, you can simply skip this step:

 Click Continue

Twitter will probably still display some suggestions. If you do not want to use these suggestions, you can do this:

☞ **Uncheck the box** ✔ **by**
Select all ──────

☞ **Click** Continue

In the next window you can add a photo to your *Twitter* account. In this example we will skip this step. If you actually want to add a photo, you can read how to do this in a *Tip* at the end of this chapter.

☞ **Click** Skip this step for now

You can let the program search for your contacts. For now, this will not be necessary:

☞ **Click** Skip this step

You have created a *Twitter* account. A confirmation email has been sent to your mail address. This email contains a hyperlink with which you can activate your account.

☞ **Open the email message from *Twitter* in your email program**

 HELP! No email message.
It may take a while for you to receive the *Twitter* email message. If you have not received a message after some time, you should check the folder with unwanted (junk) email messages. Sometimes the confirmation email message ends up in the junk bin.

In the email:

☞ **Click**

A new tab will be opened. You can close this:

Click ✕

You will see the *Twitter* window and you can log out:

In the upper right corner of the window:

Click ⬤

Click Log out

🩹 HELP! I see a login window.

If you see the *Twitter* login window, you will need to enter your user name and password to log in to your account. You can read how to do that in the following section.

☞ Close the windows of your email program ✂1

In the next section you will sign in with *Twitter* and start using the social network.

7.2 Sign In

If you want to use *Twitter*, you will need to sign in with your account information. You can do that in the *Twitter* window that is still open:

Click

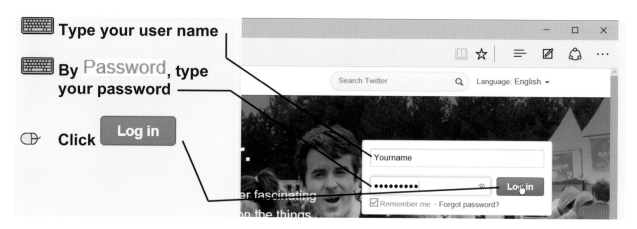

⌨ **Type your user name**

⌨ **By** Password **, type your password**

🖰 **Click** Log in

You may be asked whether you want *Edge* to remember the password. In this example we will choose not to let the program store the password. If you let the program store your data, other people who use your computer may be able to use your *Twitter* account without you knowing it.

In the message bar:

🖰 **If necessary, click** No

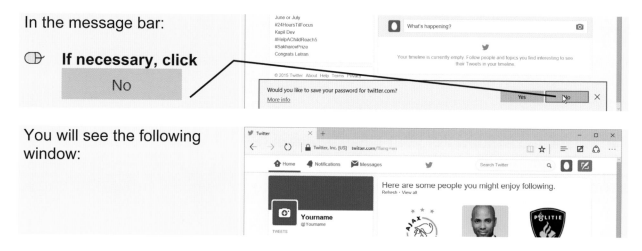

You will see the following window:

7.3 Deciding Who to Follow

Following people who post interesting messages on *Twitter* is a lot of fun. Visual Steps also has a *Twitter page*. By way of practice, you can follow Visual Steps:

In the top right of the window, in the search box:

⌨ **Type:** visual steps

🖰 **Click** 🔍

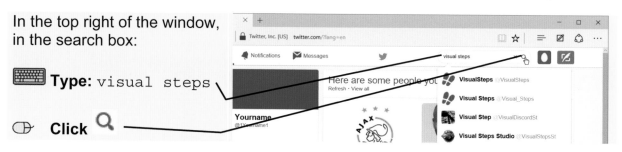

Tip

Search box
In this example you are going to search for Visual Steps. But if you want, you can also search for family members, friends, movies stars, celebrities, artists, musicians, TV programs, journalists, sports stars, etcetera.

You will see the search results:

Please note: your own screen will display different search results.

To display the *Twitter* accounts:

☞ **Click Accounts**

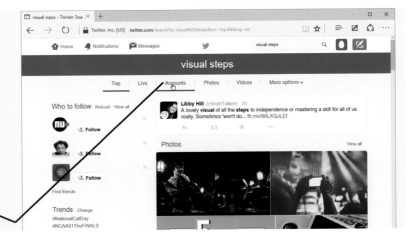

☞ **Click VisualSteps**
@VisualSteps
Publisher of the well-known Visual Steps computer books.

Please note: You can recognize Visual Steps by this image . There are two accounts, an English and a Dutch account. Select the English account **VisualSteps** @VisualSteps.

You will see a window containing the most recent messages:

To follow Visual Steps:

☞ **Click**

Now you have become a Visual Steps follower. You can tell this because you see the Following button:

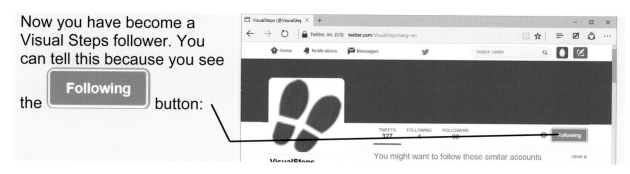

From now on, the home page will display the tweets sent by Visual Steps. This is how you open this page:

☞ **Click** 🏠 Home

Whenever Visual Steps publishes a new tweet, this tweet will be included in your timeline:

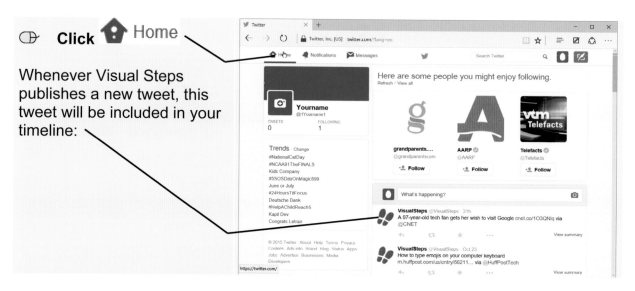

This way you can follow several other people or topics. For instance, family members, friends, movie stars, artists, TV shows or a sports star. In this book we will follow at least four tweeters. If you start following four *Twitter* accounts as well, the screen shots in this book will look similar to your own computer screen.

☞ **Follow four more *Twitter* accounts** 👣¹⁷

💡 **Tip**
Waiting
Other *Twitter* users may want to accept a follower first, before he or she can read the tweets. In this case you will not see Following in your window, but Pending. If the user has accepted your request, the tweets will appear on the home page.

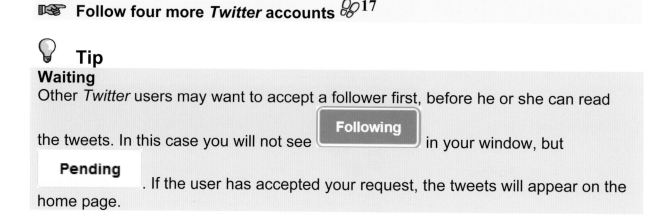

☞ **Open the home page** 🐾¹⁵

Now you will also see the tweets of the other people you are following in your window. In the next section you will learn how to post a tweet.

7.4 Publish a Tweet

It is very simple to publish a message, also called *tweet*. Here is how to do that:

⌨ **By** What's happening? **type a message, for example:** This is my first tweet!

🖱 **Click** ✍ Tweet

💡 **Tip**

140 characters
A tweet cannot contain more than 140 characters.

You will see your tweet appear:

The tweet may not appear at once. If necessary, try

clicking the button in the address bar to refresh the page.

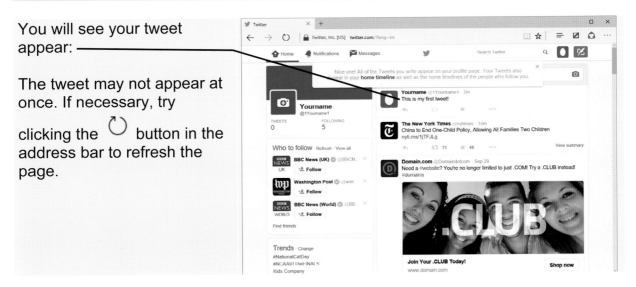

You will probably want other people to be able to read your tweets, as you will also want to read tweets from other users. In the next couple of sections, you can read more on this subject.

7.5 Reacting to Tweets by Replying to Messages

There are several ways in which you can react to other people's tweets: through a reply, mention or a direct (private) message.

You can practice sending a message by sending one to Visual Steps with the Reply function. To do this, you will need to open the Visual Steps page:

Click FOLLOWING

Drag the scroll box downwards

Click VisualSteps

Now the Visual Steps page will be opened:

By a tweet, click

If necessary, drag the scroll box downwards

Now you will see a new window. @VisualSteps has already been entered in the text box. You can type a comment:

⌨️ **Type your comment**

 Click 🖋 **Tweet**

 Please note:

A reply always starts with the user name, in this example @VisualSteps. If you place the @VisualSteps user name in the middle of the message, it will turn into a mention. In the next section, you can read more about this type of tweet.

The message is sent to @VisualSteps. Now you can return to your own *Twitter* page:

👆 **Click** 🏠 **Home**

In the tweets list, you will see the message you have sent:

Your followers will also see this message appear in their timeline.

 Please note:

A reply that is sent in this way is not just visible to Visual Steps. The tweet also appears in your timeline. The people who follow you on *Twitter* will see your reply in their timeline.

💡 **Tip**

Direct message

If you want to send a message that is only intended for Visual Steps, it is better to send a private message. See *section 7.7 Sending a Direct Message*.

Tip

Where can I find the message?
Visual Steps will only see this message appear in their timeline if they follow you. If they do not follow you, they will only see the replies to tweets in the mentions. You can view these by clicking 🔔 Notifications , Mentions.

If you react to a tweet in the manner described above, you will get a reaction quite soon. Since this is just a practice tweet to Visual Steps, you will not receive a reaction.

7.6 React to Tweets with Mentions

Another way of replying to the tweets from another *Twitter* user is by using the mentions option anywhere in the body of the message. You can use mentions when you reply to a tweet, or when creating a new tweet yourself:

⌨️ **By** What's happening?,
**type a tweet which
contains the words:**
@VisualSteps

⊕ **Click** 🖊 **Tweet**

Please note: in this case
your message cannot start
with @VisualSteps.

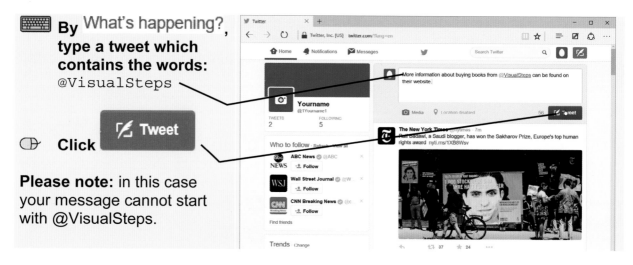

The message will be sent and is included in your timeline. This means all your followers will also see this message in their timeline. If the person mentioned by you in your tweet with the mention option is not following you, he will be able to find the tweet through 🔔 Notifications , Mentions.

 Please note:

A reply to a tweet and a mention name will both be listed on the Mentions page. You will not get a message when a mention or a reply to a tweet have been received. So you will need to regularly click Mentions to see whether you have received a reply or are mentioned in someone else's tweets.

7.7 Sending a Direct Message

You can also send a direct message to the people who are following you on *Twitter*. This is a type of message that can only be viewed by the recipient.

 Please note:
If you have not yet acquired any followers, you can just read through this section.

This is how you send a direct message:

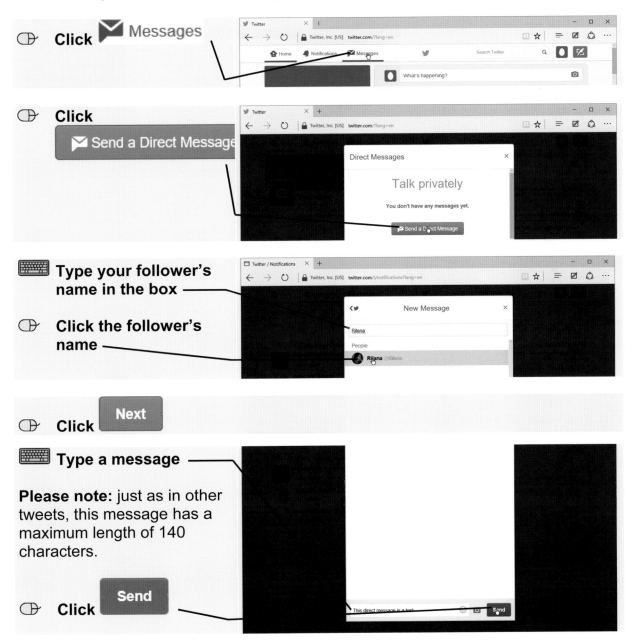

Click ✉ Messages

Click
✉ Send a Direct Message

Type your follower's name in the box

Click the follower's name

Click **Next**

Type a message

Please note: just as in other tweets, this message has a maximum length of 140 characters.

Click **Send**

HELP! Error message.

Do you see this message?

You can't send a message to a user who is not following you.   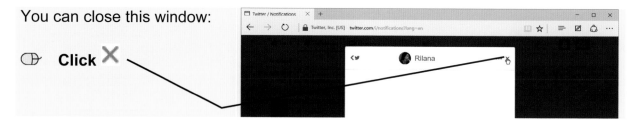,

then you have mistakenly selected someone you follow yourself, instead of a follower. You can only send a direct message to your own followers.

Now a conversation will be opened. This way, the follower will be able to react to your message right away:

You can close this window:

  Click ✕

 Tip

View the Direct Messages you have received

Here is how to view the Direct Messages you have received:

  Click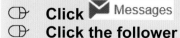
  Click the follower

You will see the conversation. You can react to a message in the same way you learned earlier in this section.

 Tip

Delete message

Both the sender and recipient will be able to delete the message. If the recipient deletes the message, this message will also disappear from the sender's inbox; and vice versa. This is how you delete a message:

  Position the pointer on a direct message in the conversation

  To the left of the direct message, click 🗑

  Click

Tip

Direct message through a tweet

You can also send a direct message to your followers by using the text box of your regular tweets. A direct message always has the following structure:

DM @name message or dm @name message

DM stands for *Direct Message*, or in other words, a private message.
If you start a tweet with 'DM @VisualSteps', the message will be delivered as a direct message to the Visual Steps address.

Please note: do not forget to type DM or dm, followed by a blank space. If you do, the message will be displayed as a regular message, in all the timelines.

7.8 Retweet

When you have stumbled upon an interesting or funny tweet, you may want all your followers to read this tweet too. You can do this by *retweeting* the message. This means you are going to forward the message as if it were your own tweet. Your followers will see this tweet appear in their timeline. Here is how to retweet:

☞ **Open the www.twitter.com/visualsteps website** ✇²

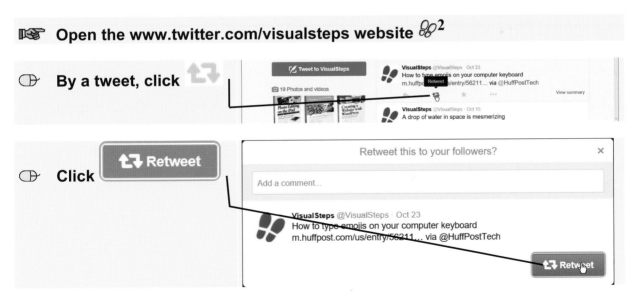

Now the message has been sent and can be viewed by all your followers. Next to the message you will see this symbol: ↿⇂.

You have now learned how to send messages in a variety of different ways. In the next section you will read about deleting messages.

7.9 Deleting a Tweet

Since there are many people reading this guide, Visual Steps receives regularly a large number of tweets. That is why it is a good idea to learn how to delete a tweet. Here is how to that:

Click 🏠 Home

Click your user name, for example Yourname

If necessary, click Tweets & replies

By the tweet, click ●●●

Click Delete Tweet

You will be asked to confirm the deletion:

Click **Delete**

The message has been deleted and it will also be deleted by @VisualSteps.

👉 **Delete the mention too** 👣16

You can also delete the retweet:

By the retweet, click 🔁

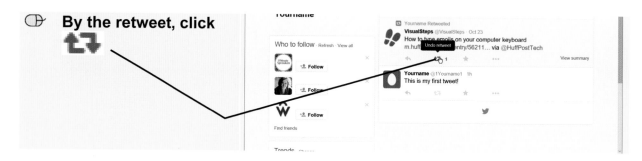

The retweet has been undone:

In a short time, your retweet will also disappear from the tweet list of your followers.

⊕ **Click**  Home

💡 **Tip**

Other retweets
In order to see who has retweeted your tweets, you open the page by clicking 🔔 Notifications , Notifications.

7.10 Add a Photo to Your Tweet

You can also add a photo to your tweet:

⌨ **By** What's happening?, **type a message, for instance:** Here's another picture of our ski vacation!

To add the photo:

⊕ **Click** 📷 Media

☞ **Add the desired photo** 🐾²⁷

Now the photo has been added. The tweet can be sent:

⊕ **Click** 📝 Tweet

The uploading process may take a while. Once the upload has finished, you will see the tweet with the photo:

⊕ **Click the photo**

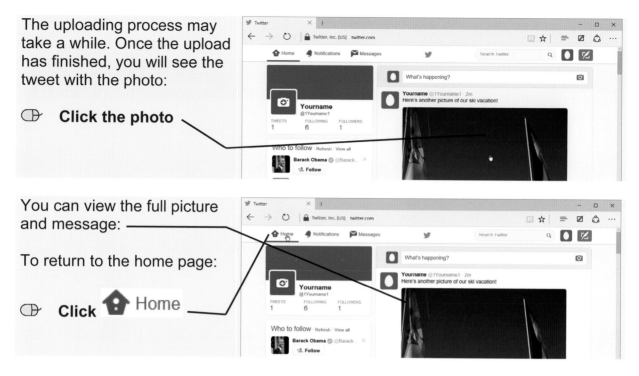

You can view the full picture and message:

To return to the home page:

⊕ **Click** 🏠 Home

You have mastered the basic operations in *Twitter*. At the end of this chapter you can read some tips.

☞ **Close the window** 👣¹

If you no longer want to use *Twitter*, you can read the last *Tip* at the end of this chapter to find out how to delete your account.

7.11 Background Information

Dictionary

Direct message	Messages you can send to other *Twitter* users without others being able to read the message.
Favorites	Each tweet contains a small star at the bottom. If you want to save a tweet, you can do this by clicking the star. Your favorites will be visible to everyone
Followers	A list of the twitterers who follow you.
Following	A list of the twitterers you follow.
Hashtag	The # sign. This symbol is used to indicate the specific subject you have tweeted about.
Home page	On the home page you will see the timeline containing the messages (tweets) from the twitterers you follow as well as your own tweets. This page is visible to you only, once you have signed in.
Profile	Page with information about yourself.
Retweet	Retweets are messages that have been forwarded by the people you follow, or they can be your own retweets and retweets of your messages.
Tweet	A message posted via *Twitter*.
Tweeting	The act of posting messages (tweets) on *Twitter*.
Mentions	Mentions are all the retweets, replies and messages in which your user name is mentioned.

Source: Twitter

Hashtag
In tweets you often see the # symbol. This is called a *hashtag*. A hashtag is a simple way of marking a keyword or topic by appending a *tag* (label) to the message, so you can make sure that other *Twitter* users will find the message. For example, if you are going to organize an event and send tweets about this event, you can include the #bookfair hashtag in your tweets. If somebody is looking for #bookfair, he or she will find all the messages about this topic, including your tweets.

A well-known hashtag is #daretoask. If you search for #daretoask you will see all sorts of questions asked by other twitterers. You can react to these questions, if you know the answers.

7.12 Tips

Tip
Add a profile photo
If you want to add a profile photo, follow these steps:

☞ **Click** ⬛, View profile

To add a profile photo:

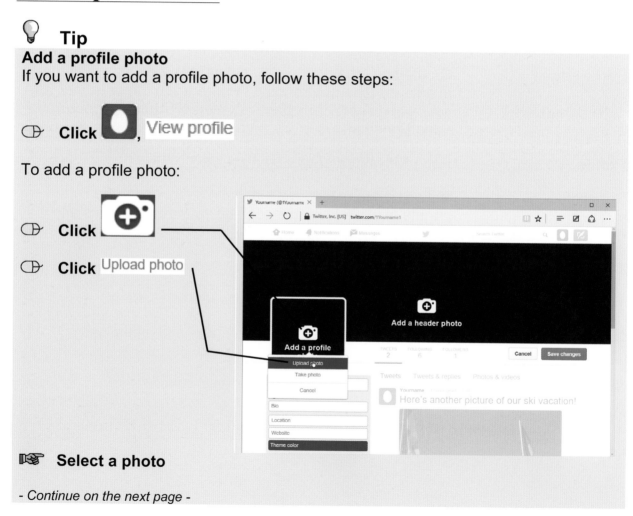

☞ **Click** 📷

☞ **Click** Upload photo

☞ **Select a photo**

- Continue on the next page -

👆 **Click**

The photo will be added:

👉 **Select the desired position and size of the photo**

👆 **Click** Apply

💡 **Tip**

Search the list of contacts

You can let *Twitter* search your list of contacts by your *Gmail*, *Yahoo*, and *Outlook* (*Hotmail*) accounts to see if any of them also have a *Twitter* account.

This option is only available if you have an email address with one of these services. If you are using one of these services, here is what you do:

👆 **Click** , Settings

👆 **Click** Find friends

👆 **By the desired service, click** Search contacts

👉 **Follow the instructions in the next few windows**

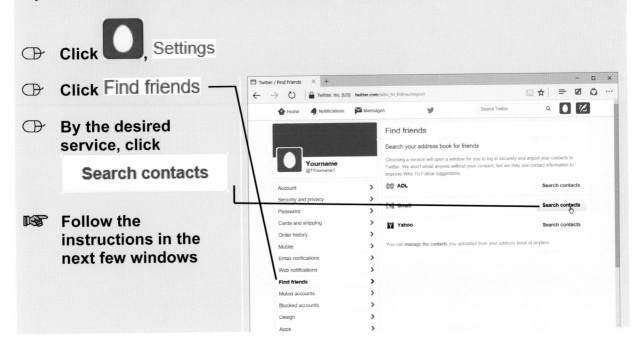

💡 **Tip**

Hyperlinks in a tweet

You can also insert a hyperlink (URL) into your tweet. When you insert a URL into the tweet, *Twitter* will automatically shorten it.

Tip

Favorites
Below each tweet you will see a star. If you want to save a tweet, you can store it by clicking this star. Your favorites will be visible to everyone.

☞ **By the tweet, click** ⭐

The tweet will be marked with a ⭐.

You can find your favorites by your profile page:

☞ **Click** 🏠 Home

☞ **Click your user name**

☞ **Click** FAVORITES

You will see your favorite tweets:

 Tip

Unfollow
Do you no longer wish to follow a certain person or company you have been following on *Twitter*? Then go to your home page and do the following:

☞ **Click** 🏠 Home

☞ **Click** FOLLOWING

By the relevant twitterer:

☞ **Position the pointer on** Following

☞ **Click** Unfollow

💡 Tip

Change the visibility of your tweets

If you have a *Twitter* account, the default setting is that anybody who visits your *Twitter* page can follow your tweets. If you only want people of whom you approve to read your tweets, you can change this default setting:

👆 **Click** ⬤ , Settings, Security and privacy

👆 **Drag the scroll box downwards**

👆 **Check the box** ☑ **next to** Protect my Tweets

👆 **Drag the scroll box downwards**

👆 **Click** Save changes

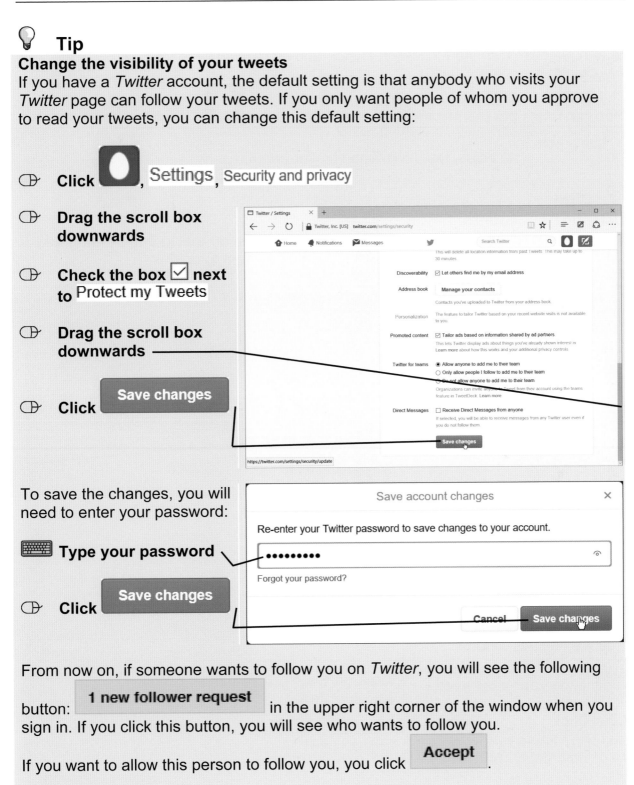

To save the changes, you will need to enter your password:

⌨ **Type your password**

👆 **Click** Save changes

From now on, if someone wants to follow you on *Twitter*, you will see the following button: **1 new follower request** in the upper right corner of the window when you sign in. If you click this button, you will see who wants to follow you.

If you want to allow this person to follow you, you click Accept .

- Continue on the next page -

In turn, you can also start following this person by clicking 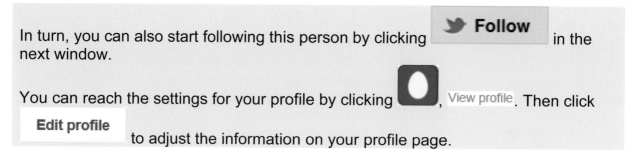 in the next window.

You can reach the settings for your profile by clicking , View profile. Then click

Edit profile to adjust the information on your profile page.

⚙ Tip

Deleting an account

If you want to delete (deactivate) your account, you can do that in the following way. You can just read through this section, if you do not want to do this.

Please note: once your account has been deleted, you will not be able to create a new account with the same email address.

☞ **Click** , Settings

☞ **Drag the scroll box downwards** ──────

☞ **Click** Deactivate my account

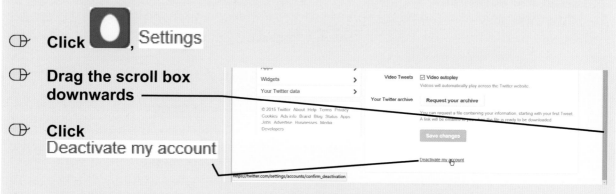

You will be asked if you want to permanently delete your account.

If you are sure:

☞ **Click** Deactivate

You will see this window:

⌨ **Type your password**

☞ **Click**

Deactivate account

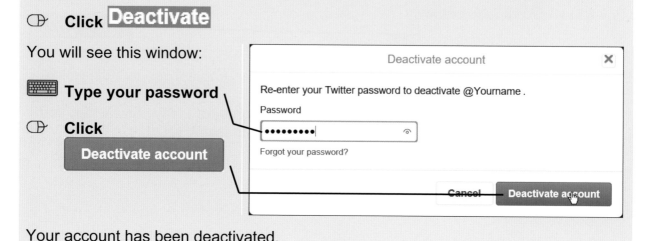

Your account has been deactivated.

8. Video Calls with Skype

Skype is a program that enables you to make free phone calls over an Internet connection.

You can use *Skype* to make a phone call to other *Skype* users, when they are online. During a call, you speak into a microphone and you hear the other person's voice through your head phones or your computer's speakers.

If you have a webcam, you can make a video call instead of a regular phone call. You will be able to see each other through the webcam. This makes it very easy to communicate with distant family members or even nearby friends and colleagues.

This service is available throughout the entire world. The location of your contact is of no importance, the only requirement is that both parties have a fast Internet connection and the free *Skype* program is already installed.

In this chapter, you will learn how to download *Skype* for free, and create a *Skype* account. Next, you will learn how to make a video call.

In this chapter you will learn how to:

- download and install the *Skype* program;
- create a *Skype* account;
- sign in with *Skype*;
- add contacts;
- set up the image and sound;
- run a sound check;
- make a video call with a contact.

 Tip

Other Skype users

In this chapter you will learn how to add contacts. It is a good idea to ask your family and friends if they already use *Skype*, and write down their *Skype* user name. If this does not work, you can just read through the following sections so you will be able to use *Skype* in the future.

8.1 Downloading and Installing Skype

In this section you will be downloading and installing *Skype*. In *Windows 10* you can find an option for this using the search function:

Click 🔍

⌨️ **Type:** skype

Click

S Get **Skype**
Trusted Windows Store

🔁 **Please note:**

If *Skype* has already been installed on your computer, you can continue with *section 8.2 Creating a Skype Account*. If the program is not yet installed, and you do not see the option **S** Get **Skype** Trusted Windows Store app, you will need to go to the website www.skype.com and continue with the next step.

You will see this window and you start the download:

Click

Download Skype ⬇

Skype keeps the world talking. Call, message and share whatever you want for free.

Download Skype ⬇

At the bottom of the window you will see an information bar:

⊕ **Click** Run ⎤　　Skype for Windows desktop setup

 HELP! The web page looks different.

By the time you read this book, the web page may look a little different on your own computer. Web pages are changed on a regular basis. If this is the case, just look for buttons that are similar to the ones described in this book.

Now the screen turn dark and you will see a window in which you need to give permission to continue:

☞ **Give permission to continue**

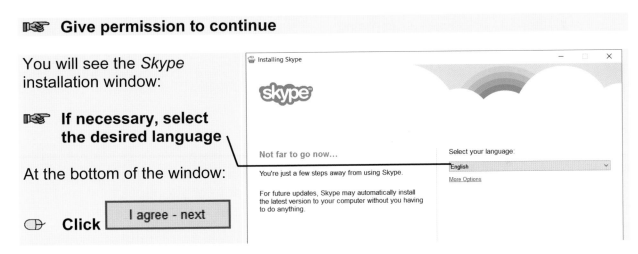

You will see the *Skype* installation window:

☞ **If necessary, select the desired language**

At the bottom of the window:

⊕ **Click** I agree - next

You will see the *Skype Click-to-Call* window. This window offers an extra option that requires just a single mouse click to switch from surfing the web to calling a phone number.

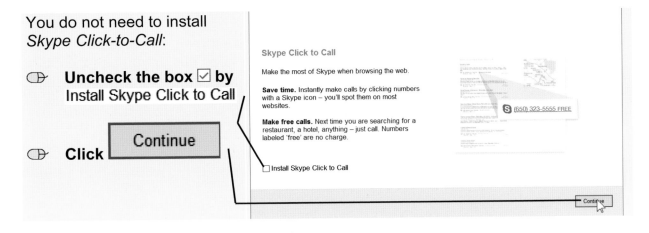

You do not need to install *Skype Click-to-Call*:

⊕ **Uncheck the box ☑ by** Install Skype Click to Call

⊕ **Click** Continue

You can see the progress of the installation:

After a few seconds you will
see the sign in window from
Skype:

During the installation
procedure, a new shortcut
has been placed on the
desktop. You can use this
shortcut to open the program.

This installation of *Skype* is now complete.

 Close the windows 🦶¹

8.2 Creating a Skype Account

You can register with *Skype* by using your *Microsoft* account. A *Microsoft* account
consists of a free email address ending with @hotmail.com or @outlook.com and a
password. If you do not have a *Microsoft* account or prefer to use another email
address, you can register with that.

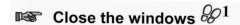 **Please note:**

If you already have a *Microsoft* account or a *Skype* account, you do not need to
follow the steps in this section. You can continue with *section 8.3 Signing In with
Skype*.

If the *Skype* window has not yet been opened on your computer, you will need to
open *Skype*. You can use the shortcut on your desktop to do this or you use the Start
menu:

Open *Skype* 🦶¹⁸

This is how you create a *Skype* account:

👈 **Click**
Create an account >

The *Skype* website will open on the page where you can create an account. Enter your own name and email address in the first couple of fields:

⌨ By **First name***, type your first name

⌨ By **Last name***, type your last name

⌨ By **Your email address***, type your email address

⌨ By **Repeat email***, re-type your email address

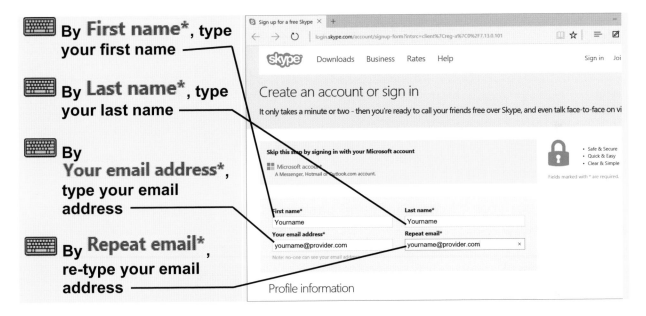

Next, you enter your profile information. This information is visible to all other *Skype* users. In this example we will only fill in the required data:

👈 **Drag the scroll box downwards**

👈 **If necessary, select your country by Country/Region***

👈 **If necessary, select English by Language***

If you wish you can also enter information in the other fields.

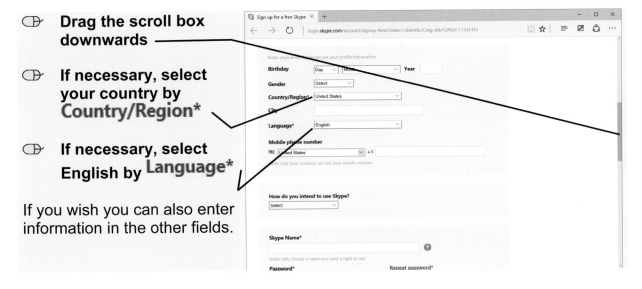

The next two required fields are a Skype name (you can make this up yourself) and a password. A Skype name needs to be 6 to 32 characters long. It must start with a letter, and can only consist of letters and numbers. The password can be from 6 to 20 characters long and again, can only consist of letters and numbers.

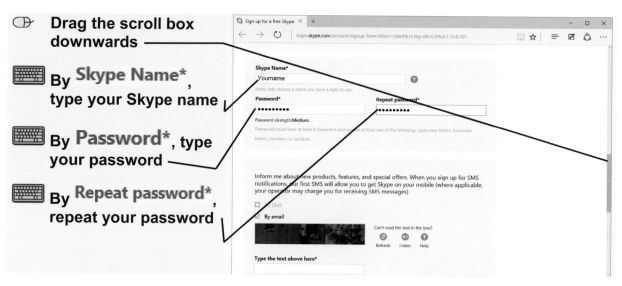

☞ **Drag the scroll box downwards**

⌨ **By Skype Name*, type your Skype name**

⌨ **By Password*, type your password**

⌨ **By Repeat password*, repeat your password**

☞ **Remember your Skype name and password. Be sure to write it down and keep it safe.**

HELP! Not available.

If the Skype name you want to use is not available, you will see this notification:
Skype Name not available.

⌨ **Type a different Skype name**
Or:

☞ **Click the radio button  by one of the suggested names**

☞ **Drag the scroll box downwards**

If you do not want to receive any emails from *Skype*:

☞ **Uncheck the box ☑ by By email**

You will see some characters you need to copy:

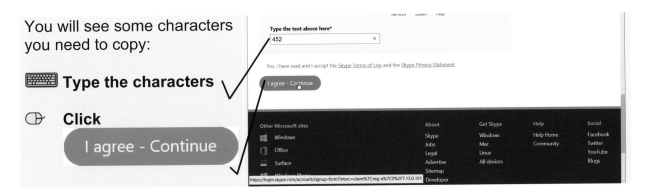

 Type the characters

⊕ **Click**

I agree - Continue

 HELP! I cannot clearly read the characters.

If the characters are difficult to read, you can let the program read the characters out loud (in English).

☞ **Turn on your speakers**

⊕ **Click**

You can also 'refresh' the characters. Do this by clicking 🔄. You will see a new set of characters.

Now you will see this window with information about your *Skype* account:

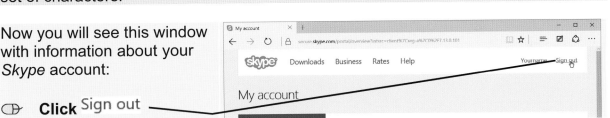

⊕ **Click** Sign out

☞ **Close the *Edge* window** 📇¹

8.3 Signing In with Skype

Before you can start using *Skype*, you need to sign in with your *Microsoft* account or your Skype name, and the matching password.

👉 **Please note:**

If you want to sign in with your Skype name, you can continue in the middle of page 227.

This is how you sign in with your *Microsoft* account:

☞ **Click**
Microsoft account

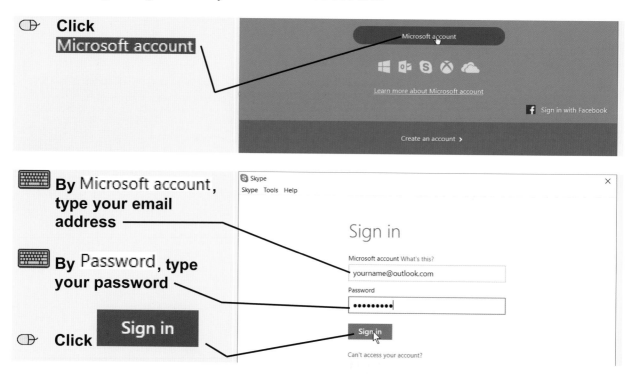

⌨ **By** Microsoft account,
**type your email
address**

⌨ **By** Password, **type
your password**

☞ **Click** **Sign in**

You will be signed in with *Skype*. Now you can continue on page 228. If your *Microsoft* account has not previously been used for *Skype*, you may see this window:

☞ **If necessary, click**

I'm new to Skype

Please note: if you already have a *Skype* account, you click

I have a Skype account

and you follow the instructions in the following windows in order to merge the accounts.

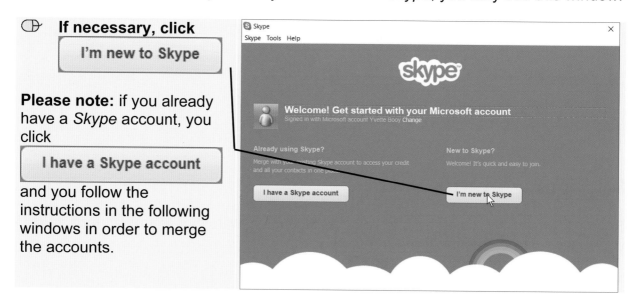

You will need to agree with the terms of use before you can continue:

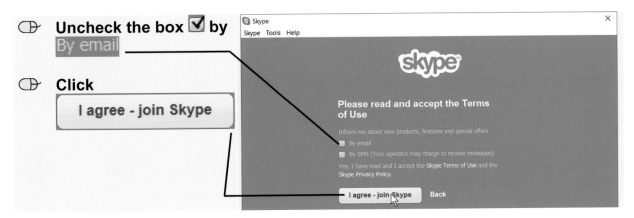

- ⏻ **Uncheck the box ☑ by** By email

- ⏻ **Click**

  I agree - join Skype

You will be signed in with *Skype* and you can continue on the next page. If you are using a *Skype* account, you can sign in like this:

- ⏻ **Click** Skype Name

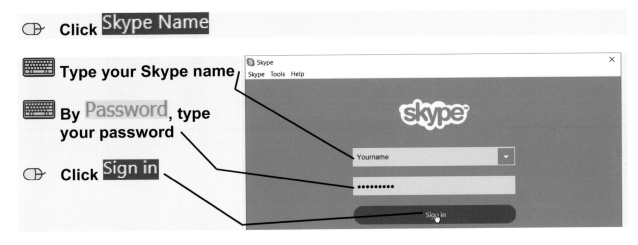

- ⌨ **Type your Skype name**

- ⌨ **By** Password**, type your password**

- ⏻ **Click** Sign in

💡 **Tip**

Automatically open and sign in

By default, the options for ☑ Sign me in when Skype starts and
☑ Sign me in when Skype starts are selected on the sign in screen. When *Skype* was installed, the Start Skype when I start Windows option has been selected. This way, *Skype* is always ready to receive a call when you are online. If this option is selected, you will never miss a call.

Do you prefer to choose when to start up *Skype*? In the *Tips* at the end of this chapter you can read how to disable the automatic startup.

You will be signed in with *Skype*. If you had not signed in with *Skype* before, you will see some additional windows where you can change settings:

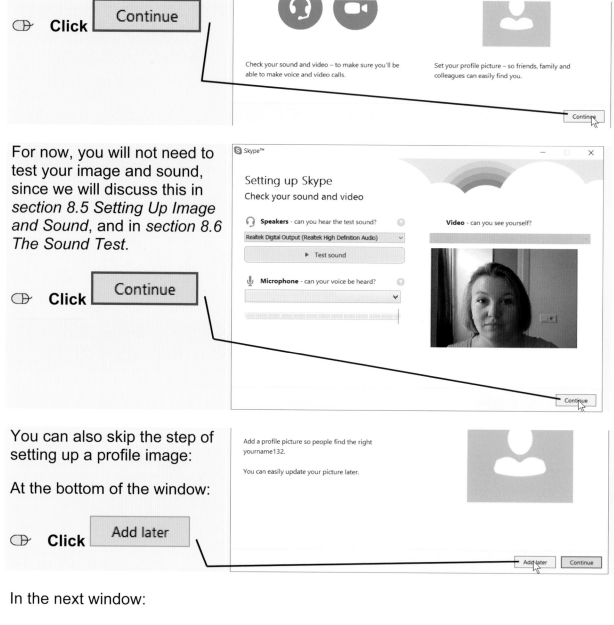

Click **Continue**

For now, you will not need to test your image and sound, since we will discuss this in *section 8.5 Setting Up Image and Sound*, and in *section 8.6 The Sound Test*.

Click **Continue**

You can also skip the step of setting up a profile image:

At the bottom of the window:

Click **Add later**

In the next window:

Click

Start using Skype

You will see the *Skype* home window:

In this example there are no contacts, except

Echo / Sound Test Service

:

If you signed in with your *Microsoft* account you may see some contacts.

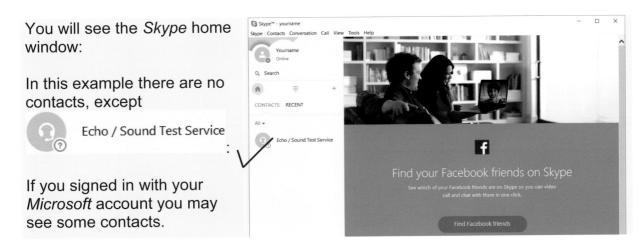

8.4 Adding a Contact

Skype allows you to contact other *Skype* users who have installed the *Skype* program or the *Skype* app to their computer, smartphone, or tablet, and who are online. You can search for *Skype* users by entering a Skype name, a full name, or an email address.

If you do not yet know the Skype name of a friend or family member, then just read through this section. If this is the case, you can ask your friends and family for their Skype names and add these later on.

Click Search

Type the information you already have about your contact

Click **Search Skype**

The fastest way of finding a contact is by using his or her Skype name:

Tip

Too many search results

If you enter only the name of your contact you may get a large number of search results, if this name occurs very often:

For example, entering the
name *John Williams* results
in a long list of users: ———

It will be difficult to find the
right John Williams with only
this minimal amount of
information.

This is why it is a good idea
to ask your contacts for their
Skype name beforehand.

If you have found your
contact:

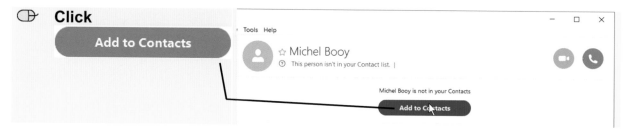

☞   **Click the name**

By default, every *Skype* user can make a call to any other *Skype* user. In the next

window you will see the ⬛ and ☎ buttons. These enable you to start a conversation right away.

But your contact may have adjusted his privacy settings and selected the option to only accept calls from (known) contacts. If this is the case, you will not be able to make a connection by using these buttons. You will need to ask this person first to accept you as a new contact, in order to make a call with *Skype*:

☞   **Click**

Add to Contacts

Tip

Privacy settings
In the *Tips* at the end of this chapter you can read more about privacy settings.

Type a message to this contact to ask whether you can add him or her to your list of contacts:

⌨ **Type your message here** ──────

Or you can use the default message that is already there.

🖰 **Click** [Send]

The message has been sent and the person has been added to the contacts list.

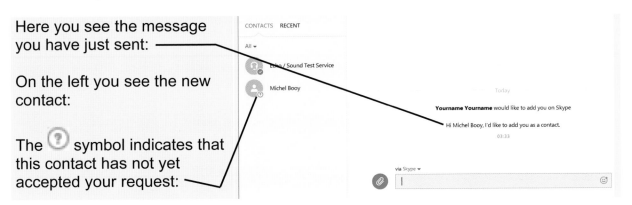

Here you see the message you have just sent: ──────

On the left you see the new contact:

The ⑦ symbol indicates that this contact has not yet accepted your request: ──────

Now your contact will see that there is a new contact request. If you receive a contact request yourself, you will see a message on the *Recent* tab:

🖰 **Click** RECENT ──────

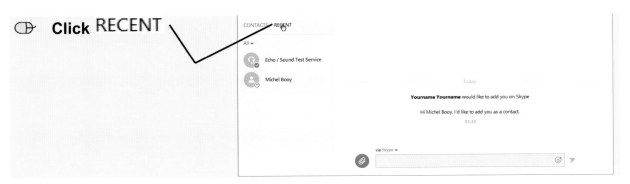

This is how you accept a contact:

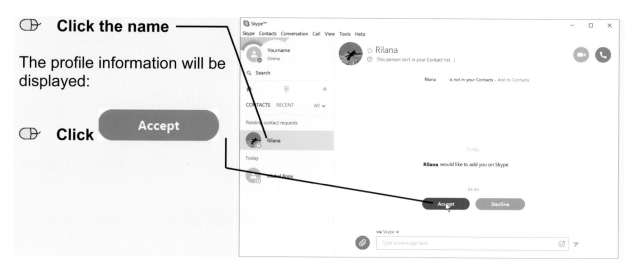

Click the name

The profile information will be displayed:

Click Accept

Tip

Unknown person

If you do not know the person who has sent the contact request, you can click their name in order to view more information. If you want to refuse the contact request:

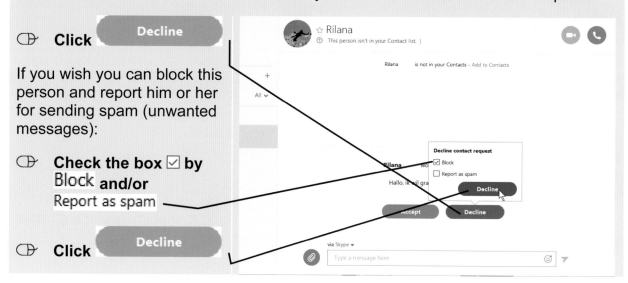

Click Decline

If you wish you can block this person and report him or her for sending spam (unwanted messages):

Check the box ☑ **by**
 and/or
Report as spam

Click Decline

⬠ **Click** CONTACTS

In this example, the contact has accepted the request:

The indicates that this person is now online and available for a call:

💡 **Tip**

Change status
By changing your status, you can show others whether you are available for a call or not. You do that like this:

⬠ **Click** ✅

You will see the five status options you can choose from:

⬠ **Click the desired status**

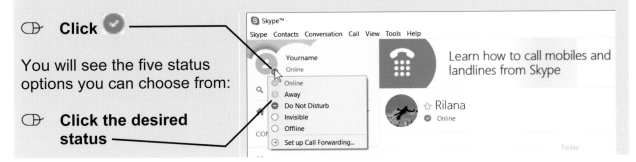

8.5 Setting Up Image and Sound

Before you make a video call it is recommended to check the settings of your webcam, speakers, and headset or microphone.

☞ **Close all the other programs that can play images and/or sounds**

☞ **Check if your webcam, speakers, and microphone or headset are connected**

First you open the sound settings:

⬠ **Click** Call

⬠ **Click** Audio Settings...

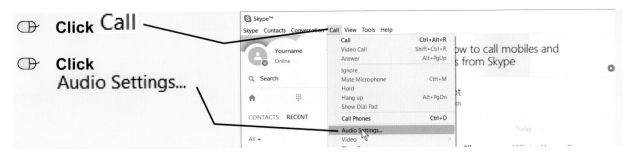

The *Options* window will be opened. Test the sound by speaking into the microphone:

If you see the green bar move while you speak, the microphone is correctly placed and set up:

If the computer is connected to multiple microphones, you can select another microphone by 🎤 **Microphone**.

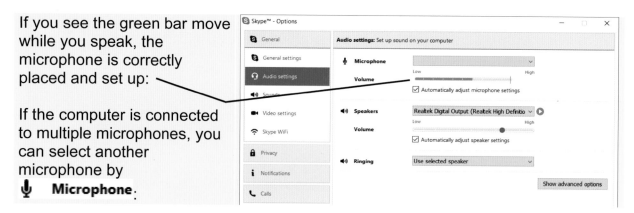

You can also move the microphone and put it a bit closer, if you need to. If the volume of the microphone is set correctly, you can now set the correct volume for your speakers:

🖱 **Click** ▶

You will hear music.

If the sound is too loud or too soft, you can use the slider to adjust the volume:

If multiple devices are connected to the computers, you can select other speakers or another headset by 🔊 **Speakers**.

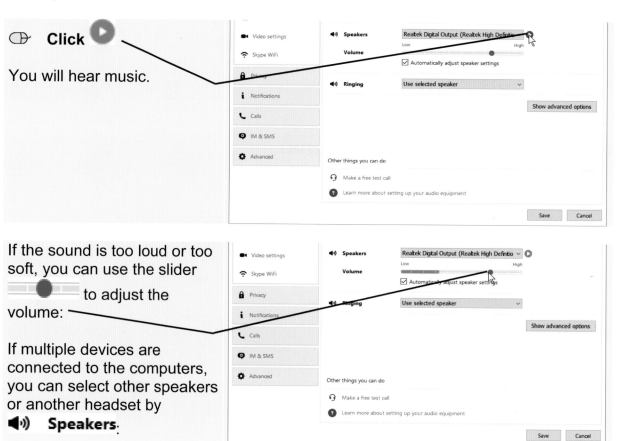

The final step is for setting up your webcam:

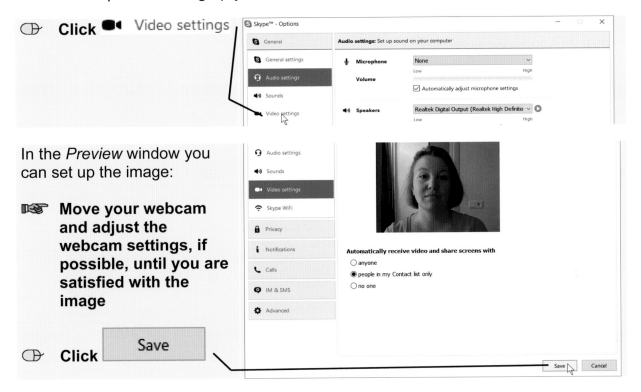

☞ **Click** 🎥 *Video settings*

In the *Preview* window you can set up the image:

👉 **Move your webcam and adjust the webcam settings, if possible, until you are satisfied with the image**

☞ **Click** Save

The *Options* window will be closed.

💡 **Tip**

Webcam settings
Depending on the brand and type of your webcam, you may be able to change even more settings by clicking the *Webcam settings* button.

8.6 The Sound Test

Before you actually make a video call to your contact, you need to test the sound, to check if all your devices are working together properly. The sound test consists of three elements. After you have clicked the green phone button, you will hear a brief explanation. Then you will hear a 'ping'. Immediately record a short sentence (just say a few words). In just a few seconds, you will hear your own voice recording.

If you have connected a webcam with a built-in microphone or a separate microphone, speakers and/or a headset, you can run the sound test:

⊕ **Click** 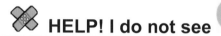 Echo / Sound Test Service

⊕ **Click** ●

⊗ **HELP! I do not see** ⬤ Echo / Sound Test Service .

If you do not see ⬤ Echo / Sound Test Service in your window, it is best to sign off and then sign in again with *Skype*:

⊕ **Click** Skype, Sign Out

You will see the *Skype* sign in window again:

☞ **Sign in with your Skype name, or your email address and password**

☞ **Try to connect to** ⬤ Echo / Sound Test Service **once again**

☞ **Listen to the voice and wait for the ringer**

☞ **Say a few words**

☞ **Listen to your own voice**

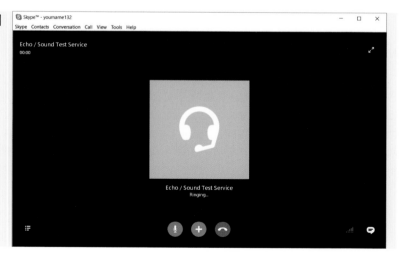

If you can hear your own voice, the test has been successful. To end the test:

☞ **Click**

HELP! Sound test was unsuccessful.

If the sound test was unsuccessful:

☞ **Work through *section 8.5 Setting Up Image and Sound* once more**

8.7 Making a Video Call with a Contact

If you have added a contact who is online and is using a computer with a webcam, a tablet or a smartphone, you can hold a video conversation together. This is how you start a video call:

☞ **Click the desired contact**

☞ **Click**

If you want to call without seeing an image, you can use

the ⟨⟩ button.

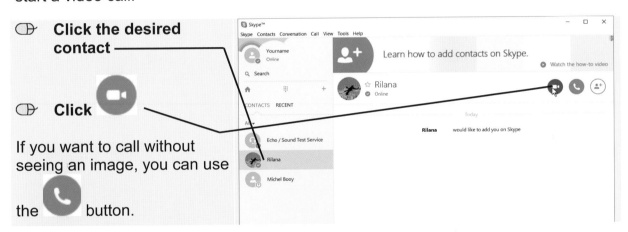

You will hear a ringtone until someone at the other end picks up the phone:

You will see the image of your own webcam:

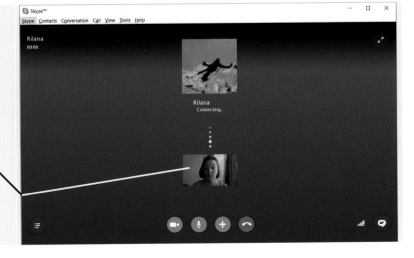

If the person you have called is online and available, they will see this window on their screen:

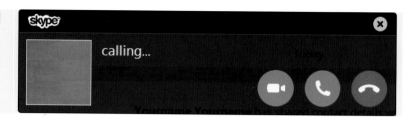

💡 Tip

Video call or phone call

If you receive a video call yourself, you can choose to hold a video conversation or a 'regular' phone call. If you click [video icon], your webcam will be activated.

If you click [phone icon], your webcam will not be activated and you will only have a voice connection from your side. But you will still see the image of your contact's webcam.

You can refuse to take a call by clicking [end call icon].

Please note: if you make a video call and your contact clicks [phone icon], the image of your webcam will be visible to him.

Once the connection has been made, you can hold a conversation:

☞ **Hold the conversation**

If you want to end the call:

👉 **Click** [end call icon]

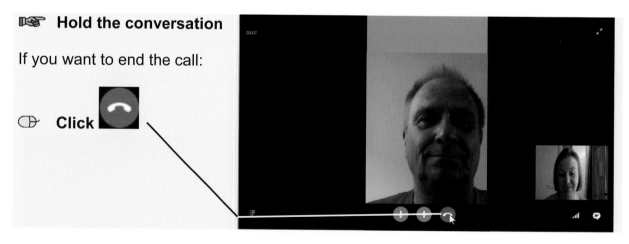

A video call is a fun way of contacting your friends and family, and can be very useful. You see each other while you are talking, even if you are on opposite sides of the world.

8.8 Closing Skype

If you want to stop using *Skype*, just closing the window will not suffice. This is what will happen:

Click ✕

The *Skype* window will be minimized and placed on the taskbar, but the program will still be active. On the taskbar:

Click

Now *Skype* is opened again. If you really want to stop using the program, you will need to sign off and close the program. You do that like this:

Click Skype

Click Sign Out

You will see the sign in window again. This is how to completely close *Skype*:

On the taskbar:

Right-click

Click Quit Skype

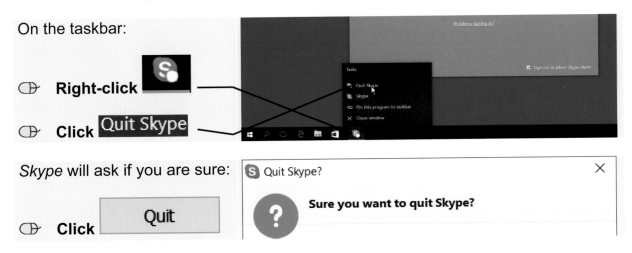

Skype will ask if you are sure:

Click Quit

Now the program is closed and you are signed off with *Skype*. In this chapter you have learned to work with *Skype*. Now you can use your computer to make free phone calls to family and friends, no matter where they live.

8.9 Background Information

Dictionary

Account	An account provides user access to a certain service. It consists of a user name and a password. If you want to use *Skype* you need to have an account.
Contacts	The persons you have added to your list of people with whom you want to communicate.
Headset	A combination of a headphone and a microphone.
Internet calls	A system that allows you to make phone calls through the Internet.
Status	This allows you to indicate your availability in *Skype*.
Video call	A conversation with a contact through an image and a sound connection.

Source: Skype Help, Wikipedia

8.10 Tips

 Tip

Check for updates
Skype is regularly updated and enhanced. The updates will be installed automatically, so you do not need to worry about this. If you still want to check for new updates yourself, this is what you do:

☞ **Click** Help , Check for Updates

Have you already installed the most recent version?

☞ **Click** | OK |

Do you see a message that there is a new update available?

☞ **Follow the instructions in the next few windows to install the update**

 Tip

Adjust settings
By default, *Skype* automatically opens when you start up the computer, and anyone with a *Skype* account can contact you. You can disable this setting, if you want:

☞ **Click** Tools, Options...

By default, *Skype* automatically opens when the computer is turned on. If you do not want this:

☞ **Uncheck the box** ☑ **by** Start Skype when I start

Go to the privacy settings:

☞ **Click** 🔒 Privacy

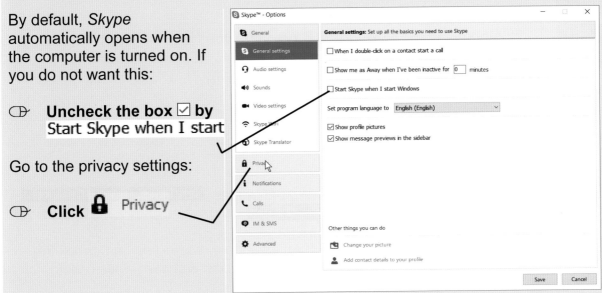

- Continue on the next page -

By default, anyone who has a *Skype* account can contact you. You can disable this setting:

☞   **Click the radio button** **by** people in my Contact list only

The default setting is for *Skype* to accept browser cookies. A cookie is a small text file that is stored on your computer by a website, in order to save certain information. If you do not want this to happen, you can uncheck ☑ the box by Accept Skype browser cookies Learn more. Click | Clear Skype cookies | if you want to delete all stored Skype cookies:

As you have seen, the *Skype* windows will frequently display ads. These ads are selected on the basis of your profile data and your surfing behavior. If you no longer wish to see these ads that are especially selected for you, you can uncheck the box ☑ by Allow Microsoft targeted ads, including use of Skype profile age and gender.. If you have made any changes to the settings, be sure to click | Save | to apply them.

 Tip

Buttons in the call window

When you make a regular call or a video call, you will see a number of buttons in the call window. These are their functions:

   End the call.

   Open and close the sidebar with the contacts list.

   Open a chat window in which you can send text messages to your conversation partner.

   Disable and enable the webcam.

   Mute the microphone and activate it again.

   Open a menu with the following options as: Send files..., Send Contacts..., Add people to this call... and Show dial pad.

   You can click this button to open a window where you can check the settings for your microphone, speakers, and webcam while calling.

   Switch to full screen mode or back again to regular screen mode.

9. Managing and Editing Digital Photos with Picasa

Picasa, the photo editing program from *Google*, has become very popular. Not only is it available as a free download, it is loaded with many options and is simple to use. It also lends a feeling of extra security, knowing that no matter how many edits you make in *Picasa*, your original photos will always be preserved.

In this chapter you will learn all of the basic operations necessary for simple photo editing. *Picasa* allows you to adjust and correct photos that you ordinarily would have deleted because of a mistaken exposure or a slanted subject. In many cases the corrections are so successful that you can even print the photo, or use it in a slideshow.

Picasa uses its own system for sorting photos. You will see how this works by looking at the *Library*. The advantage of this, is that you can see all the folders with photos and other images right away.

In this chapter you will get acquainted with *Picasa*. You will soon discover that photo editing can be quite simple and easy.

In this chapter you will learn how to:

- download and install *Picasa*;
- manage *Picasa* folders;
- work with the *Library* and create albums;
- view, move, and delete photos;
- automatically correct, contrast, color, and exposure using automatic correction;
- adjust shape and size of a photo, and straighten a skewed photo;
- correct red eye;
- create a web album.

Please note:

This chapter uses practice files. These can be downloaded from the website that goes with this book. Be sure you download the files first before you download and install the *Picasa* program.

9.1 Downloading and Installing Picasa

Before you download *Picasa* make sure you have the practice files that will be used in this chapter available. In *Appendix B Downloading the Practice Files* you can read how to download them:

☞ **Download the practice files for *Picasa* to the *Pictures* folder of your computer, as explained in *Appendix B Downloading the Practice Files***

Now you can download *Picasa*:

☞ **Go to picasa.google.com** 👣²

Note that you do not need to type 'www' at the beginning of the web address.

You will see a brief explanation regarding *Picasa*:

👆 **Click**

Download Picasa

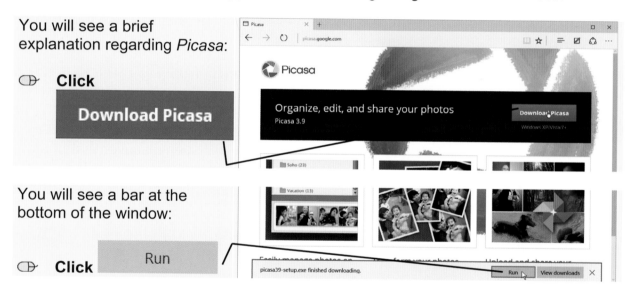

You will see a bar at the bottom of the window:

👆 **Click** Run

Your computer screen will turn dark and you will need to give permission to continue:

☞ **Give permission to continue**

A window will now be displayed where you need to agree to the terms and conditions:

👆 **Click** I Agree

In the next window:

👆 **Click** Install

Just leave the checkmark ☑ by Create Shortcut on Desktop:

☞ **Uncheck** ☑ **all the other options**

☞ **Click**

  Finish

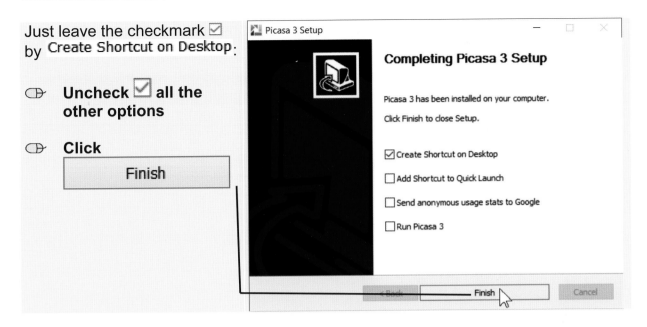

Now *Picasa* has been installed on your computer:

☞ **Close** *Edge* 👣[1]

You will see the *Picasa* icon on your desktop.

9.2 The Library

You can open *Picasa* in several ways. The easiest way is by using the icon on your desktop. On the desktop:

☞ **Double-click** Picasa 3

It is possible that an *Edge* window will now be opened. You can close this window:

☞ **If necessary, close** *Edge* 👣[1]

When you open *Picasa* for the first time, the program will want to search your computer for photos. The photos that have been found will not be moved or copied; they will only be displayed in the *Picasa Library*.

You can choose whether you want to search the entire computer or just specific folders:

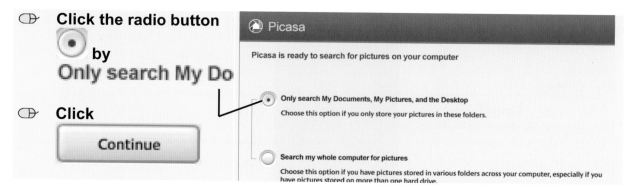

☞ **Click the radio button**
 by
Only search My Do

☞ **Click**

> Continue

> ☀ **Tip**
> **Which folders do you scan**
> If you have saved your photo folders in the *Pictures* or *Documents* folder, you can use this option. If you have saved pictures in other folders, or on other disks, you can scan the entire computer with the Search my whole computer for pictures option. Then you will see photos of other users too, and all the other pictures stored on your computer. This could be thousands of pictures, so it may take a while. That is why it is better to select the Only search My Documents, My Pictures, and the Desktop option and manually add other photo folders to *Picasa* later on (see *section 9.3 Folder Manager*).

The *Picasa* program includes a photo viewer. This is a program with which you can open and view photos on your computer. When you open *Picasa* for the first time, you can set this viewer as the default photo viewer for all your photos:

The default viewer option is enabled: ——

All file formats have been selected: ——

If your own computer displays different settings:

☞ **Check the box ☑ by all the file formats**

☞ **Click**

> Finish

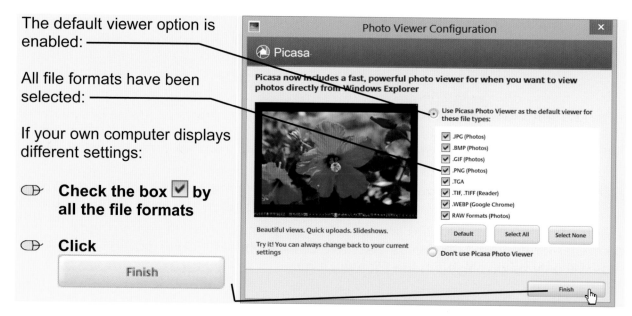

You may see a message regarding the creation of backups with *Google Photos*. For now, you do not need to do this:

☞ **If necessary, click *No thanks***

Again, it is possible that an *Edge* or *Internet Explorer* window will now be opened. You can close this window:

☞ **If necessary, close the window** ✂ 1

Picasa will now start searching the selected folders on your computer. Folders that contain images or video files will be displayed in the *Picasa Library*.

The *folder list*:

Please note: you will see different folders with photos. In the next section you will learn how to change this, so that you see the same items on your screen as you see in this book.

The *lightbox* is on the right-hand side of the screen:

The *photo tray* is on the bottom:

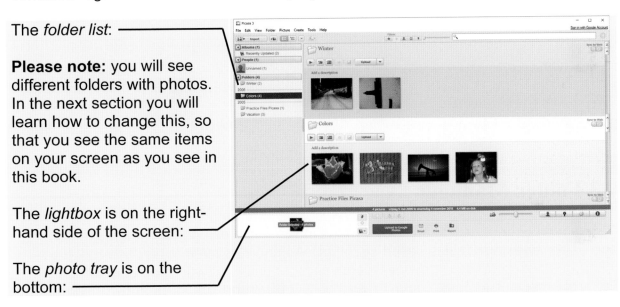

- In the folder list you see folders and albums. A folder is a storage location on your computer. Photo files are saved in folders. In *Picasa*, an album is a virtual collection of photos. Virtual means: 'not actually existing''. The albums in *Picasa* are used to display the photos you have selected in the same group. In fact, the album only contains links to the actual location of the photos on the computer. This means the photos themselves are not physically placed in the album but they can be viewed from the album. Folders and albums are ordered by the date of the first picture taken in that folder or album.
- The thumbnail overview will display small images of the photos found by *Picasa*, per album or folder. You will see the name of the folder or album, and the date of the first photo.
- In the photo tray you can carry out certain tasks on one or more photos, such as printing, sending by email, or moving.

Please note:

In the folder list you will only see the name of the folder that actually contains the photo. If a photo has been saved in a subfolder, the only name that is displayed is the name of the last (sub)folder; you will not see the name of the folder to which this subfolder belongs.

 Tip

Change the sorting order

By default, the folders are sorted by their date of creation. But you can choose a different sorting order:

In the upper left corner of the window:

☞ **Click**

☞ **Click the desired order**

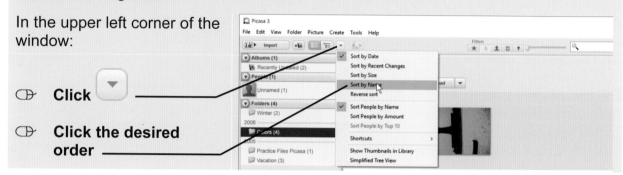

9.3 Folder Manager

Picasa will continuously search for images in the *Pictures* and *Documents* folders, and on the desktop. This is called *scanning*. As soon as something changes in a folder on your computer, the view in *Picasa* is adjusted as well. You can use the Folder Manager function to select the folders that will be scanned, and consequently displayed in *Picasa*.

If you want to delete a folder from *Picasa* but not from your computer, you will need to use this function:

☞ **Click Tools**

☞ **Click Folder Manager...**

The folders that are not scanned are indicated by an ✖. The 🔃 icon appears next to the folders you have allowed to be scanned.

You can set up only the folder with practice files to be scanned:

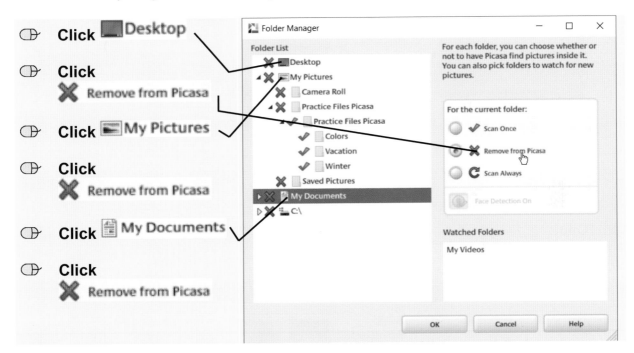

- 🖯 **Click** 🖥️**Desktop**
- 🖯 **Click** ✖ **Remove from Picasa**
- 🖯 **Click** 🖥️**My Pictures**
- 🖯 **Click** ✖ **Remove from Picasa**
- 🖯 **Click** 📄 **My Documents**
- 🖯 **Click** ✖ **Remove from Picasa**

By all the folders you will see an ✖. The folder with the practice files is a subfolder of the *Pictures* folder. This is how you change the setting to allow this folder to be displayed:

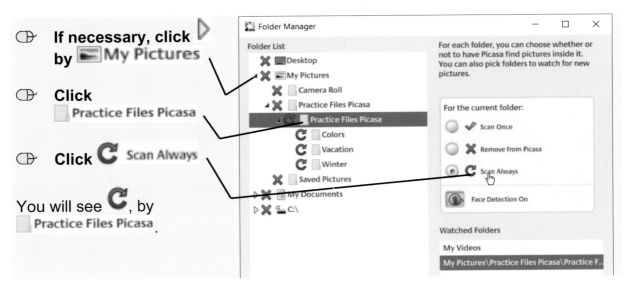

- 🖯 **If necessary, click** ▷ **by** 🖥️ **My Pictures**
- 🖯 **Click** ☐ **Practice Files Picasa**
- 🖯 **Click** 🔃 **Scan Always**

You will see 🔃, by ☐ **Practice Files Picasa**.

You may see a folder listed under Watched Folders. In this example this is the My Videos folder. You can delete that from *Picasa*:

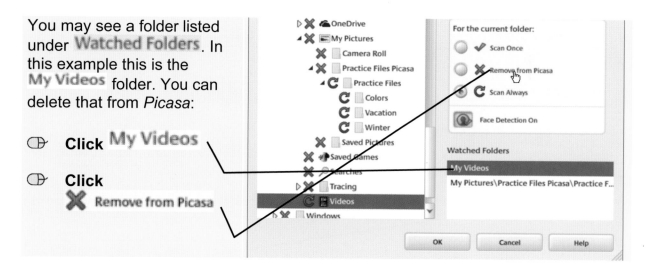

 Click My Videos

 Click
✕ Remove from Picasa

Close the window:

 Click OK

Now you only see the practice files in *Picasa*:

Tip

Your own photos
While you are working through this chapter, you will be using the sample photos you have downloaded. If you want to use your own photos, you need to add the desired folders through the Folder Manager, and then hide the exercise files.
In the *Tips* at the end of this chapter you can read how to use *Picasa* to transfer photos from your camera, tablet, or smartphone to your computer.

💡 Tip

Photos and folders in File Explorer
This is how you go to *File Explorer* from *Picasa*:

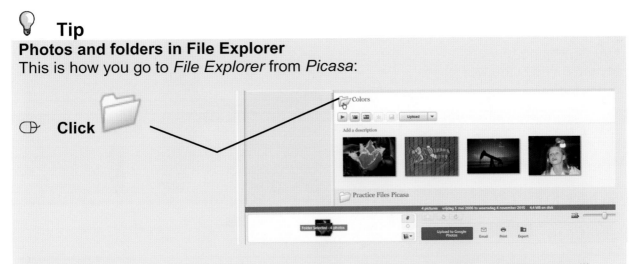

⊕ **Click**

Please note: you can only do this with folders. Further on in this chapter you will learn how to create albums. You cannot view the contents of these albums in *File Explorer*.

9.4 Viewing Photos

To take a look at a photo:

⊕ **Click** 📁 Winter

⊕ **Double-click the first photo**

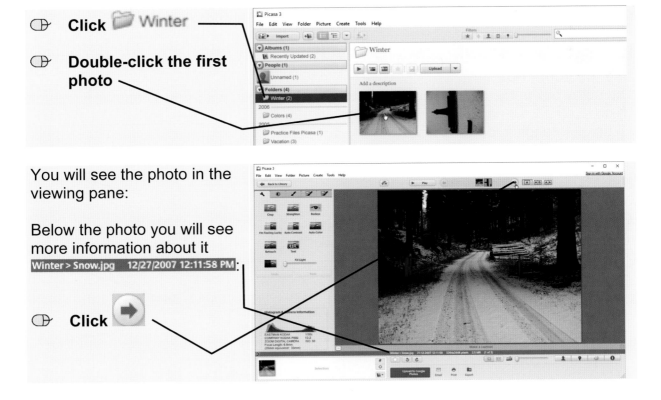

You will see the photo in the viewing pane:

Below the photo you will see more information about it

Winter > Snow.jpg   12/27/2007 12:11:58 PM:

⊕ **Click** ➡️

You see this photo:

You cannot go forward, because this is the last photo in the folder: ——

You can browse back with

this button ⬅ : ——

Go back to the *Library*:

👆 **Click**

⬅ Back to Library

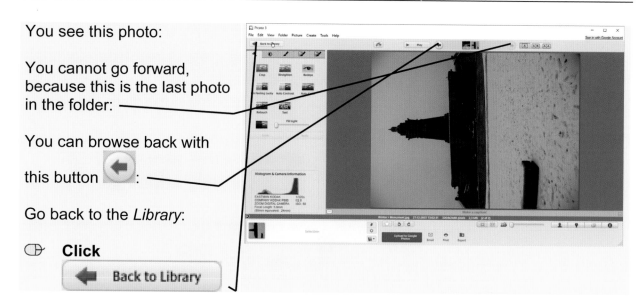

In order to view a photo in another folder, you need to click the folder in the folder list:

👆 **Click the folder**
📁 Practice Files Picasa (1)

You will see the photo in this folder: ——

💡 **Tip**

Use the scroll box
The scroll box in the Lightbox works a bit differently from the usual *Windows* scroll boxs.
To scroll through folders:

👆 **Click ▲ or ▼** ——

To scroll through photos:

👆 **Click ▲ or ▼** ——

To scroll manually:

👆 **Drag the scroll box downwards or upwards** ——

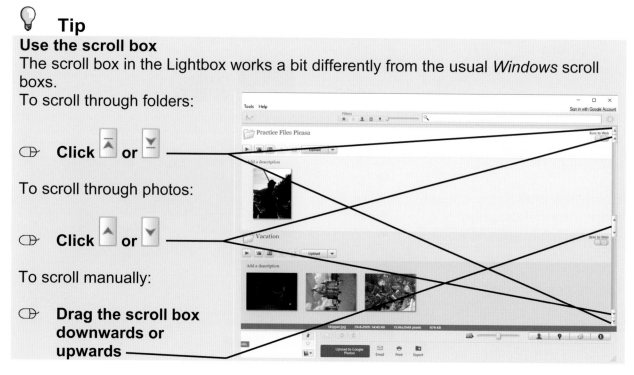

9.5 Moving Photos

When *Picasa* scans the photos, the program takes the same arrangement of the photos in the folders as you have saved them. If you want to change this arrangement, you can do the following:

☞ **Place the pointer on the photo**

☞ **Drag the photo to the folder** Colors (4)

You will see the window *Confirm Move*:

☞ **Click** | **Move Files** |

 Please note:

The photos you move in *Picasa* will also be moved on your computer. Because the Practice Files Picasa folder is now empty, you will no longer see this folder in the folder list. The folder will still exist on your computer, but it no longer contains any photos.

In order to move multiple photos at once, you need to select them first:

☞ **Open the folder** Colors (5) &&[19]

Click the second photo

Press Ctrl **and hold it down**

Click the moved photo

Release Ctrl

Now both photos have been selected. You will see the photos in the tray:

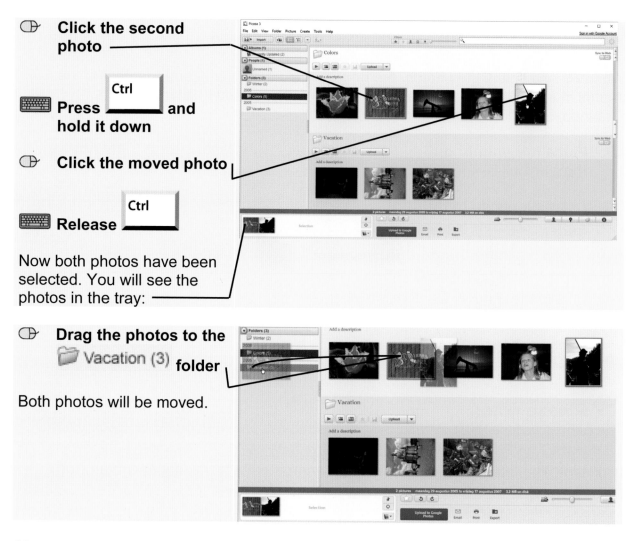

Drag the photos to the 📁 Vacation (3) **folder**

Both photos will be moved.

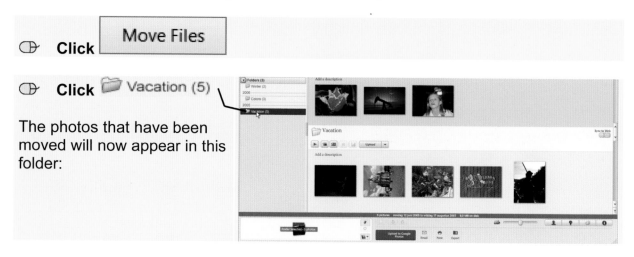

You will see a window where you will be asked for permission:

Click Move Files

Click 📁 Vacation (5)

The photos that have been moved will now appear in this folder:

9.6 Delete Photos

Deleting photos works like this:

☞ **Click the photo**

Delete

⌨ **Press**

You will need to confirm this action:

☞ **Click** | Delete Image

Delete Items ✕

Are you sure you want to send the selected file to the Recycle Bin?
(It will also be removed from any albums in which it appears)

☐ Don't ask again, always remove

Delete Image | Cancel

 Please note:

The photos you delete in *Picasa* will also be deleted from your computer. If you accidentally delete the wrong photo, you can always restore it by going to the *Windows Recycle Bin*. See *section 2.12 Empty the Recycle Bin*.

9.7 Albums in Picasa

An album is a particular type of folder used by *Picasa* to collect the photos you have selected and display them all together. A *Picasa* album actually only contains links to the locations on your computer where the photos are physically saved. The working is similar to a *Library* in *Windows*. So the photos will not really be moved to an album, they will only be *displayed* in the album. You can include the same photo in multiple albums. For example, in the ⋆ Starred Photos album, you can collect your best or most important photos. You can place the photos in an album by following the methods learned in this chapter.

You can also assemble the photos from various folders first, and then place them all at once in an album. You do that like this:

⊕   **Click the second photo**

Now the photo is displayed in the tray:

⊕   **Click**

In the bottom left corner of the photo you see the ◉ icon:

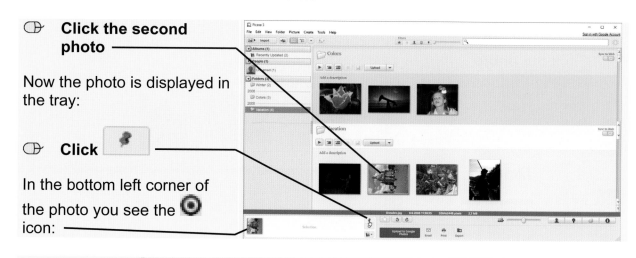

☞   **Open the** 📁 Winter (2) **folder** 🦶19

⊕   **Click the first photo**

Now this photo will be displayed in the tray as well:

In the bottom left corner of the window:

⊕   **Click**

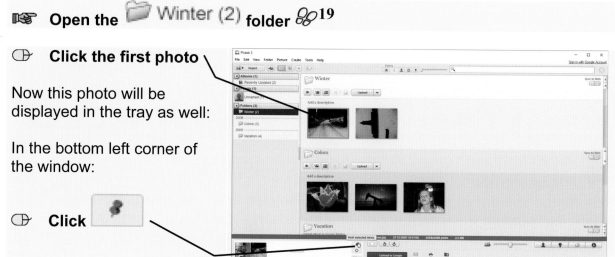

Now place the photos in the |✱ Starred Photos album.

In the bottom left corner of the window:

⊕   **Click**

⊕   **Click the album** |✱ Starred Photos

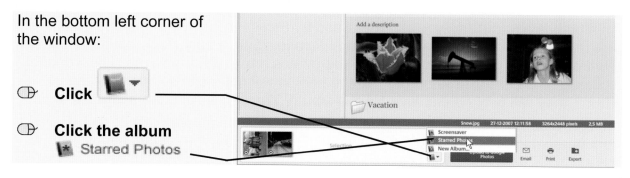

⊕   **By Albums, click**
        ⭐ Starred Photos (2)

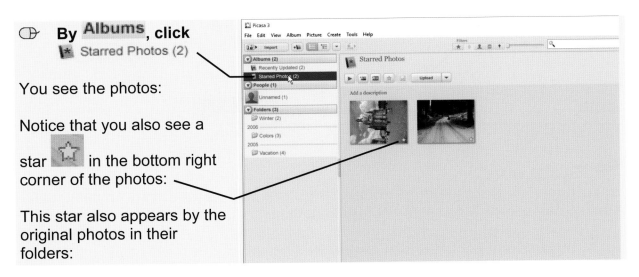

You see the photos:

Notice that you also see a

star in the bottom right
corner of the photos:

This star also appears by the
original photos in their
folders:

Albums are especially suited for collecting photos from different folders that concern a single subject. If you would like to do this, you start by creating a new album.

Please note:

In order to create a new album, the photo tray needs to contain one or more photos.

In the bottom left corner of
the window:

⊕   **Click** [folder icon ▼]

⊕   **Click** [+ New Album...]

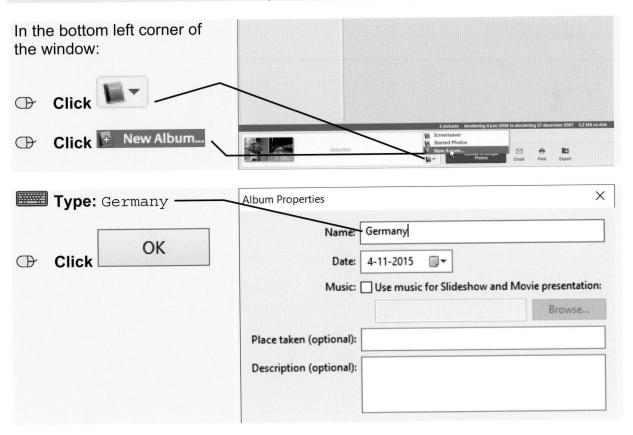

⌨ **Type:** Germany

⊕   **Click** [OK]

Click the album
🖰 **Germany (2)**

You see the photos in this album:

☞ **Please note:**

You can remove photos from an album in the same way as you remove photos from a folder (see *section 9.6 Delete Photos*). But, there are some important differences:

- If you remove a photo from an album, the original photo will still be saved. The photo will not be deleted from the computer.
- If you remove/delete a photo from a folder, the photo will actually be deleted and moved to the *Windows Recycle Bin*. If the photo has also been placed in an album or in multiple albums, the photo will also be removed from those albums.

This is how you delete an album:

🖰 **Right-click**
🖰 **Germany (2)**

🖰 **Click** Delete Album

You will need to confirm this action:

🖰 **Click**

Delete Album

The album will be deleted, but the photos will remain stored in the folders on your computer.

Please note:

The ⭐ Starred Photos album cannot be deleted, as it is one of the default albums that comes with the *Picasa* program.

Once you have finished with the photos in the tray, you can delete them:

In the bottom left corner of the window:

☞ **Click** ⬭

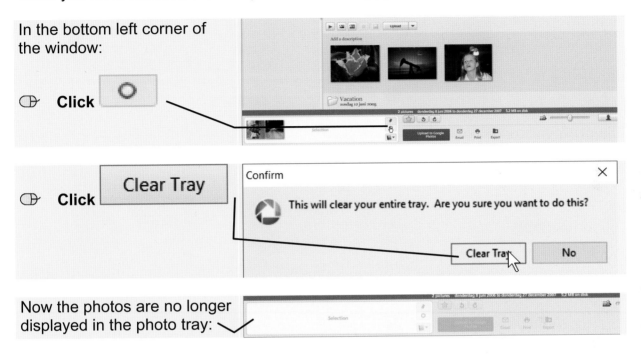

☞ **Click** Clear Tray

Now the photos are no longer displayed in the photo tray:

You have learned the basic methods for using the *Picasa Library*. In the next sections you will learn how to edit the photos.

9.8 Automatic Correction

Picasa provides several options to correct a photo automatically. Take a look at some of the options you can try:

☞ **Click** 📁 Vacation

☞ **Double-click the first**

photo

You will see the photo in the viewing pane:

This photo is underexposed and normally, you would probably not want to use it.

☞ **Click** I'm Feeling Lucky

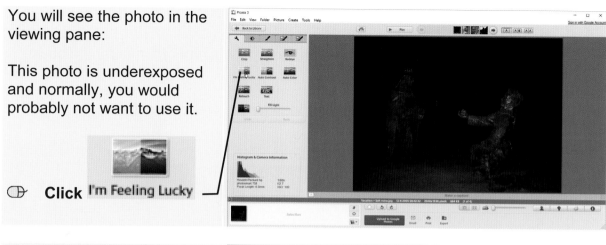

The photo has become clearer. You will see much more detail:

The I'm Feeling Lucky button is no longer active. You can use this button just once for each photo:

You can also further enhance the quality of regular photos in this way, as you can see in the next photo:

☞ **Click** ➡ **twice**

Now you see a photo of a city. This photo is a bit blurry:

☞ **Click** I'm Feeling Lucky

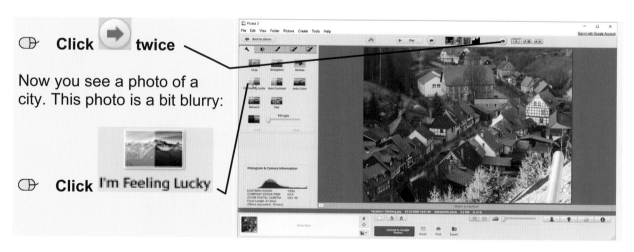

The photo has become a bit clearer:

If you do not like the result, you can undo the edit, like this:

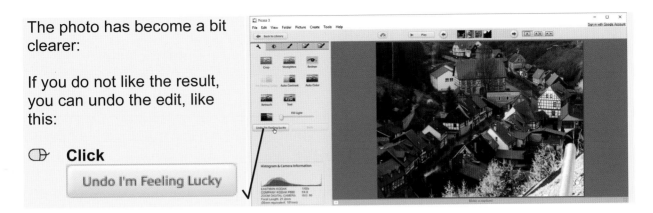

☞ **Click**

> Undo I'm Feeling Lucky

9.9 Correcting Contrast, Color and Exposure

When you use the I'm Feeling Lucky button, *Picasa* will attempt to correct the contrast, color and exposure of the photo, all at once. If you are not satisfied with the result, you can always correct the photo manually after the automatic correction:

☞ **Click** ➡️

This picture was taken with backlight.

☞ **Click** I'm Feeling Lucky

The difference is hardly noticeable. See what happens, if you add some extra light yourself:

☞ **Drag the slider** 🖱️ **by** Fill Light **to the middle**

Now the details in the photo have become clearer:

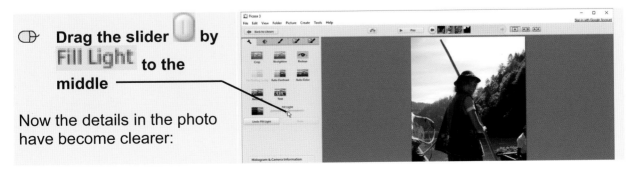

⚕ HELP! I do not like the result.

Have you edited the photo but are not happy with the result? Then click the

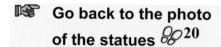 or **Undo Fill Light**   button. You can use this button to go several steps backwards and undo all previous edits. Even if you close *Picasa* and open the program again later on, you can still use this button. But once you have saved a photo by clicking File, Save, this button will no longer be active.

You can fill the light even more accurately, by using the slider. But the contrast and the color can only be corrected automatically. Usually, both the contrast and the color

will be corrected by using the **I'm Feeling Lucky** button, but if you just want to correct one of these two elements you can use separate buttons. And in some cases you can also enhance the result of the auto-correct tool even further.

☞ **Go back to the photo of the statues** 👣²⁰

You have already corrected this photo with

I'm Feeling Lucky.

↪ **Click** **Auto Color** ─────

The picture was taken in a salt mine.

Now the salt on the ground has become whiter:

The selection of the right color also depends on the mood of the photo.

If the color of a photo is already pretty accurate, it is better not to use the

I'm Feeling Lucky tool. In such a case you only need to correct the exposure or the contrast, for example:

☞ **Go to the photo** 👣 **20**

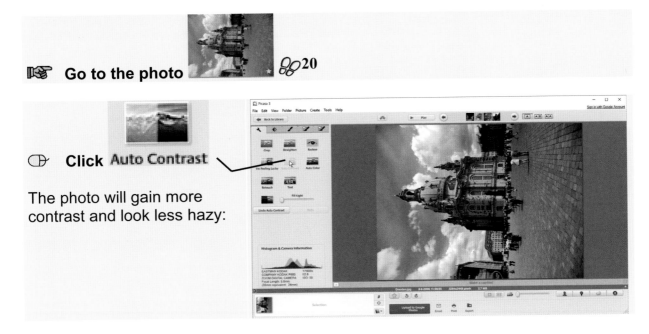

👆 **Click Auto Contrast**

The photo will gain more contrast and look less hazy:

9.10 Adjusting the Shape and Size

If you want to use a photo in a slideshow (see the *Tip* at the end of this chapter) it should be positioned the same way (have the same orientation) as the other photos. This is how you rotate a photo:

At the bottom of the window:

👆 **Click** 🔄

The photo has been rotated:

With 🔄 you can rotate the photo the other way round.

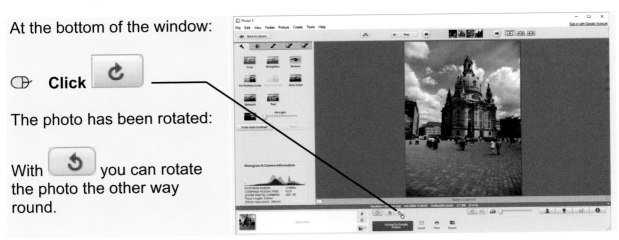

In front of the church you see a big square. In order to get a better view of the church, you can try cropping the photo:

  Click Crop

You can select one of the frequently used photo sizes, or crop the photo to your own taste. **Manual** has been selected by default:

  Place the pointer above the top left side of the church

  Press and hold the mouse button down, while dragging to the bottom right

  Release the mouse button

Please note:

Do not start too close to the top of the church, but include a large part of the sky. In the next section you will see why this is important.

HELP! I cannot fit the church in the frame properly.

If you do not like the result, click the   Reset   button to try again.

Please note:

If you select a standard size, you are not completely free in choosing the size of the box. The box will need to have the height-width ratio that goes with the size you have chosen. You can only select your own height-width aspect ratio while using the **Manual** option.

The default setting is for the photo to be in portrait mode, but by clicking the **Rotate** button you can cut out a horizontal box. The 10 x 15 measurement will then change to 15 x 10.

⊕ **Click**

Preview

You will briefly see what the cropped picture will look like:

Then the original picture will be shown once more.

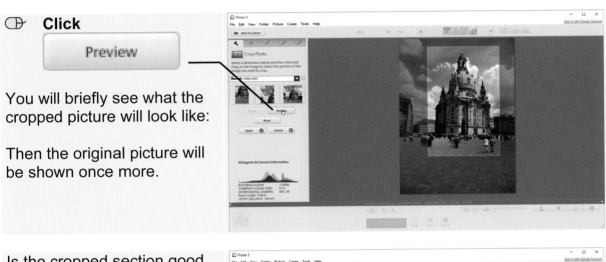

Is the cropped section good enough?

⊕ **Click**

Apply ✓

If you are not satisfied, click **Reset** and try again.

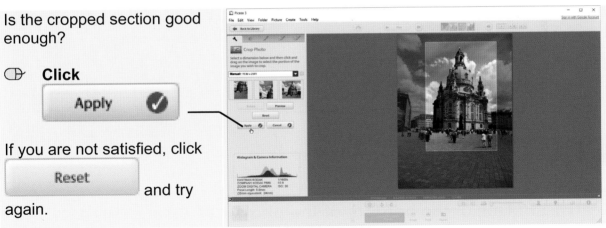

9.11 Straightening a Photo

Because the photo has been rotated and enlarged, you can see more clearly that the photo is skewed. You can correct this with the *Straighten* tool:

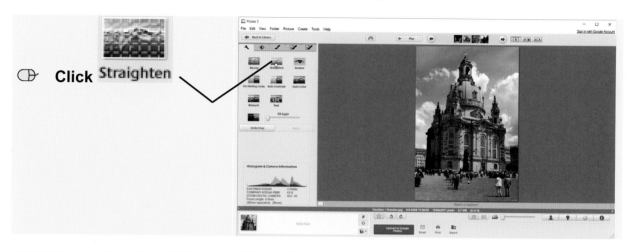

☞ **Click Straighten**

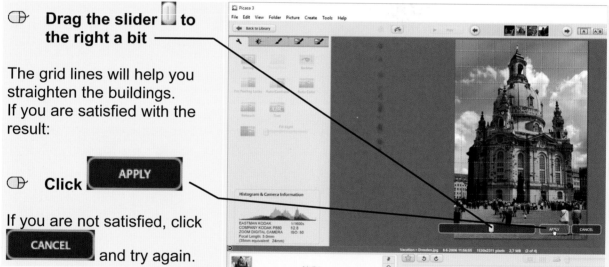

☞ **Drag the slider [ ] to the right a bit** ────

The grid lines will help you straighten the buildings.
If you are satisfied with the result:

☞ **Click [APPLY]**

If you are not satisfied, click [CANCEL] and try again.

✕✕ HELP! One of the borders of the photo has disappeared.

When the photo is straightened it will be rotated a little. The photo will no longer completely fill the selected size. *Picasa* will then zoom in a bit, and crop the photo on all sides, until the photo fills the selected size again. This will result in a slight loss of a part of the photo. Keep this in mind before using the *Straighten* tool.

The section of the photo that you have cropped, will still be saved in *Picasa*. If you decide to restore the entire photo later on, you will need to undo the straightening action first.

Click **Undo Straighten**

Now the church is skewed again.

Click Recrop

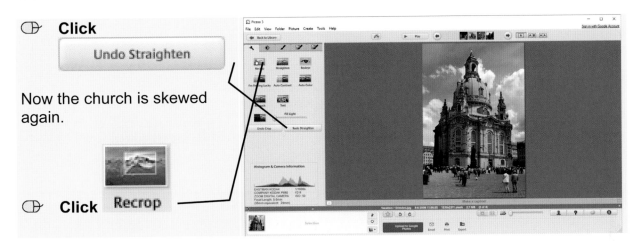

💡 Tip

Straighten the middle of the photo
Depending on your position and the lens of your camera, a photo is sometimes more skewed on the sides. Try to pay attention to the center of the photo then, if you attempt to straighten it.

Click Reset

You will see the original photo:

Click Apply ✓

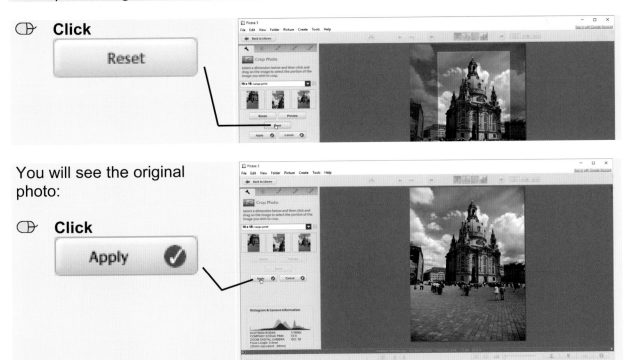

9.12 Correcting Red Eyes

A frequently occurring problem is the 'red eye' effect when using flash photography. *Picasa* has a special button to correct this. First, you can use the search function to find the photo in the *Library*:

☞ **Open the *Library*** ✔✔²¹

💡 **Tip**

Quickly getting to the Library

Esc

By pressing ▬▬▬▬ you will also return to the *Library*.

👆 **Click the search box**

⌨ **Type:** red

The photo will appear:

You can see that the photo has been saved in the *Colors* folder: ———

To view all the photos again, click ❌ :

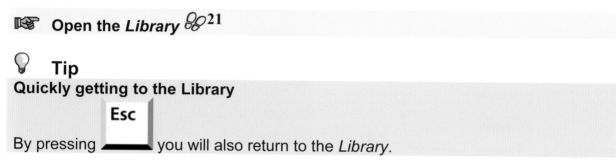

☞ **Open the photo** ✔✔²²

👆 **Click** **Redeye**

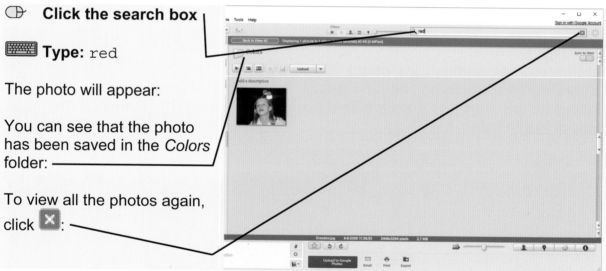

Picasa analyzes the photo and searches for red eyes. This may take a few seconds. Afterwards, both red eyes will be corrected:

You will see that both red eyes have been corrected:

Sometimes *Picasa* will not be able to find the eyes. In such a case you can correct the eyes manually:

⊕ **Click**

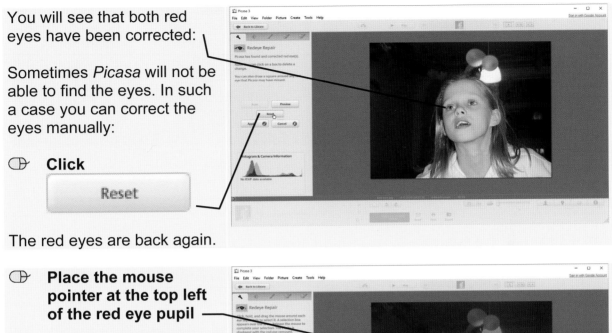

The red eyes are back again.

⊕ **Place the mouse pointer at the top left of the red eye pupil**

⊕ **Drag across the eye until the whole pupil is**

in the frame

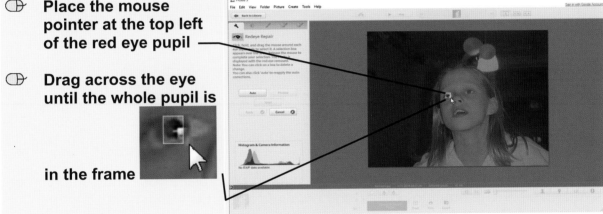

If you release the mouse button, you will see the eye without the red pupil:

☞ **Correct the other eye in the same way**

If you are satisfied:

⊕   **Click**

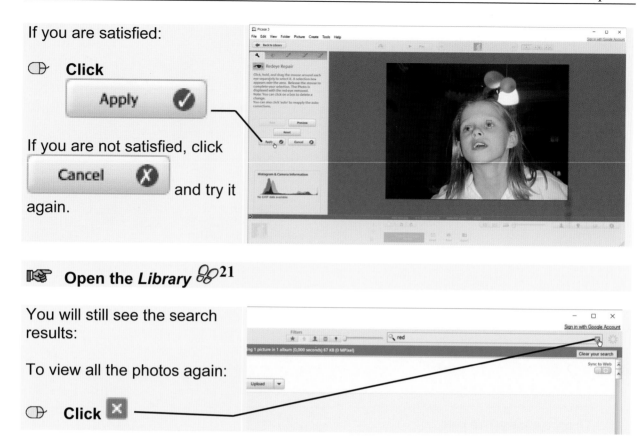

If you are not satisfied, click

and try it again.

☞   **Open the *Library*** ∞²¹

You will still see the search results:

To view all the photos again:

⊕   **Click** ☒

9.13 Web album

A web album is a location on the Internet where you can place your photos and share them with others. In order to do this, you will need to sign in with a web album service first. You can place the photos you have edited in *Picasa* in a web album on the Internet. Once you have a *Picasa* web album, you can upload the photos directly:

At the bottom of the window:

⊕   **Click**

Upload to Google Photos

Now you can sign in and
send your photos:

If you do not yet have a
Google account, you can click
Create an account and
follow the instructions in the
next window:

Or close the window:

 Click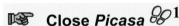

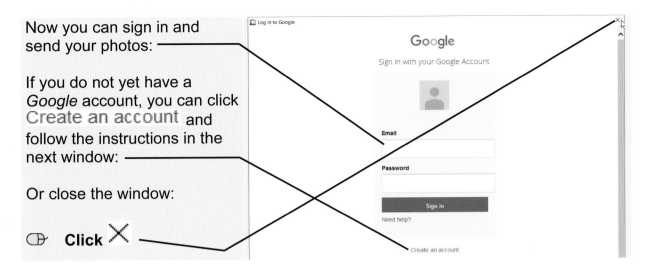

In this chapter you have become acquainted with some of the basic photo editing
tasks that can be done in *Picasa*. Now you can start working on your own photos.

☞ Close *Picasa* ⚘¹

💡 **Tip**

Learn more about Picasa
In this chapter you have learned the basics of using *Picasa*. If you want to learn
more about the *Picasa* photo editing program, you will find the book ***Digital Photo
Editing with Picasa for Seniors*** quite interesting.

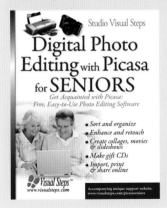

Learn how to:
- Sort and organize photos into albums
- Enhance and retouch photos
- Create collages and make gift CDs
- Create movies and slideshows
- Print and share photos online
- Import photos

More information about this book:
www.visualsteps.com/picasaseniors

9.14 Background Information

Dictionary

Album	Albums are virtual groups of photos that only exist within the *Picasa* software. You can combine photos in one album, and you can use a single photo in multiple albums without taking up any extra computer space. If you delete photos in an album or delete the entire album, the original photo files will still be saved.
Brightness	The amount of light that can be perceived in a photo. If the brightness is low the colors will fade, if the brightness is high they will become clearer.
Contrast	The difference in color between adjoining parts of a photo.
Crop	Cut off a portion of the photo you do not want to see.
Folder list	An overview of all the folders on your computer containing photos, and of all the albums you have created. The folder list is displayed on the left side of the *Library*.
Library	A window that presents an overview of all the photos, folders and albums in *Picasa*.
Photo tray	The photo tray allows you to collect photos as a group so that you can perform certain actions on the group at once, such as printing, sending by email or moving.
Red eyes	The pupil of an eye reflects a red color. This may be visible on pictures taken with the use of a flash.
Star	You can use the *Star* rating function to mark your favorite photos in your collection.
Thumbnail overview	Miniature view of the photos on the right side of the *Library* pane.
Viewing pane	A window in which an opened photo is displayed. On the left side of this window you will see an assortment of buttons and tabs that can be used to perform various photo editing tasks.
Web album	A location on the Internet, where you can share your pictures with others.

Source: Picasa Help

9.15 Tips

 Tip

Viewing photos in a slideshow

Instead of viewing the photos in a folder in the *Library* one by one, you can also view them in a slideshow.

⊕ **Click a photo**

⊕ **Click**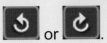

You will see the slides in that folder as a full-screen slideshow. The slideshow begins with the currently selected photo. If you place the pointer on the bottom side of the slide, you will see a bar with buttons. The slideshow will be paused.

With ⬅️ and ➡️ you can skip to the previous/next slide.

With ▶️ you start or continue playing. You should not move the mouse pointer while the slideshow plays.

You rotate a slide with ↺ or ↻.

By clicking ⭐ you can star the photo.

With 🖼️ you display or hide the titles of photos.

With 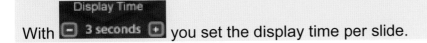 you set the display time per slide.

Tip

Import photos from your camera

You can import photos from your camera directly into *Picasa*. Most digital cameras can be connected to the computer through a USB cable. You can also easily connect tablets or smartphones with the cable that is included. This is how you do it:

☞ **Connect the USB cable to the camera**

Usually, the terminal for this cable on a camera is hidden behind a flap.

☞ **Connect your camera to your computer's USB port**

☞ **Turn the camera on**

⊕ **Click**

> 🔘▶ **Import**

☞ **By Import from:, select the camera**

⌨ **Type the name of the desired folder**

To import all the photos:

⊕ **Click**

> **Import All** ✓

If you do not want to import all the photos, you can select the desired photos first. When you are done:

⊕ **Click** **Import Selected (1)**

The photos will now appear in *Picasa*.

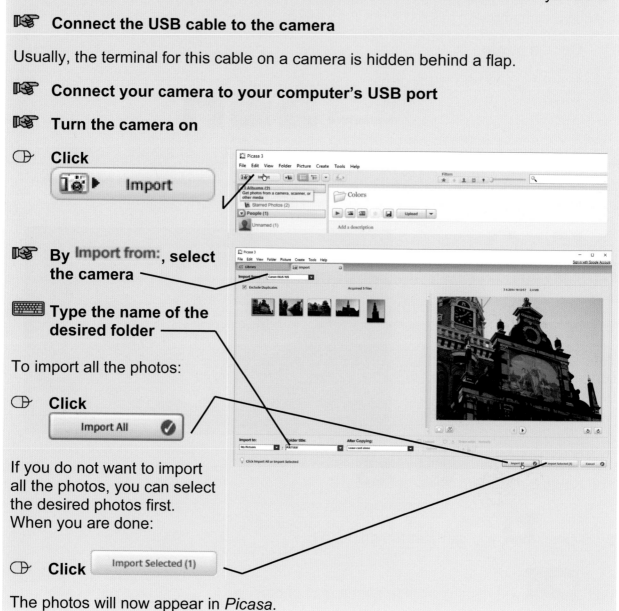

10. Video Editing with Movie Maker

In this chapter you will learn the basic operations for editing videos. First, you will need to place the videos on your computer. This is called *importing*.

Modern digital (HD) cameras, cell phones, iPads and other tablets can be connected to your computer with a USB cable, or you can import files from a memory card. The computer will treat the camera, cell phone, iPad or other tablet in the same way as an external hard disk drive. If your device is not recognized, you may need to install a device driver first; the driver program is usually supplied by the device's manufacturer. It may also be found on a CD or DVD that has been supplied with the product, or on the manufacturer's website.

Once you have imported the video material, the next step is to arrange the recordings so that they become an ongoing story. The first recording you made does not necessarily need to be placed at the beginning of the film. And you may not want to include all of your recorded material. You may even want to crop some scenes from the beginning or end of the video, or even from the middle section.

In this chapter you will learn how to use the options and functions in *Movie Maker*. We have used practice files for the examples in this book. These practice files consist of short clips of an African safari, and a piece of music that was played during a ride in a minibus. This is a quick and efficient method for getting to know the basics of working with *Movie Maker*. If you prefer, you can also start working directly with your own video files.

Once you have edited the material, you can save the film on your computer and upload it to the *YouTube* video website.

In this chapter you will learn how to:

- download and install *Movie Maker*;
- import video files to the computer;
- add video files;
- save a project;
- delete a video;
- crop videos;
- add effects, transitions, and music;
- save the film on your computer;
- upload the film to *YouTube*.

Please note:

In order to perform the tasks in this chapter, you will need to have the free video editing program *Movie Maker* from Microsoft installed on your computer. If you do not have this program yet, you can read how to install it in the next section.

 Please note:

While you are working through this book, you can use the practice files or your own videos. You will be creating a film from these videos. This film consists of a series of shortcuts to the original files that are stored on your computer. It is important that you do not delete or move these files. If you do, *Movie Maker* will no longer be able to find the files. As a result, the project you are working on will lose its content.

10.1 Download and Install Movie Maker

If *Movie Maker* is not on your pc, you download it from the Internet:

☞ **Open *Edge* ☏²**

 Please note:

If *Movie Maker* is already installed on your computer, you can continue with *section 10.2 Copying From an SD Card or USB Cable*.

☞ **Go to explore.live.com ☏²**

You will see this window:

 **If necessary, drag the scroll box downwards**

 **Click Movie Maker**

In the nex window:

 **Click**

Download now

At the bottom of the window you see a bar:

☞ **Click** [Run]

Your screen will turn dark and you will need to give permission to continue:

☞ **Give permission to continue**

☞ **Click**
Choose the programs you w

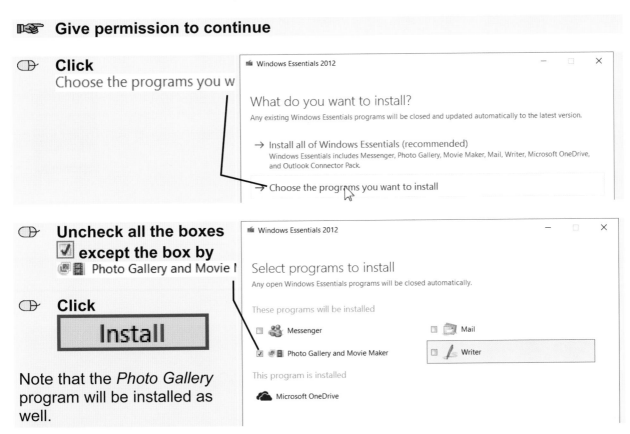

☞ **Uncheck all the boxes**
☑ **except the box by**
🖼️ Photo Gallery and Movie I

☞ **Click**
[Install]

Note that the *Photo Gallery* program will be installed as well.

You can see the progress of the installation:

Windows Live Essentials has been installed:

☞ **Click** [Close]

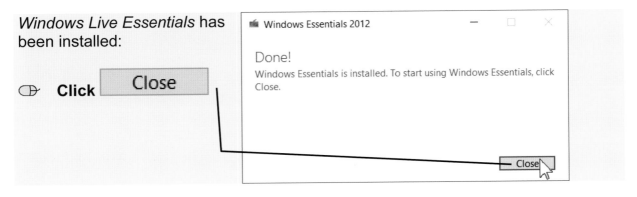

 **Close** *Edge* 🦶¹

Movie Maker has now been installed and is ready to use.

10.2 Copying From an SD Card or USB Cable

Modern video cameras, such as *camcorders* and mobile phones, often store their recordings on an SD card. If you own a card reader, you can insert the card into the reader and import the files to *Movie Maker*.

A Secure Digital card (SD card) is a memory card that can be used in portable electronic devices, such as digital cameras and cell phones. You can buy special cards with a higher *write* speed, for use in digital video and photo cameras.

For this purpose, your computer needs to be equipped with a card reader for SD cards. If your computer does not have a card reader, or if your camera does not use an SD card, you will often be able to use a USB cable to connect your computer to the camera, cell phone, iPad or other tablet.

You open *Movie Maker*:

👉 **Click** 🔍

⌨ **Type:** movie maker

👉 **Click**
    Movie Maker
    Desktop app

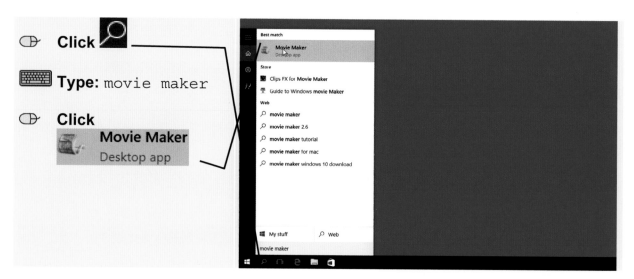

If this is the first time you open the program, you will need to agree to the user licensing terms:

👉 **If necessary, click** | Accept |

If you use a card:

☞ **Insert the card into the card reader**

If you use a camera with a USB cable:

☞ **Make sure the camera has been turned off**

☞ **Connect the camera to the power supply**

☞ **Connect the camera to your computer with the USB cable**

☞ **Turn the camera on**

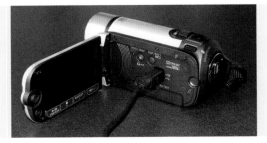

 Please note:

It is possible that your camera needs to be connected to the computer in a different way. In that case, please consult the manual that came with the camera.

☞ **Click**  File

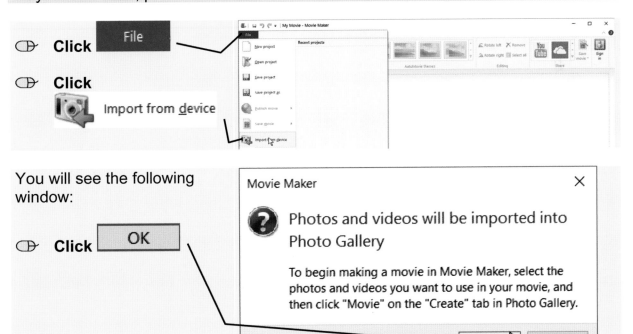

☞ **Click** Import from device

You will see the following window:

☞ **Click** OK

Movie Maker ✕

❓ Photos and videos will be imported into Photo Gallery

To begin making a movie in Movie Maker, select the photos and videos you want to use in your movie, and then click "Movie" on the "Create" tab in Photo Gallery.

☐ Don't show this message again   OK   Cancel

You will see the camera in the window:

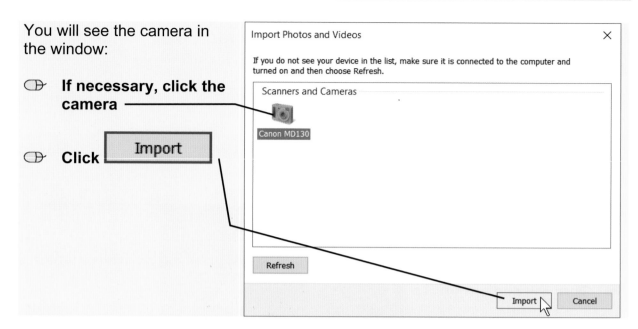

Import Photos and Videos   ✕

If you do not see your device in the list, make sure it is connected to the computer and turned on and then choose Refresh.

Scanners and Cameras

Canon MD130

Refresh

Import   Cancel

 If necessary, click the camera ——————

 Click

🩹 HELP! The camera cannot be found.

If the computer does not recognize the camera, you will see the following window:

Sometimes it takes a while for your computer to find the camera:

☞ **Wait a few minutes**

 Click [Refresh]

If your camera still is not found, this may be caused by the following reasons:
- Your digital video camera is turned off.
- Your digital video camera is in stand-by mode. With some cameras, the stand-by mode is activated while the camera is in recording mode (*Camera* mode) and while the camera contains a tape, but no video or audio data is being transferred.

You can try a number of things:
- Check if your digital video camera is connected correctly to the computer.
- Check if your camera has been turned on and in *Play* mode.
- Turn your camera off and then turn it on again in *Play* mode (also called *Player* or *VCR* mode).

 Click

The program will search for files containing photos and videos:

You will see the number of new photos and videos that have been found:

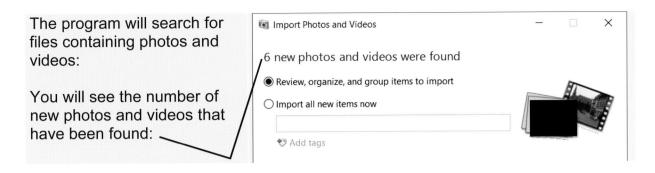

10.3 Checking the Settings

Before you start importing files, you need to check the program settings:

Click <u>More options</u>

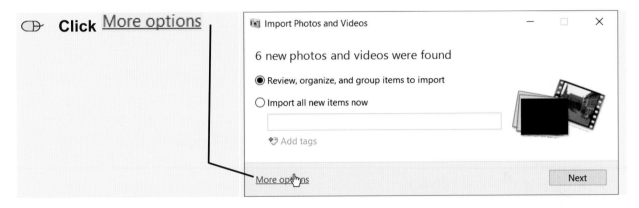

The videos and photos that you import are stored in a single folder. In this case the videos are more important, so it is a good idea to store the files in the *Videos* folder:

By Import to: click 📄 Pictures

Click 🎞 Videos

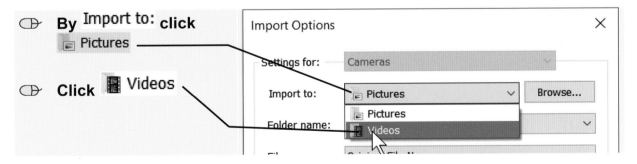

The file name starts with the date on which the file has been transferred to the computer. Usually, this is a different date from the recording date. You can also use the recording date in the file name, but if the images are recorded on different dates (for instance, during a trip) the files will be scattered among different folders.

It is better to move all recordings from the same period to the same folder:

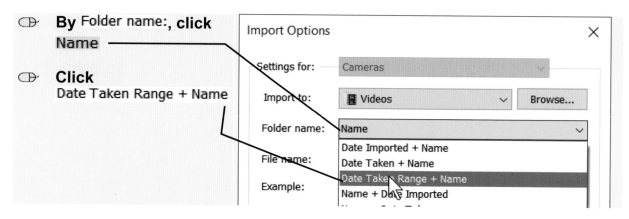

- ☞ By Folder name:, **click**
  Name

- ☞ **Click**
  Date Taken Range + Name

The day the recording was taken will be entered, starting with the earliest date.

Instead of using the original file name, you can enter a new file name yourself:

- ☞ By File name:, **click**
  Original File Name

If you select
Original File Name (Preserve Folders)
the original folders will be copied from the camera as well.

Often, the original folder and file names on the camera are not very practical, and it is easier not to use them.

- ☞ **Click** Name

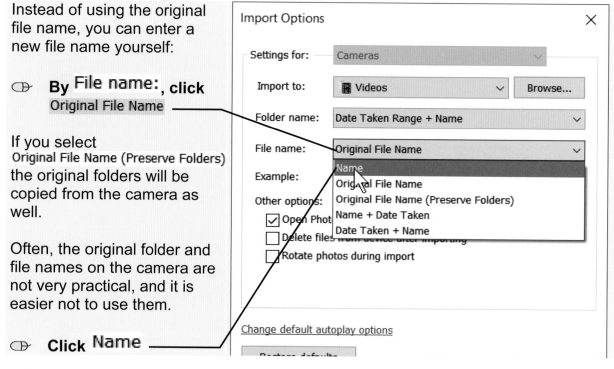

 Tip

Revert to default settings

Did you change the settings and have you forgotten what the original settings were? Then you can restore the default settings:

- ☞ **Click**  Restore defaults

In the bottom of the window:

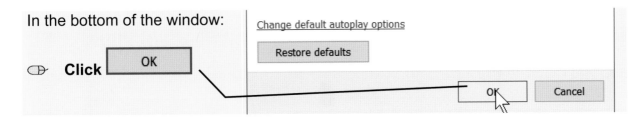

 Click OK

10.4 Importing Files

You can decide whether to import all new files, or make a selection yourself and import only the selected files. To import all new files:

☞ **Click the radio button** ⦿ **by**
Import all new items now

⌨ **Type a name**

☞ **Click** Import

If you want to select the files to import yourself, click the radio button ⦿ by
Review, organize, and group iter

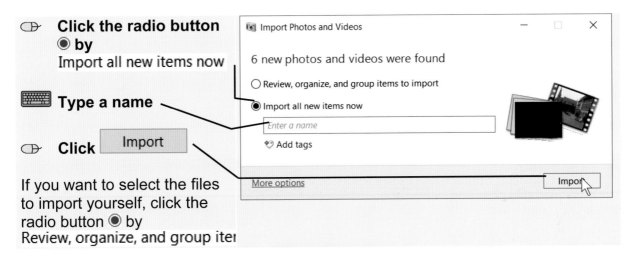

💡 **Tip**

Import everything, or only selected files?
In most cases it is wiser to import all the files at once, and then decide later which files to keep. In the first place, you will have a clearer image of the video or photo on your computer screen. You can decide on the spot if you want to save all the images or delete some of them. This will also free up more space on your device for new recordings.

The files will be imported:

You will see the imported videos and photos (if any), in *Windows Live Photo Gallery* and you may see this window:

☞ **Close the windows** 🐾¹

In this section and the previous ones, you have imported your own video files, and you can start working on them. In the next couple of sections, you will use the practice files to get acquainted with the options in *Movie Maker*.

10.5 Movie Maker Window

While you were importing the video files, you had a glimpse of the *Movie Maker* window. Now you can take a closer look at all of the components in this window:

You will see the opening window containing:

The *Quick Access* toolbar: ———

The ribbon: ————————

Various tabs: ————————

The preview window: ————

The storyboard: ————

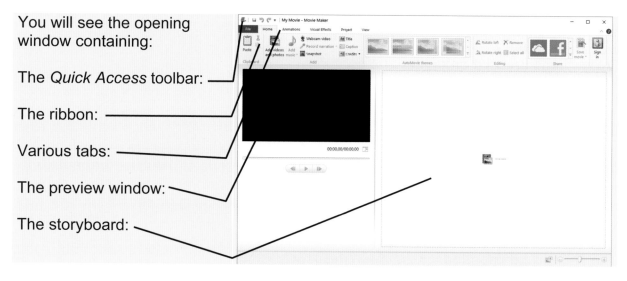

The ribbon has been designed to help you find all the necessary commands more quickly. The commands have been arranged in logical groups and tabs. Each tab is connected to a specific activity, such as changing the window settings, or adding effects.

If you want to select a command on the ribbon, you usually need to click twice. First the tab, and then the specific command or option itself. If you find that you are using the same commands over and over again, this can be a nuisance. This is where the

Quick Access toolbar comes in handy: . This toolbar contains frequently used commands, which you can activate with a single click.

10.6 Adding Video Files

A movie that is being edited in *Movie Maker* is called a *project*.
If you want to make a movie, you start by adding one or more video or photo files to your project. This is called *importing*. In this example the practice files will be used. You can download the practice files from **www.visualsteps.com/your10computer**

☞ **Download the practice files for *Movie Maker* to your computer, as explained in *Appendix B Downloading the Practice Files***

You can start now by adding the practice files:

Add videos
☞ **Click** and photos

If you want to use your own videos, you need to select the folder with your own files, instead of the *Practice Files Video* folder.

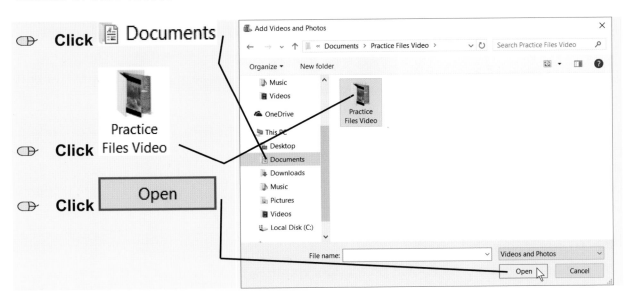

☞ **Click** 📄 Documents

Practice
☞ **Click** Files Video

☞ **Click** Open

You are going to add all the video files:

☞ **Click** Organize ▼

☞ **Click** ⊞ Select all

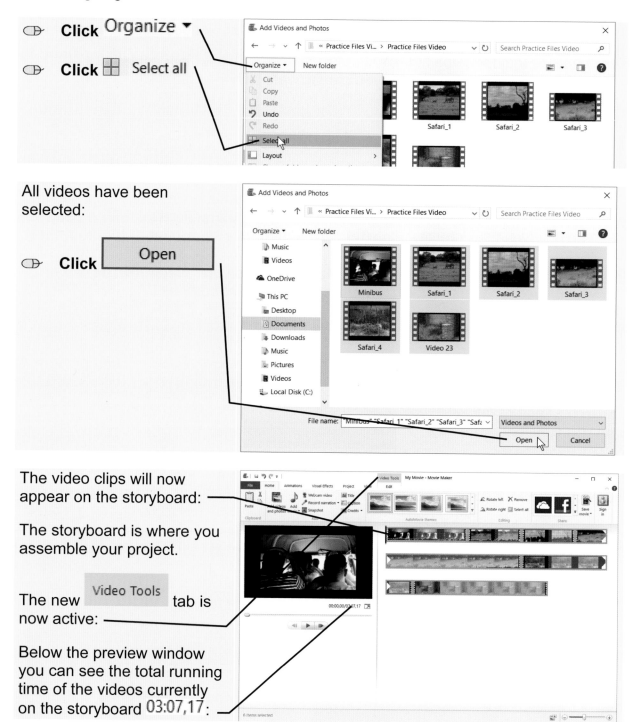

All videos have been selected:

☞ **Click** Open

The video clips will now appear on the storyboard:

The storyboard is where you assemble your project.

The new Video Tools tab is now active:

Below the preview window you can see the total running time of the videos currently on the storyboard 03:07,17:

🢒 **Please note:**

The number of video clips shown on the storyboard will depend on your screen's resolution.

You will see an image from each video clip. To view the project, you can play it in the preview window:

Click ▶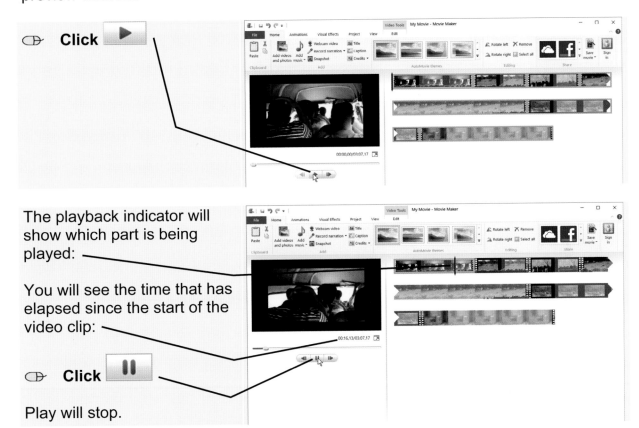

The playback indicator will show which part is being played: ⎯

You will see the time that has elapsed since the start of the video clip: ⎯

Click ⏸

Play will stop.

You can also view the video one frame at a time. A frame is the smallest unit of which a video clip is composed. A frame is also called an image. Click ▶ a few times. Depending on the video clip you might see the image changing a bit. But you will be able to see the playback indicator move along with the frames.

To view a video clip directly, click a clip. A quick way to skip to a specific spot in the project is by dragging the playback indicator.

10.7 Saving a Project

It is wise to save the project from time to time:

In the top left of the window:

Click 💾

Save the file in the
🎬 Videos folder:

☞ **Click** 🎬 **Videos** ⎯⎯⎯

⌨ **By** File name:, **type:**
        Africa ⎯⎯⎯

If you are using your own
video, you can type a
different name.

The file will be saved as a
Movie Maker project, with the
file extension .WLMP.

☞ **Click** | Save |

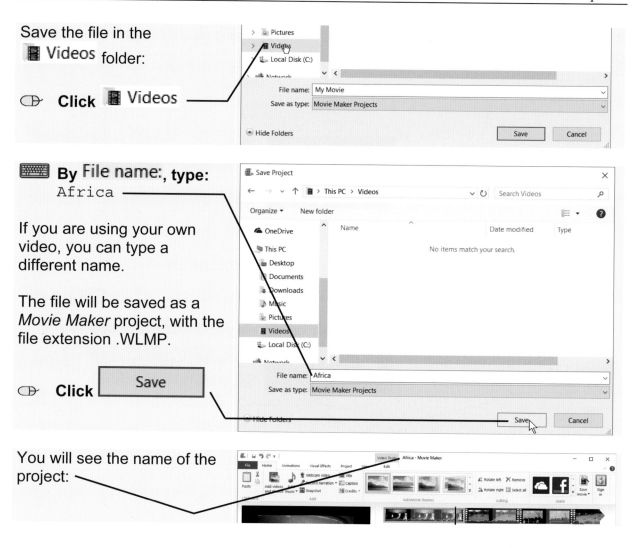

You will see the name of the
project:

10.8 Deleting Videos

The scenes you have recorded will form the basis of your movie. This is your
project's rough material. Take a look at what you have so far.

☞ **Play the entire project** ✂23

Now that you have gathered together the material you will need for your movie, you
can begin making a *movie plan*. A movie plan is a general plan that states the
content of the movie, and the scenes you plan to use.

Before you begin putting your scenes in order, it is a good idea to delete the video clips from the storyboard that you know you will not be using. Return to the beginning of the movie:

Click

Click ✗

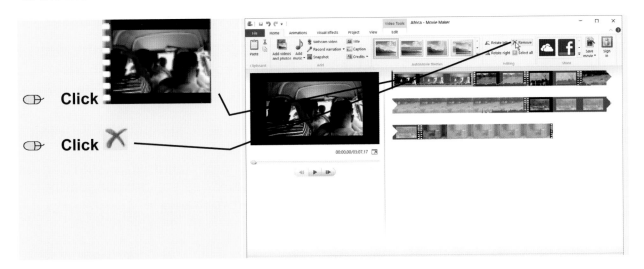

 Please note:

When you delete a video from a project, it is not deleted from your computer. It still remains in the folder where it was originally imported.

The video has been removed:

Click

Click ✗

The video has been deleted.

The overall length of the movie is now shorter:

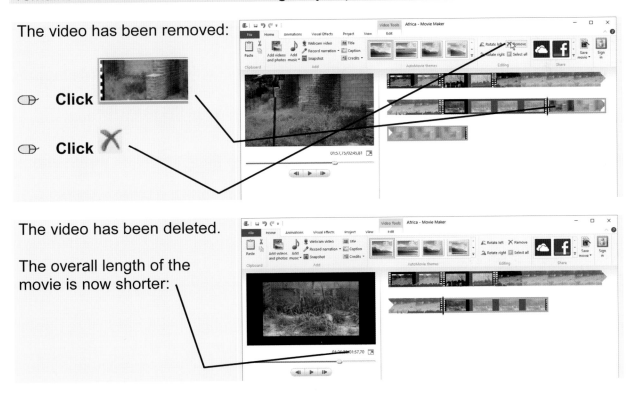

HELP! I have deleted the wrong video.

Did you accidentally delete the wrong video but have not changed anything else yet?

Then just use the Undo button to restore the deleted video. Did you delete the

wrong video and are you unable to restore it with the Undo button ? The videos that you remove from a project are not deleted from your computer. You can retrieve

the video once more by clicking the **Add videos and photos** button.

Now you have removed the videos that you do not need. While you are assembling the movie, you can still delete other unwanted scenes, if you need to.

 Tip

Moving videos
If the clips are not in the right order, you can easily move the videos. In the *Tips* at the end of this chapter you can read more about this.

10.9 Trimming Videos

The section of the project with the leopard is quite long and dreary, and the last video with the monkey could also do with some trimming. After approximately one minute, the leopard lies down and the video can be trimmed. Here is how to do that:

☞ **Drag the playtime slider until you see something like 01:00,23. below the preview window**

While you are dragging, you will see the images in the preview window:

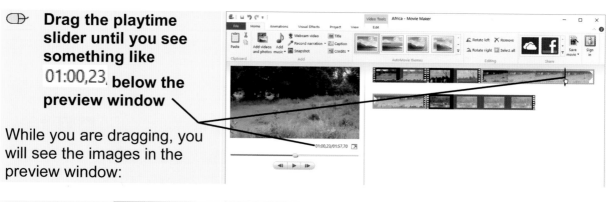

☞ **Click the Edit tab**

☞ **Click ⊢⊣ Set end point**

The video has been trimmed on the spot you have set.

 HELP! This was not the correct spot.

The video will only be trimmed within this project. The original file will not be edited.

If you have trimmed the video in the wrong spot, then click ↶ to undo the trimming.

You can also trim the end section of the video with the monkey. For this you can use the *Trim* tool as well. You can define the section you want to trim by elapsed time, or by the images:

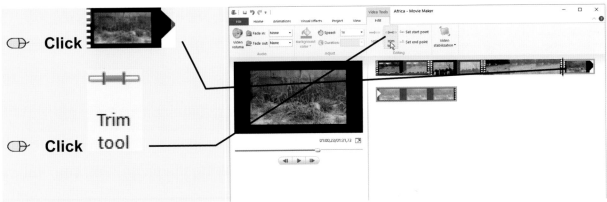

Click ▣

Trim

Click **tool**

You will see two trim markers below the preview window:

By dragging the trim marker on the right, you can move the ending point.

☞ **Drag the right trim**

marker to the left,

up to around 00:25,05

If you have a fragment that needs to go on for a certain amount of time, you can set the starting and ending points at the top of the window, by Start point: and End point:.

The time for the ending point is 00:25,05:

Save

☞ **Click** trim ────

The video has been trimmed. It is wise to save the project in between various operations. If something goes wrong while you are applying further edits, you can always go back to the version you saved.

In the top left of the window:

☞ **Click** 💾 ────

You have a succession of animals that were spotted during the safari. You can now add some effects and transitions.

10.10 Adding Effects and Transitions

Movie Maker contains a number of effects and transitions that can be added to your film. You can take a look at some of these effects:

☞ **Click the**

    Visual Effects

    tab ────

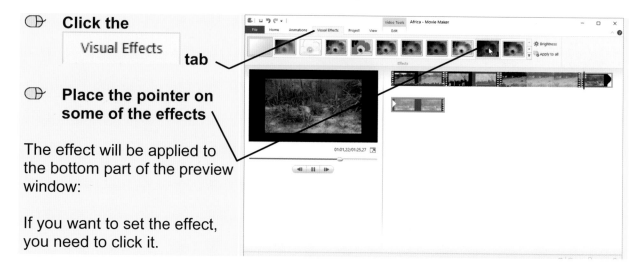

☞ **Place the pointer on**
   some of the effects

The effect will be applied to the bottom part of the preview window:

If you want to set the effect, you need to click it.

There are different kinds of effects. For instance, you can mirror videos, render them in black-and-white, make them look older, fade in and out, and add movement. If you want to see more effects, you click ▼.

You can also apply a transition. A transition determines the way in which one video changes over into another one. Without using transitions, this may be quite abrupt sometimes, especially if there is a lot of difference in brightness. You can choose from various transitions:

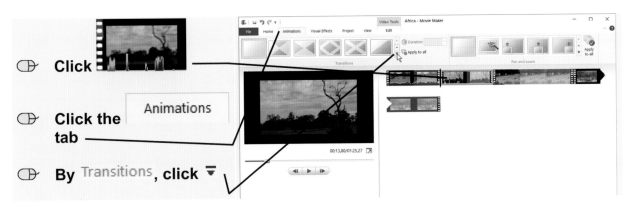

⊕ **Click**

⊕ **Click the** Animations **tab**

⊕ **By** Transitions**, click** ▼

The transitions have been grouped by category, just like the effects. If you place the pointer on a transition, you will see it appear in the preview window:

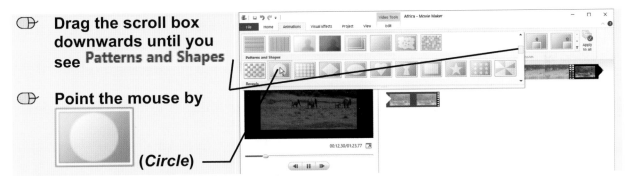

⊕ **Drag the scroll box downwards until you see** Patterns and Shapes

⊕ **Point the mouse by** *(Circle)*

☞ **Take a look at some of the other examples in this category, and in the other categories**

Now you can apply the *Circle* transition:

⊕ **By** Patterns and Shapes**, click** *(Circle)*

☞ **Play the project from the first image** ✄23

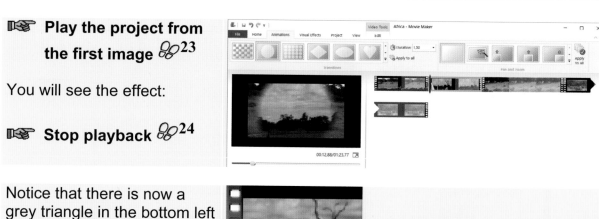

You will see the effect:

☞ **Stop playback** ✄24

Notice that there is now a grey triangle in the bottom left corner by the video where the transition has been set:

You can also set the transition for the whole project. This will ensure that the project becomes a unified video clip. To do this, you need to select all the videos:

🖱 **Click the** **Home** **tab**

🖱 **Click** ▢

All videos have been selected.

🖱 **Click the** *Animations* **tab**

🖱 **By** Transitions**, click** ▼

🖱 **Drag the scroll box downwards until you see** **Patterns and Shapes**

🖱 **Click** ⬤ (*Circle*)

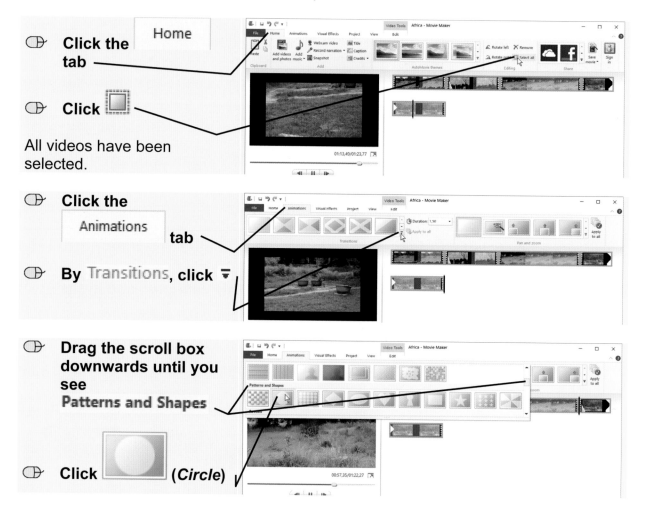

☞ **Go to the start of the project** 👣²⁵

☞ **Play the whole project** 👣²³

You will see the transitions:

Usually, a transition takes 1.5 seconds. If that is too long or too short, you can change its duration by ⏱ Duration: .

☞ **Save the project** 👣²⁶

10.11 Adding Music

Many films use background music to create a certain atmosphere, or to enliven silent sections or parts that do not have a lot of sound. You can practice adding music to the project with the tune that was played during the trip in an African minibus:

👉 **Click the** Home **tab**

👉 **Click** ♪

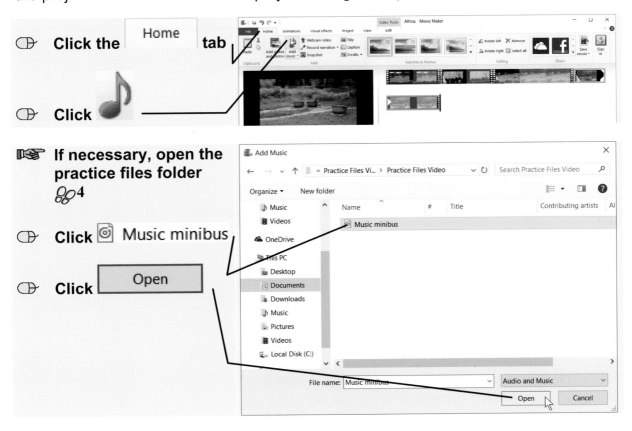

☞ **If necessary, open the practice files folder** 👣⁴

👉 **Click** 🎵 Music minibus

👉 **Click** Open

An extra music track has been added, the so-called soundtrack:

This track is displayed below the video files.

You can also edit the music you have added. For example, you can fade the music in and out. This means that you let the music start very slowly and at the end you let the music die down. Fading out can also be useful in a case where the music has not yet finished when the last slide is displayed.

This is how to set up the fade in and fade out options:

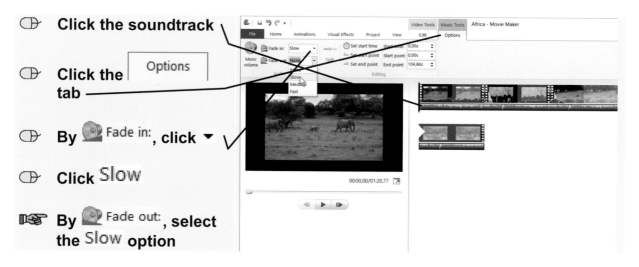

⊕ **Click the soundtrack**

⊕ **Click the** | **Options** | **tab**

⊕ **By** 🎵 **Fade in:, click ▾**

⊕ **Click** Slow

☞ **By** 🎵 **Fade out:, select the** Slow **option**

☞ **Play the entire project** ♋²³

You will hear the music begin very softly and then become louder later on. At the end of the film, the volume of the music track has faded away.

In this example you have also played the background noise of the video. You can still hear this very low noise during the elephant video. You can mute this sound too, if you wish. In the *Tips* at the end of this chapter you can read more about this.

☞ **Save the project** ♋²⁶

You have now learned how to make a film with *Movie Maker*. In the next couple of sections, you will learn how to finalize the film, and upload it to *YouTube*, if you wish.

10.12 Store the Movie on your Computer

If you want to be able to watch the movie for example, in *Windows Media Player*, the files will need to be stored on your computer. You can choose one of the following formats, depending on the quality you want:
- HD video with a resolution of 1920 x 1080 pixels
- HD video with a resolution of 1280 x 720 pixels
- Wide-screen format with a resolution of 720 x 480 pixels
- Standard format with a resolution of van 640 x 480 pixels

HD stands for *High Definition*. The higher the resolution, the higher the quality; but this also means the file size will increase as well.

The quality you need to choose depends on a number of things:
- If you own an HD camera and the movie is recorded in HD quality, then it is best to choose an HD resolution.
- If the movie is not recorded in HD quality, and you will be mainly watching the movie on your computer, then you can choose the wide-screen or the standard format.
- If the movie is recorded in the wide-screen format, or the standard 4:3 format, then choose the corresponding quality.

In your camera's specifications you will find the recording quality of the camera. Sometimes the camera has various options to set the recording quality. High quality recordings will produce a better image, but will take up much more space on your camera's internal memory or memory card. This means you will have less recording time. The quality level you need to use depends on the way you are going to view the movie. Not all equipment is suitable for movies in HD quality.

You can save your film on your computer:

☞ **Make sure your speakers are turned on and the volume is not muted**

In this example we have chosen to save the project with the recommended settings. For the Africa project, the setting is 960 x 720 pixels, and the default 4:3 image size. Your own project may have different settings, depending on the original video material.

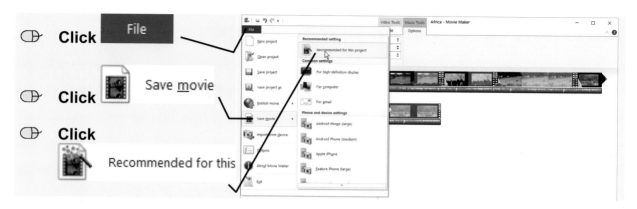

Click File

Click Save movie

Click Recommended for this

In this example you will be saving the movie in the *Videos* folder:

Click Videos

☞ **If necessary, enter a file name by** File name:

Click Save

A small window appears, indicating the progress of the rendering (saving) process:

If the movie is long and the quality is high, this may take more than ten minutes.

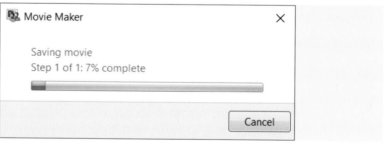

Now the film is stored on your computer. To view the film directly:

Click Play

You may see a window in which you are asked with which program you want to watch the movie:

You can watch the movie. When the movie has finished:

☞ **Close the window** 🦶¹

Now you will see the project once again.

10.13 Publishing Your Movie on YouTube

This is how to publish your movie on *YouTube*:

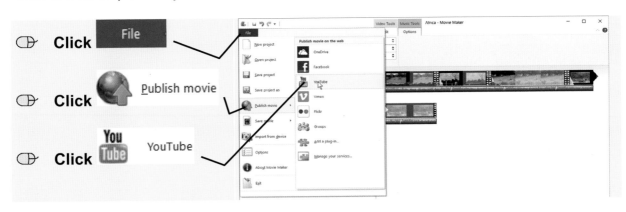

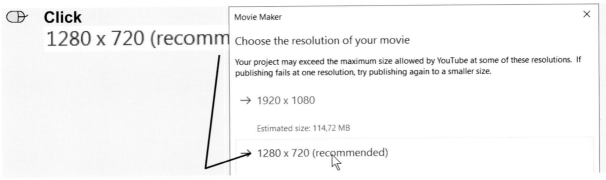

You will need to sign in with your *Microsoft* account. This is a combination of an email address ending in hotmail.com or outlook.com, and a password:

 Type your *Microsoft* account email address

 Type your password

⊕ **Click** Sign in

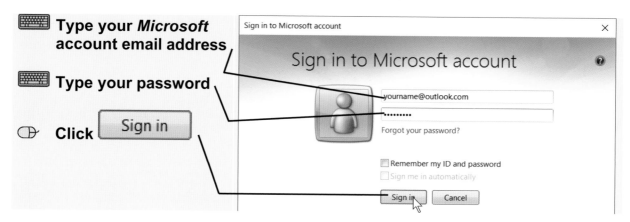

 HELP! I do not have a Microsoft account.

If you do not have a *Microsoft* account, you can create one on the web page signup.live.com.

Now you can sign in to *YouTube*:

 Type your *YouTube* user name

Please note: depending on prior use of your account, this may be a user name or an email address.

 Type your password

⊕ **Click** Sign In

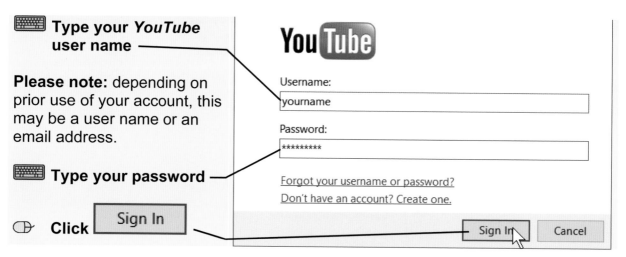

 HELP! I do not have a YouTube account.

If you do not have a *YouTube* account and wish to create one, you can do this on the http://accounts.google.com web page.

☞ **Change the title, if you want to** ————

⌨ **By** Description:**, type a description** ————

⌨ **By** Tags:**, type the desired tags** ————

Tags are keywords that allow other *YouTube* visitors to look for movies.

🖱 **By** Category:**, click** Select a category... ————

🖱 **Click** Travel & Events

If you want to allow anyone to be able to watch your movie, then do not change the Public **permission:** ————

Select the Private **option to publish a video that is only available to your friends.**

🖱 **Click** Publish

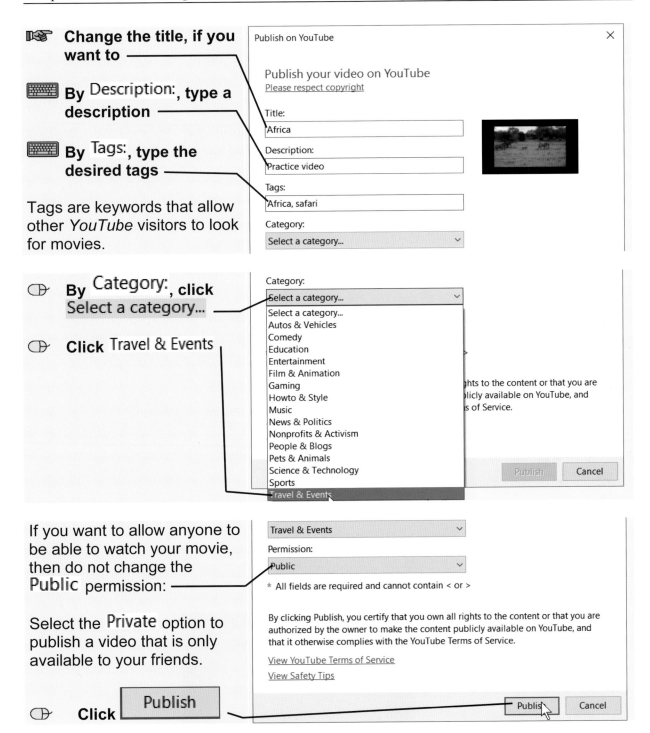

Now the movie will be rendered for use on *YouTube*:

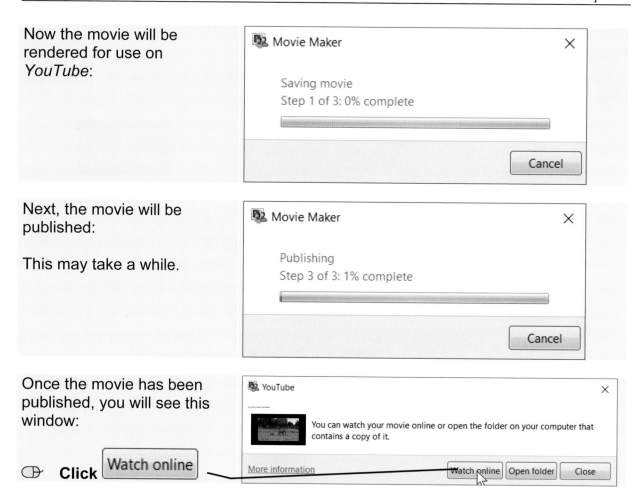

Next, the movie will be published:

This may take a while.

Once the movie has been published, you will see this window:

☞ **Click** [Watch online]

Sometimes, the movie will not be available on *YouTube* right away. Then you will see a message. Wait for a couple of minutes and click ↻.

Now the movie will be played:

After the movie has finished, and a blue checkmark **Autoplay** has appeared by its side, the next movie is announced.

☞ **Click** Cancel

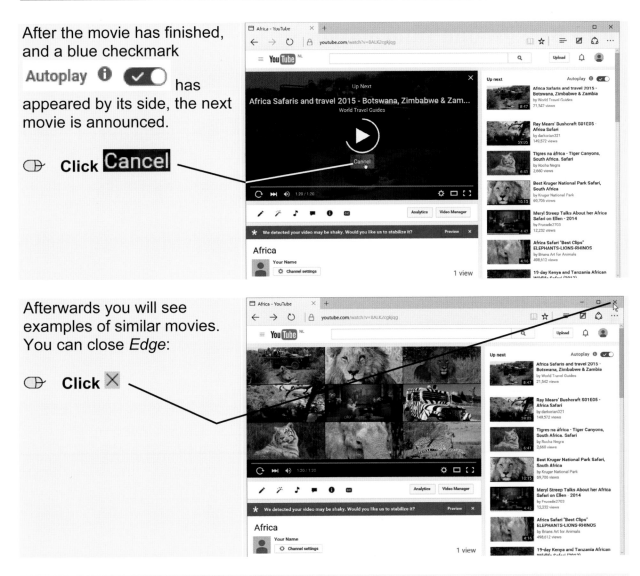

Afterwards you will see examples of similar movies. You can close *Edge*:

☞ **Click** ✕

☞ **Close all windows** ¹

Now the movie has been published on *YouTube.* If you have made the movie available to the public, anyone can watch this movie, even people who do not have a *YouTube* account.

In this chapter you have learned how to import, edit, and save video material on your computer. You have also read how to publish your video on *YouTube*.

10.14 Background Information

Dictionary

Assembling	Arranging and trimming the videos and photos within a project.
Effects	Changes in the colors or motion of the original recording, in order to create a particular atmosphere, or correct recording errors.
Fade	Type of transition where the scene *fades out* at the end, or slowly *fades in* at the beginning.
Frame	A frame is the smallest unit of which a video is composed.
HD video	HD stands for High Definition. This is a standard format for recording, saving and playing high quality videos.
Import	Transferring digital media files to *Movie Maker*, so you will be able to use these files in various projects.
Microsoft account	A *Microsoft* account consists of an email address and a password that you can use to sign in with various Microsoft services.
Movie	The final result of a project is a movie. A movie has the file type called .WMV.
Movie Maker	With *Movie Maker* you can create a movie of your photos and videos. You can save the movie to your computer or publish it online.
Movie plan	An overview of all the available videos and photos.
Playback indicator	A black line on the storyboard that indicates the position in the project when the project is played or edited.
Preview window	The section in *Movie Maker* that lets you display (part of) your project.
Project	A project is stored as a .WMLP file and contains links to all the videos, photos, and audio files that are used in the project. The project also contains the edits and the effects.

- Continue on the next page -

Rendering	Assembling a movie. In this process, the actual video images are created, including the titles, sounds and transitions. This is the stage that follows the editing stage. Rendering requires a lot of computing power and may take a little while.
Scene	Parts of a movie that belong together. Often a single event.
SD card	A Secure Digital card (SD card) is a memory card that can be used in portable electronic devices, such as digital cameras and mobile phones. You can buy special cards with a higher write speed and use them with your digital video and photo camera.
Soundtrack	The section above the video in the editing pane, where you can view the background music and sounds.
Storyboard	The section in *Movie Maker* that displays the order of the photos, videos, audio files, and text in the current project. Here you can edit the photos, videos, music, and text.
Track	An overview that displays all the titles that have been added to the movie, in chronological order (title track). It can also provide an overview of all the sound clips that are added to the movie (sound track). A track may be displayed above or below the video images, in the preview window.
Transitions	Special image effects that can be inserted between consecutive scenes. You can use them to take a time leap, to display a different angle, or to soften large differences in brightness.
Trim mark	A slider on the timeline, used to set the start or end point of a video.
USB	USB connections (Universal Serial Bus) are often used for connecting external devices to your computer, for example a mouse, keyboard, scanner, printer, webcam, digital camera, mobile phone or an external hard drive.
Video	A file that contains a recording.
Windows Live Photo Gallery	With *Windows Live Photo Gallery* you can arrange, edit, and share photos. You can also use *Photo Gallery* to import photos from an external device, such as a digital camera, a USB stick, or an external hard drive.

- Continue on the next page -

YouTube	*YouTube* is a website where you can upload, view, and share videos for free; all the videos are created by the users.
YouTube account	With this account you can use all the options on *YouTube*.

Source: Movie Maker Help

Audio files

Movie Maker supports the following audio file types:

Audio file types (format)	**File extension**
Windows Media Audio files (WMA)	.ASF, .WM and .WMA
Pulse-code Modulation files (PCM)	.AIF, .AIFF and .WAV
Advanced Audio Coding files (AAC)	.M4A
MP3 audio files	.MP3
MPEG-4 video files	.MP4, .MOV, .M4V

Comments:

- Video and music files which are protected by DRM (Digital Rights Management), cannot be used in *Movie Maker*.

Source: Movie Maker Help

10.15 Tips

💡 **Tip**

Open project
If you want to continue working on your project later on, you can open it like this:

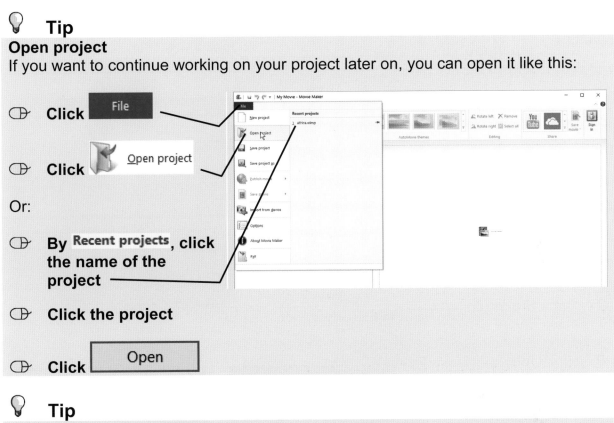

👆 **Click** File

👆 **Click** Open project

Or:

👆 **By** Recent projects, **click the name of the project**

👆 **Click the project**

👆 **Click** Open

💡 **Tip**

Adjust the music volume
If you think the volume of the music is too loud or too soft, you can adjust it:

👆 **Click** Music volume

👆 **Drag the slider ▼ to the left or to the right**

Tip

Move videos
If the video recordings are not in the right order, you can move them like this:

⊕ **Click the video you**
    want to move ————

⊕ **Drag the video to the**
    desired location ⟍

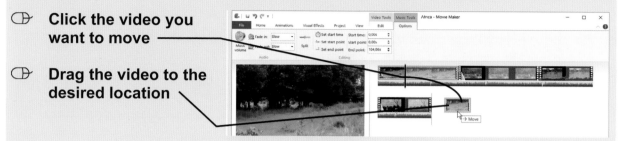

The video has been moved.

 Tip

Adjust the volume of the video
If you want to mute the background noise on the video, you can do that like this:

⊕ **Click the video** ————

⊕ **Click the** [Edit]
    tab ⟍

⊕ **Click** Video volume ————

⊕ **Drag the slider ▼ to the**
    left ————

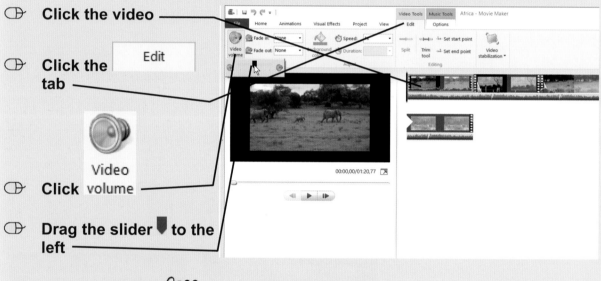

☞ **Play the project** 𝄞23

Now you will no longer hear the background sounds from the video. But the soundtrack of the other videos will still be played. You can also adjust the sound for each video separately.

11. Computer Maintenance

Security is essential for all computers connected to the Internet. A good security system minimizes the risk of acquiring *viruses* or other harmful software on your computer. A virus is a program that tries to distribute itself from one computer to another, and causes damage by deleting or damaging data. Another type of virus will annoy users by displaying unwanted messages, or alter the information that is displayed on screen.

It can be very frustrating to work on a computer that has been infected with a virus. Not just for you, but for others too. If your computer is infected, it may infect other computers too. This happens without you noticing it, for example, when you send an email or a (chat) message, or when you share files from a CD, DVD, Blu-ray disk, external hard drive, or USB stick. You are responsible for the security of the computer you work on as a user. With a recently updated *antivirus program* you can make sure that your computer is regularly scanned for viruses or other harmful software.

After a period of time, you will probably have installed new programs to your computer. Among these may be programs you no longer use. It is wise to uninstall the programs you no longer use. This not only helps to free up space but keeps your computer better organized.

Finally, we want to mention how important backups are. You have many personal files stored on your computer. For instance, precious photos of important moments in your life, important documents, addresses, and favorite websites. You can easily create a backup copy of these files. You need to store a safety copy somewhere outside of the computer, in a secure location. This is an effective method of preventing the loss of important data if your computer malfunctions one day.

In this chapter you will learn how to:

- update *Windows* and apps;
- scan your computer with an antivirus program;
- remove programs in the correct way;
- clean up your hard disk;
- create a backup copy of the entire content of your computer;
- create a backup copy of your personal files.

11.1 Windows Update

Windows Update is an important component in *Windows*. The main function is to check if you are using the most recent version of *Windows 10*. *Windows 10* is constantly being updated, extended and enhanced. It is of particular importance that you have the latest updates and revisions to the security measures. These additions and improvements are distributed by Microsoft in the form of software updates.

 Please note:

Microsoft never sends software updates through email. If you receive an email with an attachment that claims to be Microsoft software, or a *Windows Update*, you should never open the attachment. Delete the email at once, and do not forget to delete the email from the *Deleted items* folder as well. This type of email is sent by unscrupulous individuals who are trying to install harmful software on your computer.

If you want to be sure that you are using the most recent version of *Windows 10*, you need to check to see if *Automatic updates* is enabled. You do that as follows:

The *Update and Security* window will be opened on the *Windows Update* tab:

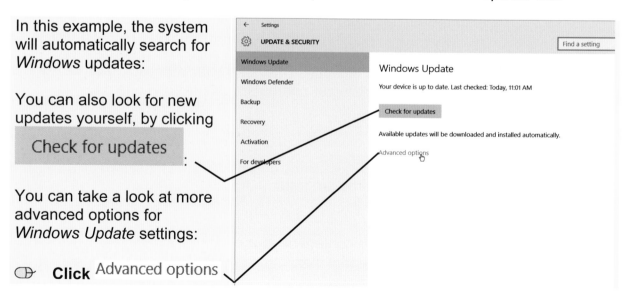

In this example, the system will automatically search for *Windows* updates:

You can also look for new updates yourself, by clicking

Check for updates :

You can take a look at more advanced options for *Windows Update* settings:

☞ **Click** Advanced options

If you see
Automatic (recommended)
in the window, the automatic
update has been enabled:

If you do not see this:

⊕ **By**
Choose how updates

click ⌄

⊕ **Click**
Automatic (recommen

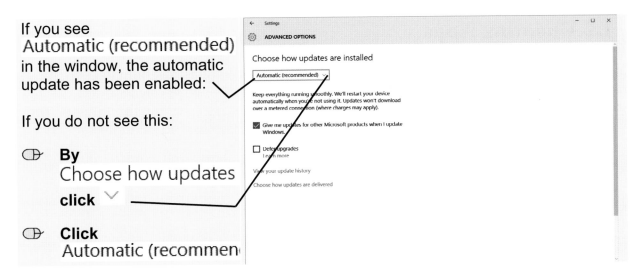

You can also enable the installation of updates for other Microsoft programs, if
desired:

⊕ **If necessary, check**
the box ☑ **by**
Give me updates for othe
Windows.

Save the settings:

⊕ **Click** ←

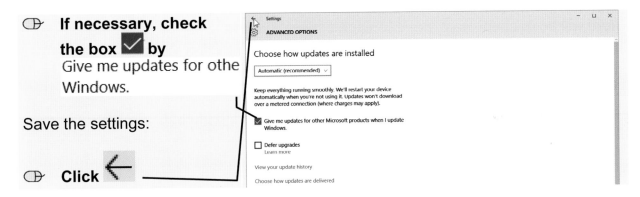

In the *Update and Security* window:

⊕ **Click** ←

Now the *Windows Update* settings have been saved.

☞ **Close** *Settings* 1

11.2 Updating Apps

The default setting in *Windows 10* for updates made to apps is for them to be downloaded automatically. However, the updates are not always downloaded immediately. Your computer may also have a different setting for these updates. You can manually search to see if updates for apps are available. You do that like this:

☞ **Open the *Store*** 👣²⁸

💡 **Tip**

Open the Store from the taskbar
You can also open the *Store* from the taskbar:

⟳ **Click** 🏪 **on the taskbar**

Store will be opened. Here you can update apps, like this:

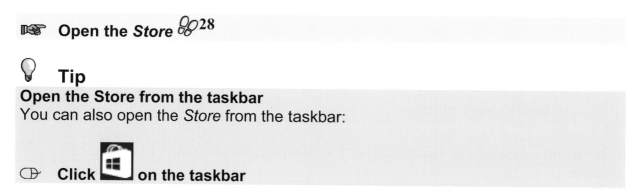

⟳ **Click** 👤

⟳ **Click** Settings

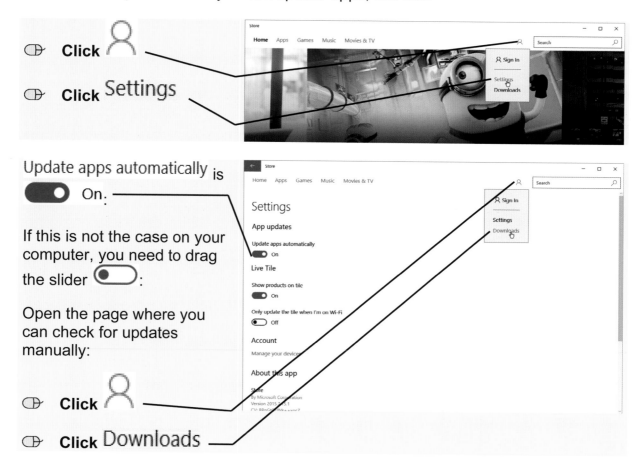

Update apps automatically is

🔘 **On**.

If this is not the case on your computer, you need to drag the slider 🔘 :

Open the page where you can check for updates manually:

⟳ **Click** 👤

⟳ **Click** Downloads

Check for updates:

⊕ Click
> Check for updates

If any updates are found, you will see ⬇ to download the updates. Just click it and follow the instructions in the window, if necessary.

Close the window:

☞ **Close the *Store* window** 🦶1

➥ **Please note:**

Windows programs will usually receive automatic updates. Programs manufactured by other companies, such as *Picasa* by *Google*, will often have an option in the Help, Extra, or Options menu with which you can check for updates. Some programs will tell you if there are any updates as soon as you open them.

11.3 Virus Protection with Windows Defender

In computer terminology, the word virus is certainly a well-known term, but in fact, viruses are just one type of the increasing threats to every computer connected to the Internet. The general term for this is *malware*. Malware is short for *malicious software*. This is software that is specifically designed to damage your computer. Viruses, worms, spyware, and Trojan horses are all types of unwanted software.

The source of an infection may be an attachment to an email, or a program you have downloaded. Your computer can also be infected when you exchange data using USB sticks that are infected with malware, or CDs, DVDs, or other storage media. Some of the malware programs are designed to be operational at unexpected moments, and not just during installation.

Windows Defender is included in the *Windows 10* software package, and helps protect the computer against malware, in two ways:

- **Real-time protection**
  With *Windows Defender* you will be warned when malicious software tries to install itself, or is installed to your computer. You will also be warned in case any apps try to change major settings.
- **Scan**
  With *Windows Defender* you can scan your computer whenever you want. For example, when your computer suddenly stops working properly, or if you have received a suspicious-looking email. You can run a scan in order to check whether you have unintentionally downloaded any malware.

Open *Windows Defender*:

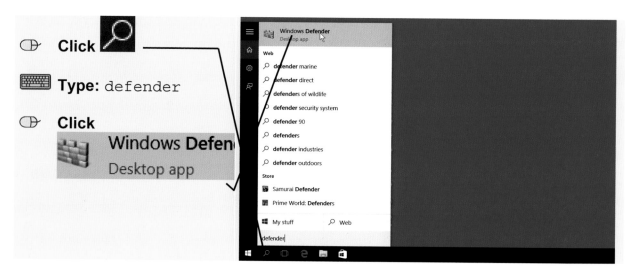

The home window of *Windows Defender* appears:

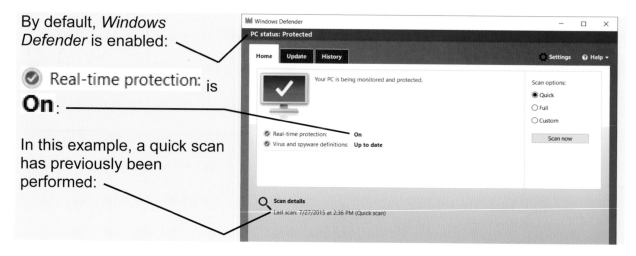

Windows Defender closely cooperates with *Windows Update*. As soon as new spyware and malware definitions become available, they are downloaded and installed automatically. In this way, the program can always dispose of the most recent information. By default, there is an extra check before a scan is carried out. You can also update *Windows Defender* yourself:

Click the **Update** **tab**

Here you see the most recent update of the definitions:

This is how you check for new definitions:

Click Update

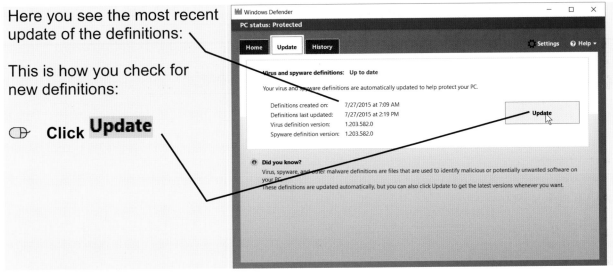

If any new definitions have been found, *Windows Defender* will be updated at once:

In this window you can view the progress of the installation of the new definitions:

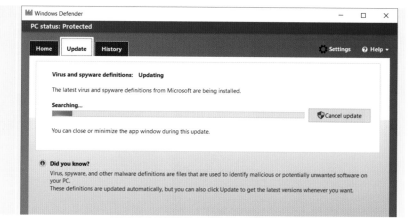

11.4 The Real-time Protection Function of Windows Defender

The real-time protection function in *Windows Defender* will warn you immediately when malware or spyware tries to install itself on your computer.

As soon as *Windows Defender* detects harmful software, you will see a message such as this one in the bottom right corner of your screen:

Malware Detected
Windows Defender is taking action to clean detected malware.

The harmful software will immediately be placed in quarantine, to prevent it from being activated. You can take a look at the quarantine information later, and decide if you want to delete or restore the item in question. To do that:

Click the

History **tab**

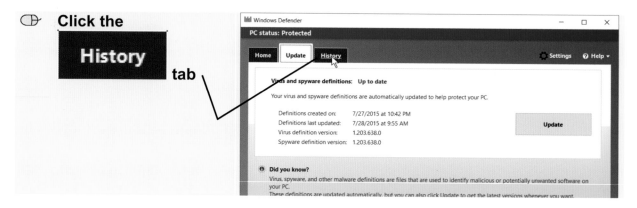

In order to protect the privacy of the user, you will not immediately see which items have been placed in quarantine:

☞ **Click**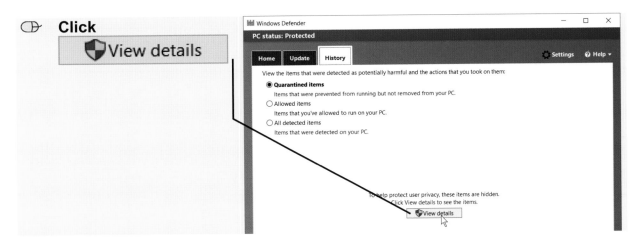

You will see an overview of the items that have been placed in quarantine. You can read more about quarantine in the next section. The list on your computer may be empty.

Here you see an overview of the items that are currently held in quarantine. You can read more about quarantine in the next section. The list on your computer may be empty.

If you see an item you know is safe, you can check the box by this item and use the

Restore button

to restore it: ——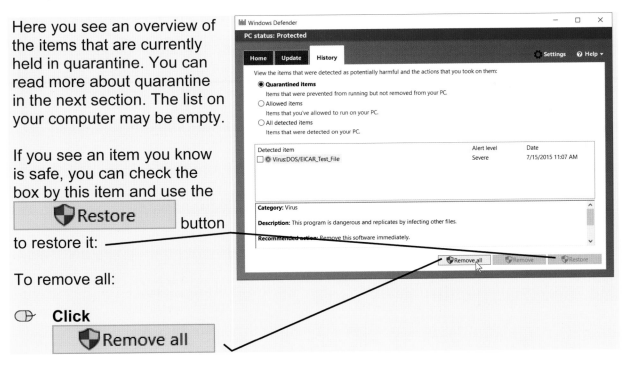

To remove all:

☞ **Click**

Remove all

All harmful software will now be deleted.

11.5 Scanning Your Computer with Windows Defender

You can scan your computer with *Windows Defender* any time you want. If for any reason, you think your computer is not functioning properly, or if you have noticed a suspicious-looking email, it may be a good time to run a scan to check if the computer has become infected by a virus or other unwanted software.

You can choose between three types of scans:

- **Quick**: only scans the locations where unwanted software is regularly found.
- **Full**: scans all the files and folders on your computer.
- **Custom**: only scans the folders you have selected.

In order to get an idea of how a scan works, you can initiate a quick scan.

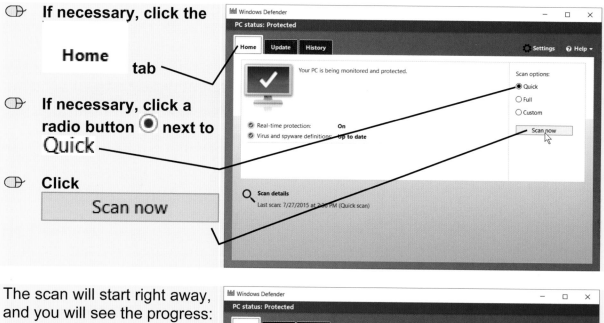

☞ **If necessary, click the**

   Home **tab**

☞ **If necessary, click a radio button ⦿ next to Quick**

☞ **Click**   Scan now

The scan will start right away, and you will see the progress:

If you want to stop the scan, you use the   Cancel scan   button:

A full scan may take up to an hour or longer, depending on the speed of your computer and the number of files. The quick scan is much faster.

Once the scan has finished, you will see a scan report:

In this example, no suspect files have been found:

If you do not open unknown email attachments, or use suspect programs, there is only a small chance of unwanted programs entering your computer. Nevertheless, *Windows Defender* will surely find a suspect file, every now and then.

If anything has been found, you will see a message. You will see a description of the malicious software, the seriousness of the threat, and the action recommended by *Windows Defender*. Here there are various options:

- **Remove**: the infected file or virus will be removed from your computer. This means the content of the file will be lost if you have not made a backup copy. This is usually the course of action if there is no other solution for the problem.
- **Quarantine**: the item will be moved to a folder where it can do no harm. If you appear to be needing this item later on, you can restore it. Select the restore option only if you are sure a false alarm has been given to the item.
- **Allow**: the item will not be detected in future scans. Select this option if you know the item is safe and are sure you want to keep it.

If no suspect files have been found on your computer, then just read through the next part of this section.

If a harmful program has been found, you will see this message:

You can view the details:

👉 **Click** <u>Show details</u>

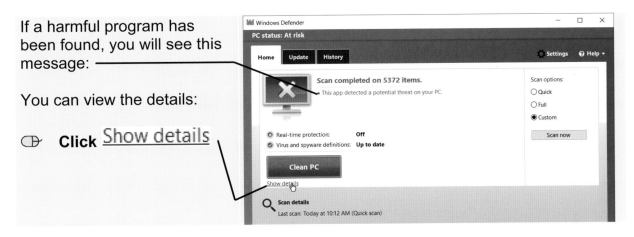

Windows Defender recommends that you **Remove** the file:

To do that:

👆 **Click**

> **Apply actions**

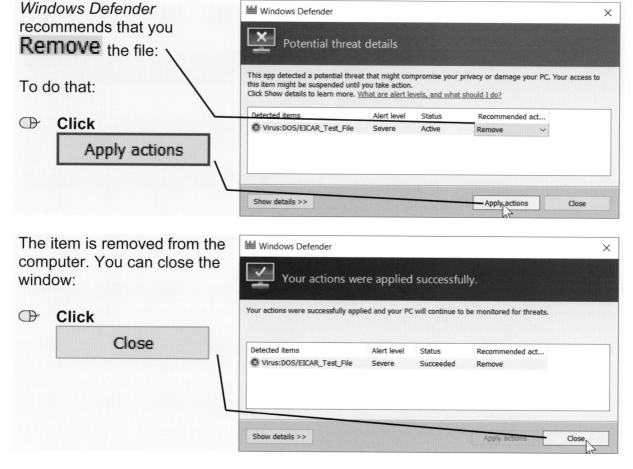

The item is removed from the computer. You can close the window:

👆 **Click**

> **Close**

You have learned about the various options in *Windows Defender*. You can close the program:

👉 **Close *Windows Defender*** 🦶¹

11.6 Uninstalling Programs

Your computer may contain some programs you seldom use or never use at all. You can easily remove these programs.

When you install a program onto your computer, you actually install both the program and an additional uninstall program at the same time. The uninstall program cleans up all the program files and will remove the program buttons or icons from the Start menu and even the desktop. This is called uninstalling.

This is how you remove a program. In this example *Skype* will be removed:

Click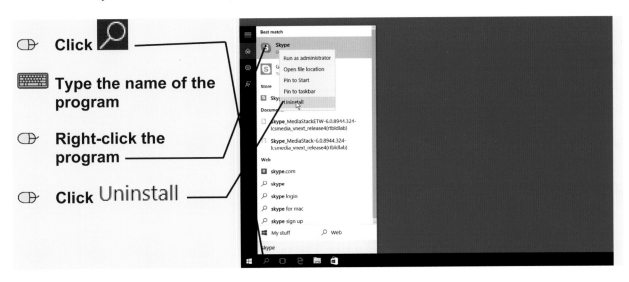

Type the name of the program

Right-click the program

Click Uninstall

You will see the *Control Panel*:

You will see the list of programs that can be uninstalled:

Click the desired program

Click Uninstall

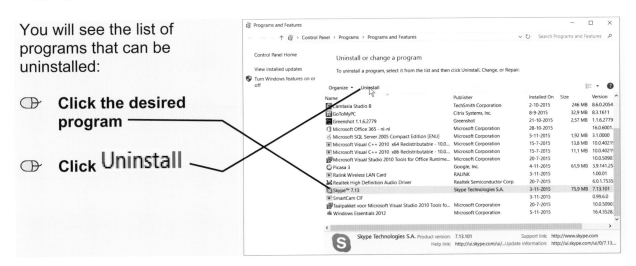

 Please note:
The list of programs often contains programs that are essential for your computer to function properly. Do you see an unfamiliar program? Do not uninstall it. First try to find out what the program's function is. You can search the Internet or try using the Help function in *Windows*, for example.

If you really want to delete the program:

Click Yes

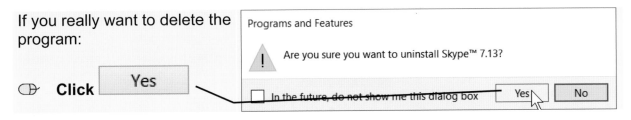

If necessary, give permission to continue

The program will be deleted.

Please note:

When you are uninstalling a certain program, you may be asked which specific components you want to uninstall, or you may see other windows with more options.

 Follow the instructions in these windows

 Close the window 🐾¹

11.7 Cleaning Up Your Hard Drive

As you use your computer, your hard drive slowly collects temporary files. For a large part, this happens automatically, for example, while you are surfing the Internet. After a while it is a good idea to do a thorough spring-cleaning and remove these temporary files. If your computer becomes too full, this is really essential.

You start by opening the *Settings*:

👆 **Click** ⊞

👆 **Click**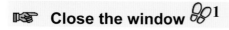

👆 **Click the search box**

⌨ **Type:** `free up disk`

👆 **Click**
Free up disk space by deleting

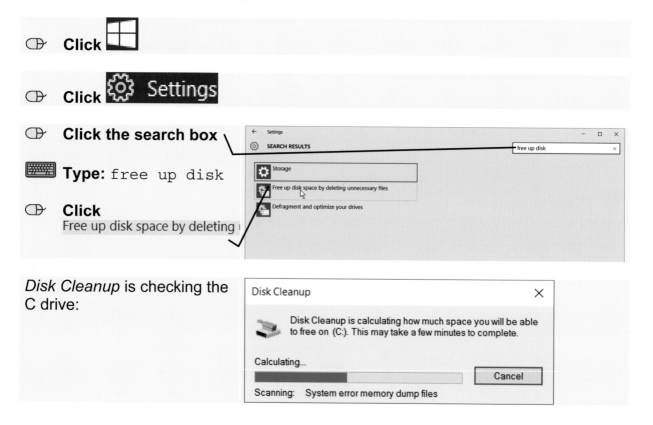

Disk Cleanup is checking the C drive:

In this window, you can see which types of files will be deleted. If you click a file type, you will see a description at the bottom of the window:

Usually you can let the program delete all of the files. If you do not want to do this, you need to uncheck the box ☑ by the files you do not want to delete:

In this example, a total of 320 MB of disk space will be freed up:

With [OK] you will only delete the files from your own user account.

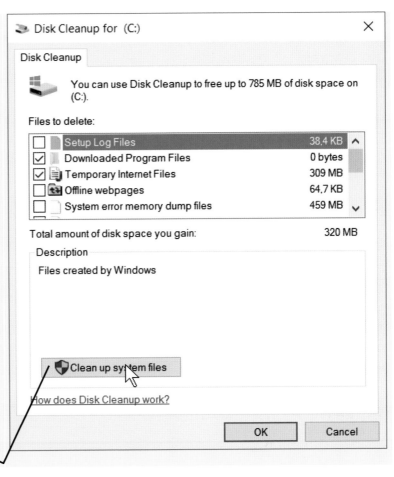

⊕ **Click**

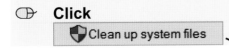

You will see the *Disk Cleanup* window once again:

Once again, you will see which types of files will be deleted. If you click a file type, you will see a description at the bottom of the window:

Usually you can let the program delete all of the files. If you do not want to do this, you need to uncheck the box ☑ by the files you do not want to delete:

In this example, a total of 320 MB of disk space will be freed up:

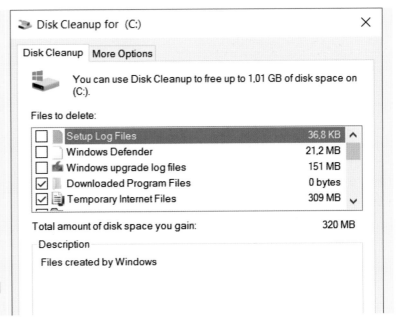

Sometimes, there are also other program files and system files that can be deleted. You can delete this type of file here:

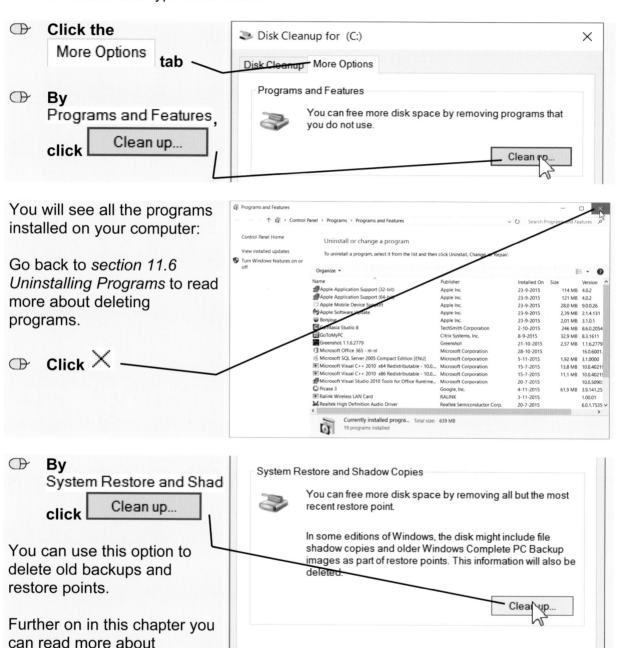

☞ **Click the** More Options **tab**

☞ **By** Programs and Features, **click** Clean up...

You will see all the programs installed on your computer:

Go back to *section 11.6 Uninstalling Programs* to read more about deleting programs.

☞ **Click** ✕

☞ **By** System Restore and Shad **click** Clean up...

You can use this option to delete old backups and restore points.

Further on in this chapter you can read more about backups.

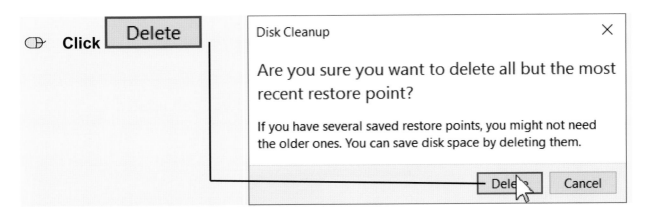

☞ **Click** the Delete button

At the bottom of the window *Disk Cleanup for (C:)*:

☞ **Click** OK

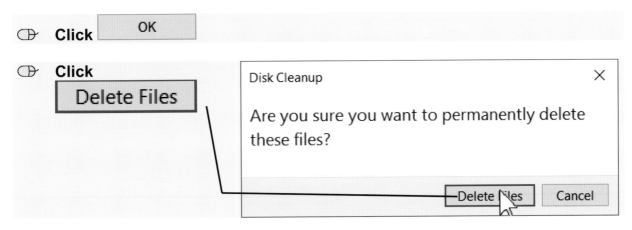

☞ **Click** Delete Files

Disk Cleanup has deleted the files you have selected.

11.8 Creating a Full Backup

In *Windows 10* you can create a full backup. This is also called a *system image*. A system image contains copies of all your programs, systems settings, and files. With this system image you can restore the entire content of your computer, in case the hard drive or the computer has stopped working.

 Please note:

The space on your hard disk may be too small for storing a system image. In that case you will automatically see a warning, and you will need to use an external hard drive.

Please note:

Creating a full backup may take several hours. That is why you should read through this section first, and only carry out this task if you really want to create a full backup.

☞ **If necessary, connect the external hard drive to your computer**

Then you need to open the *Control Panel*:

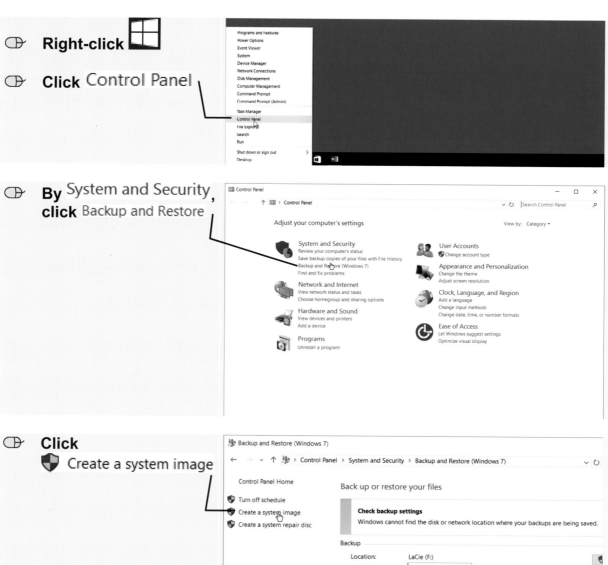

👆 **Right-click** ⊞

👆 **Click** Control Panel

👆 **By** System and Security, **click** Backup and Restore

👆 **Click** 🛡 Create a system image

You will see the *Create a system image* window. First, the system will check for the connected devices to which the image can be copied:

You can select where to save the backup, for example, on an external hard drive, or a DVD:

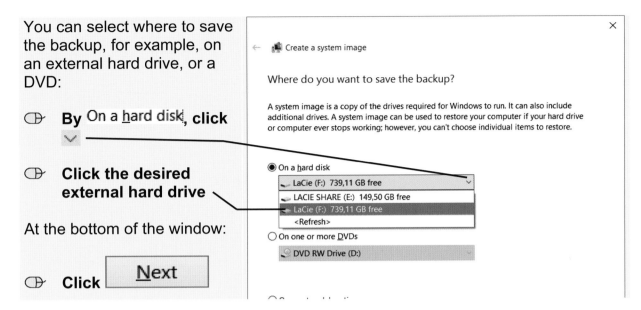

 By On a hard disk, **click** ∨

 Click the desired external hard drive

At the bottom of the window:

 Click Next

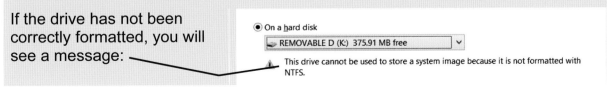 **HELP! My external hard drive is not recognized.**
If your external hard drive is not recognized in the *Create a system image* window, your drive may not be suitable for *Windows 10*.

Tip
Backup on a memory card or a USB stick
If you are using a memory stick or a USB stick instead of an external hard drive, you need to select the option On a hard disk.

HELP! The drive is not suitable.
If you want to create a system image, your external hard drive needs to be formatted for the NTFS file system. Usually, the external hard drive has already been formatted for NTFS by default. In the *Windows* help function, or in the manual that came with your external hard drive, you will find more information about this.

If the drive has not been correctly formatted, you will see a message:

○ On a hard disk
REMOVABLE D (K:) 375.91 MB free ∨
⚠ This drive cannot be used to store a system image because it is not formatted with NTFS.

If you have multiple drives on your computer, you can select which drives you want to include in the backup. By default, the drive that contains *Windows* will already be selected:

Check the box ☑ by the hard drive(s) you want to include

You will see the space required and the free space:

Click Next

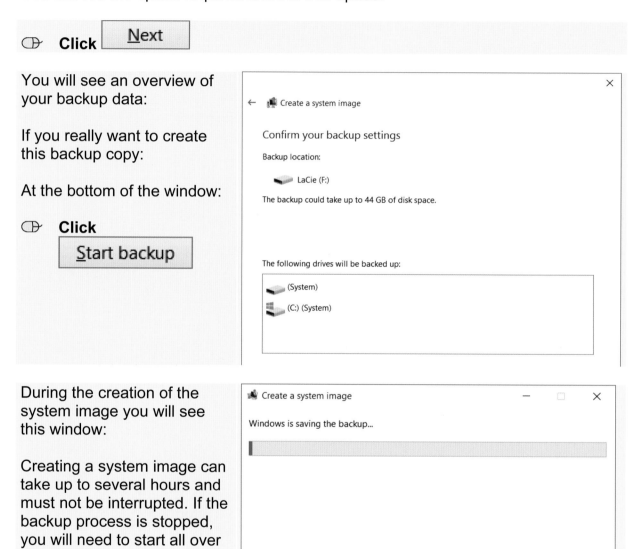

You will see an overview of your backup data:

If you really want to create this backup copy:

At the bottom of the window:

Click Start backup

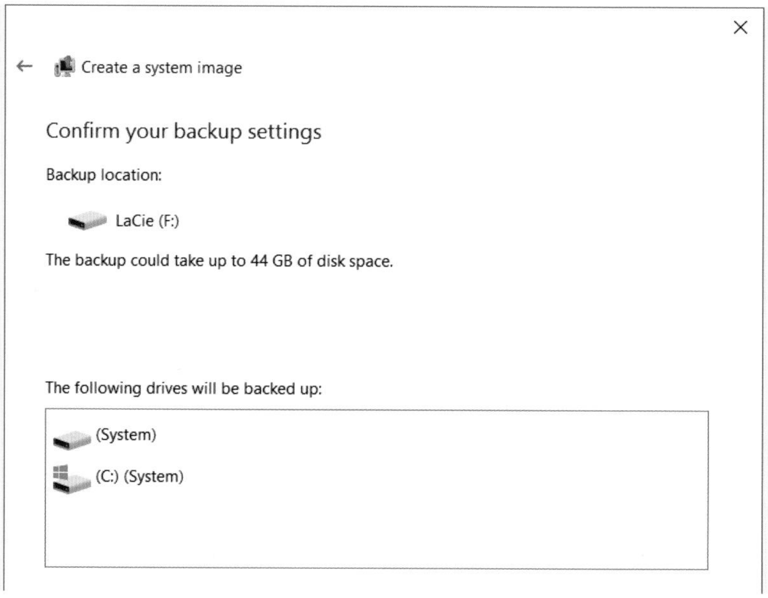
Create a system image
Confirm your backup settings
Backup location:
LaCie (F:)
The backup could take up to 44 GB of disk space.
The following drives will be backed up:
(System)
(C:) (System)

During the creation of the system image you will see this window:

Creating a system image can take up to several hours and must not be interrupted. If the backup process is stopped, you will need to start all over again.

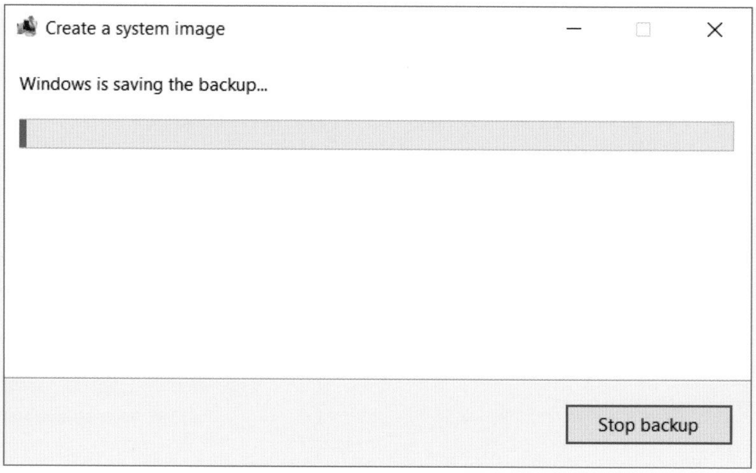
Create a system image
Windows is saving the backup...
Stop backup

After the backup copy has been made:

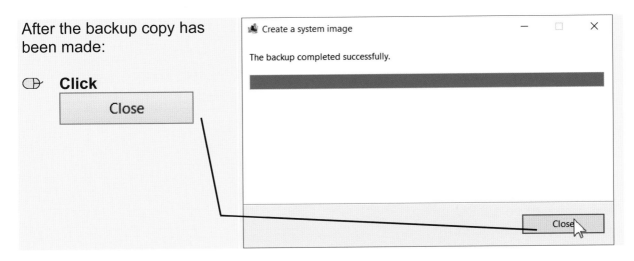

⊕ **Click**

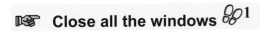

Once the backup process has finished, you will have an external hard drive with a full copy of your current system. Store this backup in a safe place.

☞ **Close all the windows** ¹

💡 **Tip**

Regularly create system images
It is recommended that you create a system image regularly. This way, you will always have a recent copy of your hard drive at your disposal.

11.9 Creating a Backup of Personal Files

In *Windows 10* you can also create a backup of your own files, such as important documents, or photos. With this method you can secure data that is important to you, in case anything happens to your computer. This can be a malfunction, for example, or your data may be damaged or deleted by fire, theft, an electrical breakdown, or some operational error on your part. It is recommended that you store this type of backup on an external hard drive.

☞ **If necessary, connect the external hard drive to your computer**

🔖 **Please note:**
Keep in mind that your external hard drive needs to have sufficient available (free) space. If the drive does not have enough free space, a warning message will be shown. In that case you will need to use another external hard drive.

☞ **Open the *Control Panel*** ³

In the search box:

Type: `file history`

 Click File History

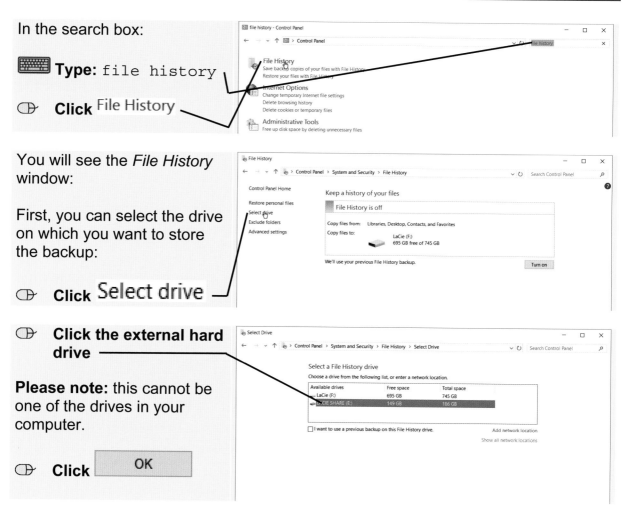

You will see the *File History* window:

First, you can select the drive on which you want to store the backup:

 Click Select drive

 Click the external hard drive

Please note: this cannot be one of the drives in your computer.

 Click OK

Tip

The name of the external hard drive
In *Windows*, the external hard drive can usually be recognized by its brand name.

You may still need to turn on the file history:

 If necessary, click

Turn on

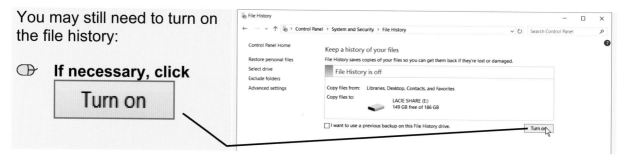

Please note:

The file history you have set up is only valid for the current user. Each user needs to turn on his or her own file history.

The backup will be created right away. During the backup process you will see Stop:

Once the backup has been made, you will see Run now:

If you do not want to create automatic backups of all the folders:

⊕ **Click** Exclude folders

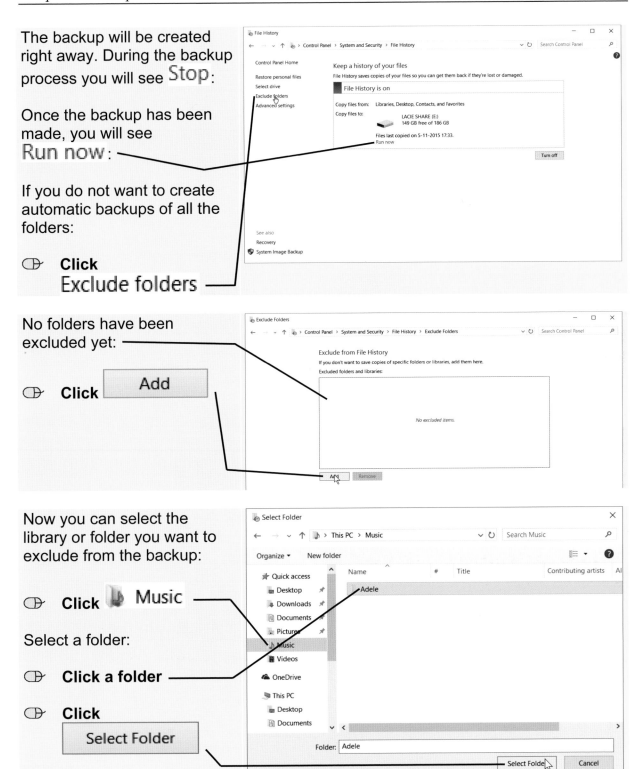

No folders have been excluded yet:

⊕ **Click** Add

Now you can select the library or folder you want to exclude from the backup:

⊕ **Click** Music

Select a folder:

⊕ **Click a folder**

⊕ **Click** Select Folder

You will see the folder that
has been excluded:

You can exclude even more
folders, if you wish.

☞ **Click**

  Save changes

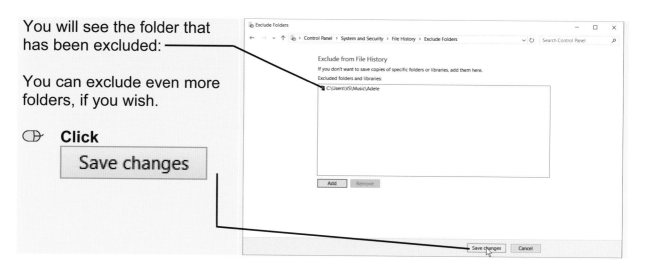

This is how you can view the advanced settings and change them, if you wish:

☞ **Click**
   Advanced settings

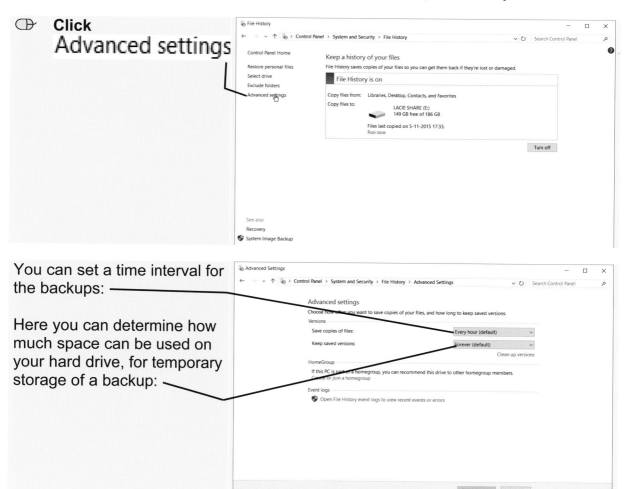

You can set a time interval for
the backups:

Here you can determine how
much space can be used on
your hard drive, for temporary
storage of a backup:

You can delete older backups yourself, in order to free up space on your backup drive:

☞ **Click**
Clean up versions

In this example you would delete all the backups older than one year:

You can select a different period, if you wish.

For now, this will not be necessary:

☞ **Click** | Cancel |

If you have changed any settings and want to save them, you click
| Save changes |.

In this example you have not changed anything:

☞ **Click** | Cancel |

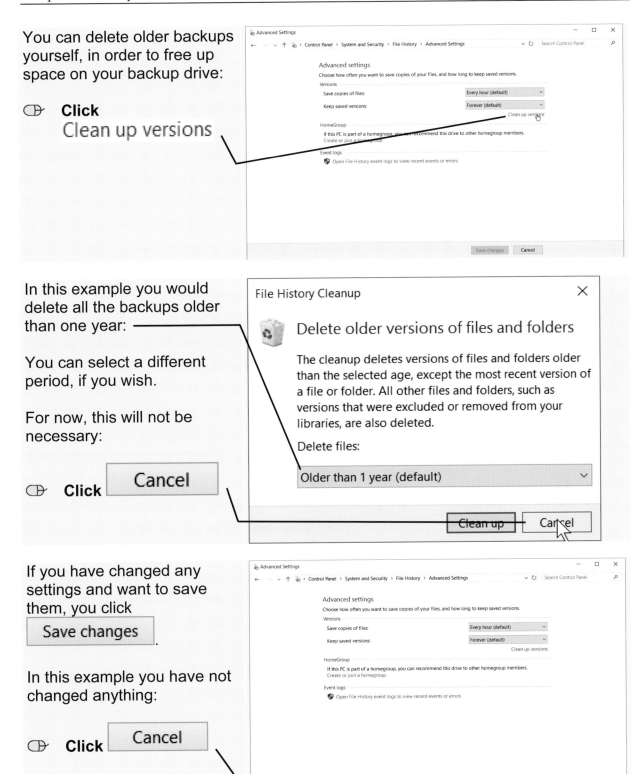

You can manually update the backup, for example, if you have changed or saved any important files:

 Click Run now

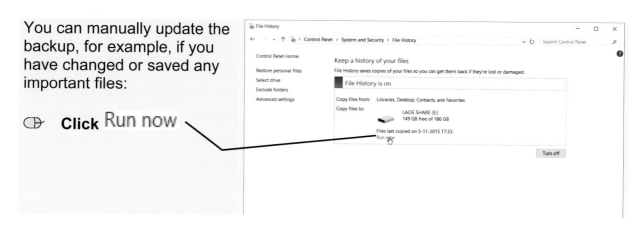

The next backups will be created automatically, according to the settings you just made.

 Please note:

In this example, a backup of any changed files is made every hour. This is called an *incremental backup*. This means that the entire hard drive is not completely backed up every time. If you wish, you can change the time period to twice a week, for example.

Please note:

The backup can only be created if the external hard drive is connected. If the drive is not connected, a temporary backup will be created on your computer's hard drive.

You will see this window:

File History

! Reconnect your drive

Your files will be temporarily copied to your hard drive until you reconnect your File History drive and run a backup.

Close

The backup will be updated. During this process you will see Stop:

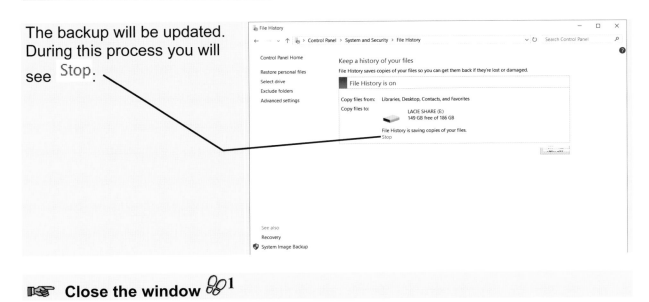

☞ **Close the window** 👣¹

You have seen how to turn on the file history, and create a backup.

11.10 Restoring Personal Files

If you want to restore personal files, you need to use the backup program as well. You can open the window directly where you can select the library or folder you want to restore:

Click 🔍 ─────

⌨ **Type:** file history

Click
🕘 Restore your files with F

The folders you have backed up are located in the *Music* library:

Select the library you want to restore:

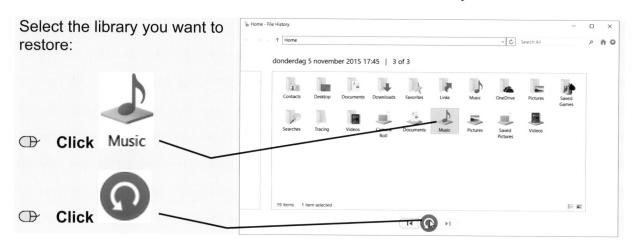

 Click Music

 Click ⟳

💡 **Tip**

Restore an older version
By default, you will be restoring the latest version. In order to restore an older version:

 At the bottom of the window, click ⟨ |◁ ⟩

💡 **Tip**

Restore multiple folders
In order to restore multiple folders or libraries, you need to select these first, with

Ctrl or **Shift** .

You will see the restored library:

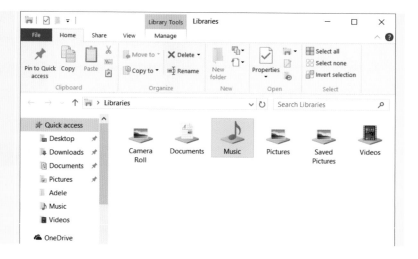

☞ **Close all the windows**

💡 **Tip**

Restore a specific folder
If you want to restore a specific folder, instead of restoring the entire library, you need to open the library by double-clicking it:

You will see the folders in this library. To restore a folder:

↪ **Click the folder**

In this chapter you have learned how to maintain and secure your computer. You have reached the end of this book. You have learned to work with various programs, options, and functions on your *Windows 10* computer.

11.11 Visual Steps Website and Newsletter

By now we hope you have noticed that the Visual Steps method is an excellent method for quickly and efficiently learning more about computers, tablets, other devices and software applications. All books published by Visual Steps use this same method.
In various series, we have published a large number of books on a wide variety of topics including *Windows*, *Mac OS X*, the iPad, iPhone, Samsung Galaxy Tab, Kindle, photo editing and many other topics.

On the **www.visualsteps.com** website you will find a full product summary by clicking the blue *Catalog* button. For each book there is an extensive description, the full table of contents and a sample chapter (PDF file). In this way, you can quickly determine if a specific title will meet your expectations. You can order a book directly online from this website or other online book retailers. All titles are also available in bookstores in the USA, Canada, United Kingdom, Australia and New Zealand.

Furthermore, the website offers many extras, among other things:
- free computer guides and booklets (PDF files) covering all sorts of subjects;
- frequently asked questions and their answers;
- information on the free Computer Certificate that you can acquire at the certificate's website **www.ccforseniors.com**;
- a free email notification service: let's you know when a new book is published.

There is always more to learn. Visual Steps offers many other books on computer-related subjects. Each Visual Steps book has been written using the same step-by-step method with short, concise instructions and screenshots illustrating every step. Would you like to be informed when a new Visual Steps title becomes available? Subscribe to the free Visual Steps newsletter (no strings attached) and you will receive this information in your inbox.

The Newsletter is sent approximately each month and includes information about
- the latest titles;
- supplemental information concerning titles previously released;
- new free computer booklets and guides;

When you subscribe to our Newsletter on the **www.visualsteps.com/newsletter.php** you will have direct access to the free booklets on the **www.visualsteps.com/info_downloads.php** web page.

11.12 Background Information

Dictionary

Automatic backup	A scheduled backup performed by the *Windows* operating system. The time and date for when the backup will take place can be set according to your own preferences.
Backup	A safety copy of the files on a computer.
Custom scan	An option in an antivirus or antispyware program which only scans the folders that you select.
Disk Cleanup	If you want to reduce the number of unnecessary files on the hard disk in order to free up disk space and speed up your computer, you can use the *Disk Cleanup* function. This function deletes temporary files, empties the *Recycle Bin*, and deletes various system files and other items you no longer need.
External hard drive	A hard disk drive that has its own casing and can be connected to the computer with a cable.
Firewall	Software or hardware that contributes to the security of a computer. A firewall can block or allow data traffic to or from your computer.
Full scan	An option in an antivirus or antispyware program that scans *all* the files and folders on your computer.
Quick scan	An option in an antivirus or antispyware program. When this type of scan is performed, only the locations where unwanted software is most often found will be scanned.
Real-time protection	This function makes sure that *Windows Defender* constantly watches all the activities while you are surfing the Internet. Attempts to install malware on your computer, will be blocked.
Spyware	This is software that can display advertisements, such as pop-ups, collect personal information about you, or change your computer settings without asking permission.

- Continue on the next page -

System image	A system image is an exact copy of a hard drive. It is essentially a full backup. A system image by default, will contain the disk drives that are essential for running *Windows*. The system image contains the *Windows* operating system and your system settings, programs and files. You can use a system image to restore the content of your computer if the hard drive crashes or the computer for some other reason has stopped working. If you decide to restore a system image to your computer, it is an all-embracing process. You cannot restore individual items. All your current programs, system settings and files will be replaced by the content of the system image.
Temporary Internet files	Web pages that are displayed in your Internet browser for the first time, are stored in a folder with temporary Internet files. Because of this, pages that you regularly visit, or that you have previously viewed, can be displayed much faster, since *Internet Explorer* will be able to open these pages from the stored files.
Trojan horse	A program that contains or installs an unwanted program. The program appears to be innocent, useful, or interesting, but it is actually harmful when activated.
Uninstall	To undo the installation of a program, by deleting the program files from the computer.
Unwanted software	Programs that are designed to damage your computer. Also known as malware.
Virus	A program that tries to distribute itself and spreads from one computer to another, thereby causing damage by deleting or corrupting data, or that annoys users by displaying messages or changing the information that is displayed on the screen.
Windows Defender	A complete solution for your Internet security, included in *Windows 10*. The program will protect your computer against all sorts of malware, such as viruses and spyware.
Windows Update	A system that checks whether you are using the most recent version of *Windows 10*.
Worm	A program that keeps copying itself, just like a virus. An unscrupulous person can use a worm to take over your computer, for instance.

Source: Windows Help

Appendix A. How Do I Do That Again?

The actions and exercises in this book are marked with footsteps:
In this appendix you can look up the numbers of the footsteps and read how to execute certain operations.

1   Close a window, program, or app
- Click ✕

2   Open *Edge* and/or web page
- Click  on the taskbar

Or:
- Click 🔍
- Type: Edge
- Click

- Click the address bar
- Type the web address
- Press **Enter** ⏎

3   Open *Control Panel*
- Right-click ⊞
- Click Control Panel

4   Open folder
- Double-click the folder

Or:
- Click the folder in the address bar

5   Moving files
- Drag the selected files to the desired folder

6   Minimize window
- Click ▬

7   Open folder on the taskbar

- Click

8   Copy file(s)
- Select the file(s)
- Drag the selected file(s) to the desired folder

9   Open *File Explorer*

- Click

10   Open *WordPad*
- Click 🔍
- Type: wordpad
- Click

11   Change the view
- Click the tab

- Click  Medium icons

12 Open *Settings*

- Click

- Click

13 Sign on with your user account

- Click your account name

- Type your password

- Click →

14 Open the *Account Settings* window

- Click ▼

- Click Settings

15 Open home page

- Click 🏠 Home

16 Delete tweet

- Place the pointer on the tweet

- Click ●●●

- Click Delete Tweet

- Click **Delete**

17 Follow *Twitter* account

- Type a search term in the search box

- Click 🔍

- Click Accounts

- Click the name of the account

- Click **+ Follow**

18 Open *Skype*

- Double-click  on the desktop

Or:

- Click 🔍

- Type: `Skype`

- Click Skype

19 Open folder
- Click the folder

20 Go to the next or previous photo

- Click ➡ to go to the next photo

- Click ⬅ to go to the previous photo

21 Open the *Library*

- Click ⬅ Back to Library

22 Open photo
- Double-click the photo

23 Play project

- Click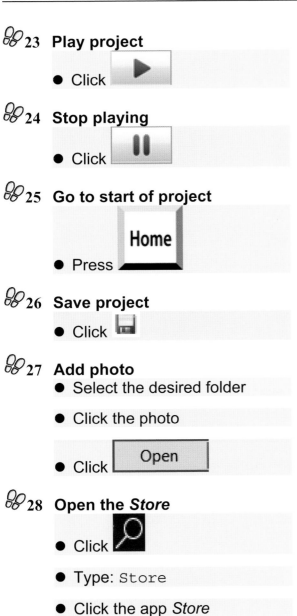

24 Stop playing

- Click

25 Go to start of project

- Press Home

26 Save project

- Click

27 Add photo
- Select the desired folder

- Click the photo

- Click Open

28 Open the *Store*

- Click

- Type: Store

- Click the app *Store*

Appendix B. Downloading the Practice Files

In some of the chapters of this book, you will need to use several practice files. You can download these files from the website accompanying this book.

☞ **Open the web page www.visualsteps.com/your10computer** %%²

You will see the website that goes with this book:

 Click Practice files

You will see the folders with the practice files. You can choose the folder for the chapter you want to work through. You can copy this folder to the *Documents* folder on your computer:

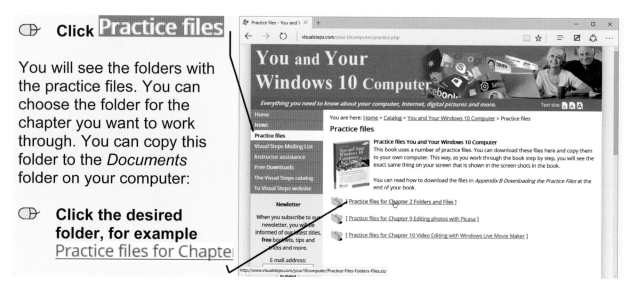

 Click the desired folder, for example Practice files for Chapter

➥ **Please note:**
The folder with practice files by *Chapter 9 Managing and Editing Digital Photos with Picasa* has to be copied to the *Pictures* folder instead of the *Documents* folder.

A bar appears at the bottom of the window:

The practice files are now being copied to the computer.

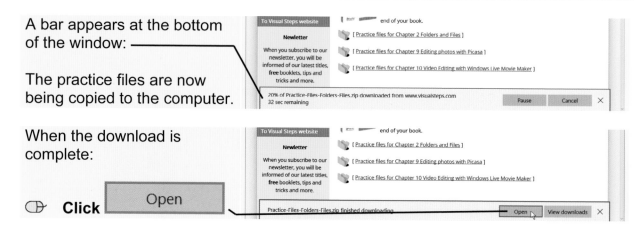

When the download is complete:

 Click Open

The folder is stored in the *Downloads* folder on the computer and this folder is now opened. This folder is a compressed folder. This means that the files in the folder are compressed so that the file size is smaller. If you want to use the files in a compressed folder, you need to unzip (or extract) them from the folder first:

Double-click the folder Practice Files Folders and Files

Click all Extract

Click Browse...

Now you can create a new folder with the name *Practice Files Folders and Files*:

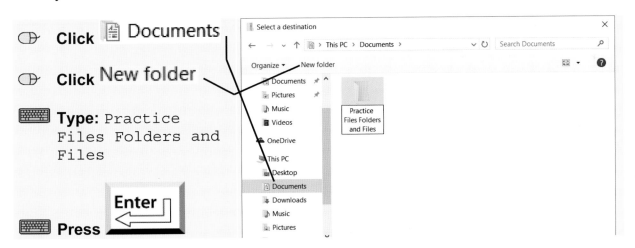

Click Documents

Click New folder

 Type: Practice Files Folders and Files

Press Enter

 Please note:
By the folder for *Chapter 9 Managing and Editing Digital Photos with Picasa* you can give the name *Practice Files Picasa*.

Please note:
The folder with practice files for *Chapter 9 Managing and Editing Digital Photos with Picasa* should be copied to the *Pictures* folder instead of the *Documents* folder.

Please note:

By the folder with practice files for *Chapter 10 Video Editing with Movie Maker* you can give the name *Practice Files Video*.

The new folder is selected:

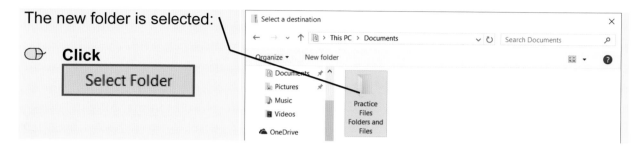

⊕ **Click**

Select Folder

Now you can extract the files to this new folder:

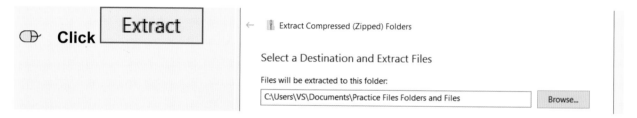

⊕ **Click** Extract

Extract Compressed (Zipped) Folders

Select a Destination and Extract Files

Files will be extracted to this folder:

C:\Users\VS\Documents\Practice Files Folders and Files   Browse...

While the files are being extracted, you see a window.

The compressed folder has been saved in the *Downloads* folder. This window is still open. You can delete the compressed folder:

⊕ **Click** ⬇ Downloads

⊕ **If necessary, click the folder**

⊕ **Click the** Home **tab**

⊕ **Click** ✕

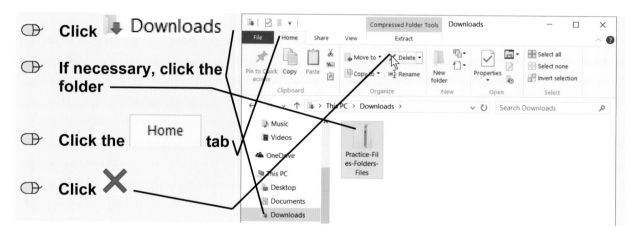

You can repeat this steps for the other folders with practice files.

☞ **Close all windows** ¹

Now you can continue with the desired chapter.

Appendix C. Index